Paradise Lost is for many the great
Composed late in the author's life, it
destiny of mankind.

This essential introductory guide:

- leads the reader into the epic poem through detailed analysis of key extracts, exploring Milton's original thought and style
- provides useful sections on 'Methods of Analysis' and 'Further Work' to aid independent study
- offers valuable information on Milton's life, times and literary legacy
- examines the development of critical opinion and discusses some recent critical views of the poem.

John Milton: Paradise Lost is ideal for anyone who is studying this complex and beautiful work for the first time. It will enable you to approach your own critical analysis of the poem with confidence.

Mike Edwards is an experienced teacher and lecturer specialising in English Literature. He is the author of several books in the *Analysing Texts* series.

Analysing Texts is dedicated to one clear belief: that we can all enjoy, understand and analyse literature for ourselves, provided we know how to do it. Readers are guided in the skills and techniques of close textual analysis used to build an insight into a richer understanding of an author's individual style, themes and concerns. An additional section on the writer's life and work and a comparison of major critical views place them in their personal and literary context.

LD 4508663 X

ANALYSING TEXTS

General Editor: Nicholas Marsh

Published

Jane Austen: The Novels *Nicholas Marsh*
Aphra Behn: The Comedies *Kate Aughterson*
William Blake: The Poems *Nicholas Marsh*
Charlotte Brontë: The Novels *Mike Edwards*
Emily Brontë: Wuthering Heights *Nicholas Marsh*
Chaucer: The Canterbury Tales *Gail Ashton*
Daniel Defoe: The Novels *Nicholas Marsh*
John Donne: The Poems *Joe Nutt*
George Eliot: The Novels *Mike Edwards*
F. Scott Fitzgerald: The Great Gatsby/Tender is the Night *Nicolas Tredell*
E. M. Forster: The Novels *Mike Edwards*
Thomas Hardy: The Novels *Norman Page*
John Keats: *John Blades*
Philip Larkin: The Poems *Nicholas Marsh*
D. H. Lawrence: The Novels *Nicholas Marsh*
Marlowe: The Plays *Stevie Simkin*
John Milton: Paradise Lost *Mike Edwards*
Shakespeare: The Comedies *R. P. Draper*
Shakespeare: The Sonnets *John Blades*
Shakespeare: The Tragedies *Nicholas Marsh*
Shakespeare: Three Problem Plays *Nicholas Marsh*
Mary Shelley: Frankenstein *Nicholas Marsh*
Webster: The Tragedies *Kate Aughterson*
Virginia Woolf: The Novels *Nicholas Marsh*
Wordsworth and Coleridge: Lyrical Ballads *John Blades*

Further titles are in preparation

Analysing Texts
Series Standing Order ISBN 978–0–333–73260–X
(*outside North America only*)

You can receive future titles in this series as they are published by placing a standing order. Please contact your bookseller or, in the case of difficulty, write to us at the address below with your name and address, the title of the series and the ISBN quoted above.

Customer Services Department, Macmillan Distribution Ltd, Houndmills, Basingstoke, Hampshire. RG21 6XS, UK

John Milton:
Paradise Lost

MIKE EDWARDS

First published 2013 by
PALGRAVE MACMILLAN

Palgrave Macmillan in the UK is an imprint of Macmillan Publishers Limited, registered in England, company number 785998, of Houndmills, Basingstoke, Hampshire RG21 6XS.

Palgrave Macmillan in the US is a division of St Martin's Press LLC, 175 Fifth Avenue, New York, NY 10010.

Palgrave Macmillan is the global academic imprint of the above companies and has companies and representatives throughout the world.

Palgrave® and Macmillan® are registered trademarks in the United States, the United Kingdom, Europe and other countries.

ISBN: 978–0–230–29328–1 hardback
ISBN: 978–0–230–29329–8 paperback

This book is printed on paper suitable for recycling and made from fully managed and sustained forest sources. Logging, pulping and manufacturing processes are expected to conform to the environmental regulations of the country of origin.

A catalogue record for this book is available from the British Library.

A catalog record for this book is available from the Library of Congress.

10 9 8 7 6 5 4 3 2 1
22 21 20 19 18 17 16 15 14 13

Printed and bound in China

Contents

General Editor's Preface

This series is dedicated to one clear belief: that we can all enjoy, understand and analyse literature for ourselves, provided we know how to do it. How can we build on close understanding of a short passage, and develop our insight into the whole work? What features do we expect to find in a text? Why do we study style in so much detail? In demystifying the study of literature, these are only some of the questions the *Analysing Texts* series addresses and answers.

The books in this series will not do all the work for you, but will provide you with the tools, and show you how to use them. Here, you will find samples of close, detailed analysis, with an explanation of the analytical techniques utilised. At the end of each chapter there are useful suggestions for further work you can do to practise, develop and hone the skills demonstrated and build confidence in your own analytical ability.

An author's individuality shows in the way they write: every work they produce bears the hallmark of that writer's personal 'style'. In the main part of each book we concentrate therefore on analysing the particular flavour and concerns of one author's work, and explain the features of their writing in connection with major themes. In Part II there are chapters about the author's life and work, assessing their contribution to developments in literature; and a sample of critics' views are summarised and discussed in comparison with each other.

Some suggestions for further reading provide a bridge towards further critical research.

Analysing Texts is designed to stimulate and encourage your critical and analytic faculty, to develop your personal insight into the author's work and individual style, and to provide you with the skills and techniques to enjoy at first hand the excitement of discovering the richness of the text.

Nicholas Marsh

How to Use this Book

The aim of this book is to show how understanding of the writer's ideas and skill emerges from close study of selected passages. These passages are identified at the beginning of each chapter. In each chapter, emphasis is placed on one specific feature of Milton's poem. The approach and techniques used are clearly demonstrated so as to help you to embark confidently on independent study of other parts of the poem. Each chapter ends with specific suggestions for your own work.

You will gain most benefit from this book if you have done some preliminary work of your own. You will need to have the relevant passage ready to hand as you read, so that you can refer back and forth easily between the analysis and the text. It will be useful to re-read the passages discussed and check on their context. There is much you can do beyond that. Study each passage in detail, first as a self-contained piece, then in the context of the poem. Think about its structure, its language, the balance of description, narrative and dialogue, and the links among these features. You will probably find it useful to make notes. In this way you can develop a feel for the atmosphere, mood and tone of the passage, and about the treatment of theme. You will also gain insight into the author's ideas and the techniques he uses.

You may have a method of study of your own that you have regularly used. By all means apply it to the passages discussed here. But remember that no programme of study is to be followed slavishly. Use all the means available to suggest approaches that may have slipped your attention, but keep an open mind and be ready to follow where your own imagination leads. Many things come to mind when you study poetry. Don't be too ready to dismiss stray thoughts as trivial or foolish. Pursue them and work out their implications. Even if they turn out in the end to be misguided, you will have gained a great deal in the process of developing them. The more you explore your ideas, the richer they will grow and the more thoroughly they will be your own.

Having done some preparatory study you will be in a better position to read the analysis in this book with understanding. There is a great deal of room for diversity of approach and interpretation in the process of analysis. You are unlikely to find your own responses mirrored precisely in the discussions, though it would be strange if there were no resemblance at all. Certainly you will now be in a position to disagree or agree for good independent reasons with what is said in the analyses that follow, and you will be able to build on them and develop further ideas of your own. Remember finally that disagreement is an essential part of the process: criticism exists to be contested.

A Note on Texts and Supplementary Materials

This book is designed to be used in conjunction with the text of *Paradise Lost*. The version used is the 1674 version, which contains 12 books. The earlier version, dating from 1667, is only slightly different in detail, but is differently organised into only ten books. Thus you may conveniently use any edition of the poem as a companion to this guide, as long as it is the 1674, 12-book version.

Editions of the 1674 version differ widely as to spelling, punctuation, capitalisation and italicisation, depending on which copies of the early editions editors prefer to adopt. Textual scholarship on the subject of *Paradise Lost* is less contentious than on the subject of Shakespeare's plays, but is nonetheless healthy and vigorous. It is saved from overexuberance, however, by the fact that although Milton was blind by the time he began composing the poem, he is known to have taken detailed interest in the niceties of spelling, punctuation and capitalisation – though he was far from consistent.

Modern editors have different goals in mind. Some modernise the spelling, others modernise the punctuation, and some do both, while others adhere rigorously to an original copy. The edition used for this guide is *The Poetical Works of John Milton, Edited after the Original Texts*, edited by H. C. Beeching (Oxford: Clarendon Press, 1900), which uses the text of the 1667 edition, but splits the material into 12 books as in the 1674 edition. This text is in the public domain and is available online.

Of several extant printed editions, three are likely to be of particular interest to students, and each has its own virtues. The authoritative Longman volume edited by Alastair Fowler (1968, revised second edition 2007) is copiously annotated, and contains an informative introduction that is enlightening particularly on the details of the composition of *Paradise Lost*. It adopts modernised spelling and punctuation. Of more recent vintage, and also generously annotated, is the Blackwell edition (2007) edited by Barbara Lewalski. It, too, boasts copious notes and additional material; unlike the Fowler edition, it adopts the original spelling, punctuation, italics and capitalisation. This edition looks most like the one that Milton's contemporaries experienced. Some students are likely to find a fully modernised edition more convenient to use. Renaissance conventions may perhaps offer an obstacle to understanding and enjoyment of the poem, and abandoning them does not affect its meaning. The Norton Critical Edition (2005) edited by Gordon Teskey answers this need, is fully annotated and contains useful additional material in the form of background information, extracts from critical essays, a glossary of names, and Milton's direct sources. Any of these, or any other 12-book edition will do as a companion for this study.

It can take time for students to tune in to the exotic music of *Paradise Lost*. For those who have difficulty with the surface meaning of Milton's verse, it may be useful to consult the Harry Blamires book on *Paradise Lost*, which explains what the poem says piece by piece. His book does not do much else, but what it does, it does well.

You can find full details of all these volumes in the Further Reading section at the end of this study.

Abbreviations and References

In references to the main extract under discussion, I have referred only to line numbers. I refer to other parts of *Paradise Lost* by book and line numbers in the form (12.300).

I refer to critical editions of the poem and critical works by editor's name and page number, as for example (Lewalski, 9), (Fowler, 9) and (Teskey, 9).

An asterisk in the text means that the word so marked has an entry in the Glossary. Only the first occurrence of such words is so marked.

PART 1

ANALYSING
PARADISE LOST

1

Milton's Conception in *Paradise Lost*

Extracts used:

Book 1. 1–26 ('Of Mans First Disobedience ... justifie the wayes of God to men')
Book 3. 1–55 ('Hail holy light ... things invisible to mortal sight')
Book 7. 1–40 ('Descend from Heav'n Urania ... shee an empty dreame')
Book 9. 1–47 ('No more of talk ... who brings it nightly to my Ear')

The subject of this chapter is the four invocations distributed at significant points in the course of the poem. The first is the most important because it begins the whole poem. The second invocation introduces Books 3 and 4 in which Satan finds his way to Eden and discovers Adam and Eve. The third invocation introduces Raphael's account of the Creation in Books 7 and 8. The fourth and final invocation changes the mood, heralding the Fall, which occupies the final four books of the poem.

These invocations are important for our study because in them Milton addresses his audience directly. They are conventionally called 'invocations'[1] because in each of them Milton invokes his 'muse', the source of his inspiration, whether Christian or pagan, to assist him in rising to the challenge of the great story he has to tell. He also tells us his intentions in the poem, and expresses what he feels about his own situation as well as how he views the events he describes.

It is not until the final invocation that Milton speaks about the genesis of the poem. This is a little surprising, but fits in rather well

with the anti-chronological ordering of the material in the poem as a
whole, which may well be an effect of the way in which the poem was
composed. Milton speaks about his muse thus:

> Of my Celestial Patroness, who deignes
> Her nightly visitation unimplor'd,
> And dictates to me slumbring, or inspires
> Easie my unpremeditated Verse:
> Since first this subject for Heroic Song
> Pleas'd me long choosing, and beginning late
>
> (9.21–6)

Here Milton presents a picture of himself as a poet from whom verse
flows effortlessly, without conscious thought ('unpremeditated') on
his part, because it springs from a superhuman source. This is an
attractive, even inspirational picture, but it is misleading. The truth
lies in the final line: Milton spent many years premeditating *Paradise
Lost*.[2] By the end of the gestation period, his conception had become a
huge project, and by the time he began to compose his poem, he was
nearly sixty years old.

In *Paradise Lost*, then, Milton undertook a large task, and he did
not attempt to minimise its demands. Indeed, the poem contains not
only the story of Adam and Eve, but also the creation and the fall of
Satan; it includes key figures and events in the biblical history of the
Old Testament, and refers to the incarnation of the Son in the New
Testament. He also refers to later events leading up to his own time.
Far from restricting his scope, he seems to be trying to incorporate the
whole of divine and human history in his poem.

Let us turn now to the first invocation, which will occupy most of
our attention in this chapter, to see how Milton chooses to introduce
his large subject. Remarkably, considering its vast scope, he manages
to encapsulate much of the whole matter of the poem in this first
paragraph:

> Of Mans First Disobedience, and the Fruit
> Of that Forbidden Tree, whose mortal tast
> Brought Death into the World, and all our woe,
> With loss of Eden, till one greater Man
> Restore us, and regain the blissful Seat,

Sing Heav'nly Muse, that on the secret top
Of Oreb, or of Sinai, didst inspire
That Shepherd, who first taught the chosen
Seed, In the Beginning how the Heav'ns and Earth
Rose out of Chaos: Or if Sion Hill   10
Delight thee more, and Siloa's Brook that flow'd
Fast by the Oracle of God; I thence
Invoke thy aid to my adventrous
Song, That with no middle flight intends to soar
Above th' Aonian Mount, while it pursues
Things unattempted yet in Prose or Rhime.
And chiefly Thou O Spirit, that dost prefer
Before all Temples th' upright heart and pure,
Instruct me, for Thou know'st; Thou from the first
Wast present, and with mighty wings outspread   20
Dove-like satst brooding on the vast Abyss
And mad'st it pregnant: What in me is dark
Illumine, what is low raise and support;
That to the highth of this great Argument
I may assert th' Eternal Providence,
And justifie the wayes of God to men.

                                                        (1.1–26)

This is a complex beginning. Few students will feel that they have a full understanding of it on their first reading As the opening paragraph of a long project, the passage demands and will repay repeated readings: here Milton tells us what he hopes to achieve in his epic poem, and we should listen carefully to what he says.

We will study the passage in several different ways, looking at the different structures that underpin it. There is, first, the verse structure – the organisation of lines and stresses. Superimposed on that there is a syntactic* structure – the order of words and its relation to meaning. Only after looking at these structures will we finally consider the thematic structure of the passage – its meaning and implications, and how it relates to the rest of the poem.

Perhaps the first things we notice about this passage are the broad features of the verse. There is no formal rhyme, and there are no regular stanzas. There is a regular metrical structure, which we might describe as 'iambic pentameter'* – the same pattern that Shakespeare adopted in his plays, and that has been a perennial choice throughout the history of English poetry. Some commentators prefer to regard these as decasyllabic* (or ten-syllable) lines on the grounds that Milton's treatment of metre* is too free to be considered iambic. Look, for example, at lines 6–7, 9–10, 11–12 and 20–1, in which the enjambement*, caesuras* and reversals of the metrical feet make it quite hard to view the metre as iambic. Nonetheless, Milton is very disciplined in his use of the decasyllabic line. In the interest of regularity, he frequently uses elisions* such as 'Th'upright' and 'th'Aonian', 'Heav'nly' and 'heav'ns', and 'adventrous', as well as the commonplace 'know'st', 'sat'st' and 'mad'st'. Milton is free in his use of metre, therefore, but strictly adheres to the basic structure of the verse.

Milton himself was clear on the subject of his verse form, adding a preface on the subject of 'The Verse' to the 1674 edition, in which he defends his use of 'English Heroic Verse without Rime'. Rhyme he dismisses as the unnecessary 'Invention of a barbarous Age' and later as a 'troublesom and modern bondage', useful only to offset weak material and poor metrical control. He prefers to follow the example of Homer and Virgil, whose verse was metrically strict and unrhymed. Perhaps the most interesting aspect of this preamble is that it was necessary at all. In fact, Milton felt compelled to defend himself against criticism levelled at him by conservatives in the literary world who were shocked at his abandoning rhyme. This was the first narrative poem in English that did not use rhyme.

Dispensing with the formal structural props of rhyme, Milton is free to develop a broad rhythmic sweep in which the ear is guided emphatically to the meaning of the verse. Although this was, perhaps, one of the first English poems, if not the first of all, composed in the knowledge and expectation that it would be read from the printed page, this verse is intended for the ear. You only have to read a few lines to feel the demand for sound. Significantly, Milton did not write it: he dictated it. Thus the poem may reasonably be seen a late flowering of the oral tradition of poetry. This point is made strongly by Philip Pullman, the title of whose trilogy, *His Dark Materials*, is drawn from *Paradise Lost*. In his Introduction to the OUP edition of the poem, he writes:

> So I begin with sound. I read *Paradise Lost* not only with my eyes, but with my mouth. I was lucky enough to study Books I and II for A

Level many years ago and to do so in a small class whose teacher, Miss Enid Jones, had the clear-eyed and old-fashioned idea that we would get a good sense of the poem if, before we did anything else to it, we read it aloud.

(pp. 1–2)

It is a good idea to follow Pullman's example and try to develop (if it does not come to you at once) a sense of the sound of the poem. There is a BBC recording available on CD of Anton Lesser reading the whole poem, which is well worth listening to.[3] Better still is to read it aloud yourself, and make the sound of the words – to read it with your mouth and ears as Pullman did.

Prosodic* Structure

Let us explore the verse structure of the invocation by trying to read it in this way, thinking about how we might speak it. There is obviously more than one way of 'performing' the poem. But if we look again at the first paragraph and split it into its natural breaths, by spacing, and using the slash symbol for brief pauses, we would, I think, probably be able to agree on something like this:

Of Mans First Disobedience,
                            and the Fruit
Of that Forbidden Tree, / whose mortal tast
Brought Death into the World, / and all our woe,

With loss of Eden,
                        till one greater Man
Restore us, and regain / the blissful Seat,

Sing / Heav'nly Muse,
                       that on the secret top
Of Oreb, / or of Sinai, / didst inspire
That Shepherd, / who first taught the chosen
Seed,
             In the Beginning how the Heav'ns and Earth
Rose out of Chaos:
                    Or if Sion Hill   10

Delight thee more,
                              and Siloa's Brook / that flow'd
Fast by the Oracle of God;
                              I thence
Invoke thy aid to my adventrous
Song, That with no middle flight intends to soar
Above th' Aonian Mount, while it pursues
Things unattempted yet in Prose or Rhime.

And chiefly Thou
                    O Spirit,
                              that dost prefer
Before all Temples th' upright heart and pure,

Instruct me,
              for Thou know'st;
                              Thou from the first
Wast present, / and with mighty wings outspread   20
Dove-like satst brooding on the vast Abyss
And mad'st it pregnant:
                              What in me is dark

Illumine,
              what is low raise and support;
That to the highth of this great Argument
I may assert th' Eternal Providence,

And justifie the wayes of God to men.

This rough-and-ready illustration is not the only way of reading
these lines, but serves to illustrate the kind of rhythmic structure
Milton develops. Within this general rhythmic structure, also, there
is a spectrum of longer and shorter cadences which may be variously
interpreted. The main point I wish to make, however, is clear: this
verse is full of cross-currents of phrasing and emphasis that engage
in a lively duet with the basic structural metre, sometimes following,
sometimes conflicting. It is not easy to read this verse in a mechanical style. Already in the first line, Milton denies the regularity of the
pentameter. A regular iambic pentameter would suggest the following
emphases:

Of *Mans* First *Dis*-o-*be*-dience, *and* the *Fruit*

Stressed this way, the line fulfils the mechanical requirements of the iambic pentameter because 'disobedience' is pronounced with four syllables, and not five.[4] Obviously, it would sound silly to speak the line this way. But as soon as we try to analyse the actual pattern of the line, we run into difficulties. What are we to make of 'Mans First'? Should we stress 'Mans', referring to Adam or Eve, or to the whole human race as opposed to Satan, whose pride was the first of all sins. Or should we stress 'First', meaning Eve's sin as distinct from Adam's, or any other sin, or anyone else's sin, or the sin of our general parents conjointly, or should we take it more generally as referring to the concept of original sin? Here, in fact, is the perfect illustration of the uneasy relationship between the form of the verse and its meaning. We will come across such ambiguities frequently in the course of our study of the poem.

Underlying the complexities of the decasyllabic line we can find a simpler structure of stresses. There are normally four stressed syllables within each line of decasyllabic verse:

> Of *Mans First* Diso*bedi*ence and the *Fruit*
> Of that For*bidd*en *Tree,* whose *mort*al *tast*
> Brought *Death* into the *World,* and *all* our *woe.*

Even here there are uncertainties. Should we in the third line not emphasise 'Brought' rather than 'all'? Or perhaps both? This is not a question I propose to answer: it is a matter for individual interpretation or performance. Suffice it to say that Milton's treatment of the decasyllabic line represents a triumph of disciplined, reasoned verse treated flexibly to develop great density of meaning. Notice, for example, as the paragraph develops, how the emphatic position of 'Sing', 'Rose' and 'Dove-like' (6, 10, 21) focuses our attention by disturbing the regularity of the basic iambic metre.

The freedom with which Milton treats metre begins in the first line of the poem, and the lack of rhyme is essential to it. Had Milton used the traditional heroic couplet – pairs of lines rhyming together – the natural effect would be to end-stop* the lines. As it is, fewer than half the lines in the whole poem are end-stopped. The abandoning of rhyme lets Milton's majestic verse roll from line to line with natural pauses wherever the sense demands.

Syntactic Structure

If we look now at the broader sweep of the opening paragraph, we will find ourselves moving on to matters of syntactic structure. Look more closely, first, at the first line. This line begins, as the whole huge poem does, with a word so insignificant that it can only have been a conscious and deliberate decision to start, as it were, at the bottom of the scale. Even among prepositions, 'of' is singularly lacking in intensity – in contrast, for example, with 'into', a much more assertive preposition.[5] 'Of' is a mere wisp of a word, lacking even the promise of an indefinite article, which comes before a noun; 'of' is a mere intermediary between two significant words, the first of which, in this case, has gone missing. All the other invocations begin in far more decisive fashion:

> Hail, holy Light, ofspring of Heav'n first-born (3.1)
>
> Descend from Heav'n, Urania... (7.1)
>
> No more of talk where God or Angel Guest (9.1)

Clearly, Milton's choice of a low-key opening is a deliberate choice: an understatement, even a small joke, given the solemnity and stateliness of what is to follow.

What actually follows is the somewhat ambiguous 'Mans First' and then the key word in the first line, dominating all other words: 'Disobedience'. It is long and Latinate*, establishing a pattern that runs throughout the poem. Milton's language in the whole poem is notably Latinate, breeding a feeling of formality and sophistication in contrast with the harder-hitting, monosyllabic vocabulary of the north European components of English. Milton's intense study of the ancient Greek and Roman writers meant that their vocabulary (and their linguistic structures) ran in his veins. In this first paragraph we have, for instance, 'mortal', 'Restore', 'regain', 'inspire', 'intends', 'pursues', 'unattempted', 'instruct', 'pregnant', 'adventrous', and so on – all words that came to us directly or indirectly (through French, particularly) from Latin. Mingled with these are words that predate the Norman conquest: 'Mans First', 'Forbidden Tree', 'Death', 'woe', 'loss', 'greater Man', 'upright heart', 'mighty wings' among others.

In general, we may say that the Latinisms, often polysyllabic, tend to generate a mood of solemnity and dignity, but remain a little detached, while the English words, frequently monosyllabic, tend to greater directness and emotional force: contrast 'mortal' with 'Death', for example.

Milton's word order is Latinate, too. In Latin, the verb generally comes at the end of the sentence. In this invocation, it takes Milton six lines to get to the main verb of the opening sentence:

> Sing Heav'nly Muse

All that precedes this is an amplification of the subject about which the muse is to sing, namely 'Mans First Disobedience'. The rest of the opening paragraph amplifies this plea until we reach the final statement of Milton's intention. In fact, we can, if we look carefully, reduce the whole complex structure of this first long paragraph to a simple framework of repeated pleas for inspiration:

> [About the Fall and everything prior to the incarnation of Christ]
> **Sing**, Heavn'ly Muse
> [who inspired the prophets]
> **Instruct** me
> [for you were instrumental in the creation]
> ... **illumine** ... **raise** ... **support**
> [So that I can explain Genesis to my fellow men]

Any sane English speaker of our time, confronted with this material, would at once split it into manageable bits and then would surely be inclined, instinctively, to start with 'sing' before going on to talk about what the singing deals with. In contrast, the basic structure Milton uses is Latinate. In Latin, the verb appears only after all the topics in the sentence have been mentioned. (You can find a shorter example below where the opening of Virgil's *Aeneid* appears.) Milton's order takes a deep breath to begin with, and launches into a long sentence, hedged about with subordinate clauses, that reaches its logical conclusion only at the end of the invocation. So, although we began by analysing out the points in this opening paragraph where the 'breaths' occur, this opening sentence is in essence all a single breath, culminating in a climactic and pointed conjunction of Latin and English vocabulary:

> ... to the highth of this great Argument
> I may assert th' Eternal Providence
> And justifie the wayes of God to men.

(24–6)

Here Milton provides the occasion for his epic poem. It presents a majestic theme – the Latinate 'Argument' is accompanied by the Old English 'great' – with a specific aim rendered in utterly Latinate terms: to 'assert th' Eternal Providence'. And here, at last in this unrhymed heroic verse is the ghost of a rhyme – or at least assonance* – in 'assert th' Eternal', giving a ponderous emphasis to a key phrase of Milton's opening statement. The Latin concludes with 'justifie', a legalistic word intended to show the author's clear intention to prove beyond reasonable doubt the message he wishes to convey; this is followed by a phrase that speaks in monosyllabic Anglo-Saxon terms straight to the heart: 'the wayes of God to men'.

In abandoning rhyme, then, and in his flexible treatment of the decasyllabic line, Milton strongly discourages mechanical reading. He focuses instead on the natural cadence of the voice, and thence on meaning. The Latinate syntactic structure favoured by Milton strengthens the effect, forcing our attention on disentangling meaning. In some instances, Milton's style blurs meaning. In particular, does that crucial and resonant phrase 'In the beginning' (9) relate to what precedes it, or what follows? In fact, we have to conclude that it could be either. The double syntax gives us pause, slows us to consider precisely what the writer intends.

Another idiosyncratic feature of the verse, the peculiarly Miltonic use of epithets*, exercises a similar effect. Consider the following list:

> First Disobedience
> Forbidden Tree
> mortal tast
> greater Man
> blissful Seat
> secret top
> chosen / Seed

adventrous / Song
middle flight
upright heart and pure
mighty wings
vast Abyss
great Argument
Eternal Providence

(1–25, passim)

Perhaps the most striking things about these epithets are first, their sheer number, and then their lack of concreteness. Even those with a physical aspect, like 'mighty' and 'vast', lack precision. For the most part, these epithets are marked by their abstraction, and often by their ambiguity. Ignoring examples discussed a little later in this chapter, let us look at, for example, the reference to the 'blissful Seat' that the Son will restore to mankind. Does it mean Paradise, the happy home from which Adam and Eve were expelled? Or does it mean heaven, to which Christians aspire? Or does it rather mean man's pre-eminent place in God's favour? All these alternative meanings fall together to a degree: the general meaning is clear enough; it is in the detail that Milton's style enforces thoughtful reading. Many of the other epithets have a similar effect. They often dip into moral or philosophical questions; they often lack concrete simplicity.

Milton's use of epithets thus has the effect of slowing down the movement of the verse, lending it a ponderous quality appropriate to its serious subject. It brings depth to the subject matter, and adds stateliness to the reading of the verse. (Contrast almost any page of Shakespeare: there we find a more active, agile, sprightly use of blank verse, with barely an epithet in sight!)

From the point of view of its appeal to the ear, what emerges from speaking the poem in the Pullman manner is not its absence of rhyme, but the profoundly musical character that emerges from its very individual style. In speaking above of the interplay of phrasing and metre above I have made deliberate use of the word 'duet'. The features of phrasing we have considered above are melodic: there is a fluid and varied arrangement of consonants and vowels; the collation of elegant Latinate and forceful Old English words has much to do with the richness of sounds Milton conjures up; the Miltonic epithets bring dignity and poise to the verse.

Clearly, however, melody is not the point of this verse, but is used to focus meaning. We find specific effects of alliteration* and assonance used – but not merely for the sake of prettiness. In the first three lines, the sequence of 'First... Fruit... Forbidden' focuses attention on the central theme of the Fall. There follows a different alliteration in 'World, and all our woe' which, allied with the three or four yawning elongated vowels, bewails the weary result of disobedience. Then, lifting the mood, the rising inflection* of 'restore... regain' points (already!) to redemption – to *Paradise Regained*. Notice, too, how the successive dentals* at the beginning of line 3, 'Brough*t* *D*eath', enforce a break between the words and thus give ominous emphasis to the introduction of mortality. As we proceed with the study of the poem, we will find evidence everywhere of the precision with which its sound supports its meaning.

One of the other sources of the Miltonic music is his frequent use of names – people and places – from many periods. Here in this first invocation alone we find Eden, Muse, Oreb, Sinai, Sion, Siloa, Aonian, and there are parts of the poem that show much denser use of proper nouns. In Book 1, there are nearly eight hundred proper nouns: that is an average of nearly one per line! Of the names in this first invocation only one, Eden, appears at first glance essential to the story Milton is telling. The others are used partly for their musical effect: they impart their own sense of grandeur and of the exotic, supporting the broad themes of the poem. There will be more to say on this subject a little later in our analysis when we come to discuss meaning in more depth.

Music is more than a characteristic of Milton's verse. It forms part of the subject matter of the poem, too. When Milton pleads – this is the actual moment of the invocation – 'Sing Heav'nly Muse', he is following a convention established in the classical epics. Virgil's Aeneid begins, 'Arms and the man I sing' (*Arma virumque cano*) and in the *Iliad*, Homer begins, in Samuel Butler's translation, 'Sing, O goddess, the anger of Achilles son of Peleus!' (*Menin aeide thea Peleiadeo Achileos*). The *Odyssey* (Butler's translation again) begins similarly, except for the lack of singing: 'Tell me, O muse, of that ingenious hero who travelled far and wide after he had sacked the famous town of Troy' (*Andra moi ennepe, mousa, polutropon hos mala polla / planchthe, epei Troies hieron ptoliethron epersen*).[6] Milton is not only following epic tradition, however: he is introducing a major feature of his epic. His poem sings throughout, though not always harmoniously. It contains the varied noises of hell, the divine harmony of heaven, the sound of the voices of angels, demons and the human characters. Milton was peculiarly sensitive to the music of language, and to the potential of verse to underpin meaning with varying metrical effects – and perhaps this sensitivity may have been accentuated in his latter years by his blindness.

In later invocations, Milton returns to the musical theme, going so far as to compare himself with the lyre-playing Orpheus (3.37, 7.34). He speaks of his verse as 'Those Notes' (9.6) and as 'Heroic Song' (9.25). In the third invocation he refers to the 'Celestial Song' (7.12) of his muse, which contrasts with the 'barbarous dissonance' of Bacchus's followers a little later (7.32), when their 'savage clamor [drowns]/ Both Harp and Voice' (7.36–7). When you go on to study the later invocations, you will be aware of further ways in which Milton not only refers repeatedly to music, but makes his own in verse.

Thematic Structure

We know already that the theme of the first invocation is Milton's request for inspiration in his intention to justify the ways of God to men. Let us explore this theme further, beginning with the use of names. Milton uses names for more than their melodious qualities. These names are references to classical or biblical or later events, and they are not chosen frivolously: each one has its place in the thematic development of the poem. Let us note, by the way, that one can read *Paradise Lost* for pleasure without reference to any notes; but if you are studying the poem, in these days when so few of us have the advantage of a classical education or a detailed knowledge of the Bible, reference to an editor's notes is probably essential for full understanding. Here we will look briefly at the meaning of the names used in the invocations.

In this first invocation, almost all the proper nouns refer to the Old Testament. Only one of these – Eden – is essential to the storyline of the poem, being the environment within which the central action occurs. The others have a broader thematic significance. Oreb and Sinai refer to the mountain on which Moses – the 'shepherd' – was called by God to receive the tablets of stone, Horeb (or Oreb) being the major peak, and Sinai a secondary peak of the same mountain. Here, then, Milton is asking for help from the same source that inspired Moses when, according to tradition, he composed the account of the Creation that we find in Genesis. A similar notion underlies the references to Sion and Siloa. Siloa refers to the spring water of Siloam, east of Jerusalem, which stands on another hill, Zion (or Sion), where King David was inspired to write the Psalms: here, again, Milton is using another form of words to ask for assistance in his own great task.

Clearly, Milton seeks inspiration from a Christian divine source. But whom precisely does Milton address? The 'Heav'nly Muse' may be a classical pagan divinity just as easily as a Christian – an idea supported when Milton refers to 'th'Aonian Mount': he means Mount Parnassus (otherwise known as Mount Helicon) in Greece, which was dedicated to the Muses (among them Calliope, the Muse of epic poetry) and the god Apollo, who was also associated with inspiration. Only later does he turn in 'O Spirit' (17) to an unequivocally Christian source of enlightenment.

Milton's address to the Muse, therefore, is ambiguous. While the name suggests the classical world, the epithet 'Heav'nly' suggests instead that Milton is thinking of the Holy Ghost (or Holy Spirit) which embodies the creative power of God, an interpretation supported by the ensuing biblical references and by the appearance of the dove, which is a conventional way of symbolising* the Holy Ghost. The reverse effect occurs in the phrase 'the Oracle of God' (12) which, though it refers to the inspiration of King David, recalls by the use of the word 'oracle' rather the pagan oracle of Apollo at Delphi. These ambiguities are pointed: they imply a comparison between the classical world and the Christian world. In adopting classical models, Milton, never short of confidence, has no intention of limiting his horizons to theirs. Rather he wishes, with the help of his Christian inspiration, to surpass those classical models – to 'soar/ Above' Mount Parnassus, spurning mere 'middle flight' in his 'adventrous song' (13–15). Indeed, he tells us, his intention is to express 'Things unattempted yet in Prose or Rhime' (16). Significantly, the line is a parody of a line from Ariosto's *Orlando Furioso* (Fowler, 59): though it is unclear precisely what Milton thinks is as yet unattempted, his consciousness of the seriousness of his work is incontestable. His intention is not merely to emulate his classical predecessors in epic poetry, but to exceed the limits of their work by focussing on the Christian theme that in his view supersedes the classical moral universe.

These proper nouns, then, add resonance to Milton's poem both on the level of sensuous impact – their sound, their associations – and in meaning. They occur throughout much of the poem. In the second of the invocations (Book 3) we find him referring to the classical world in speaking of the Muses, the 'Stygian Pool' (the river Styx of the infernal regions), Orpheus, and the blind poets Thamyris and Maeonides (meaning Homer, from his birthplace), as well as reintroducing the biblical Sion. The third invocation (Book 7) refers to Olympus, Pegasus (the winged horse, another symbol* of inspiration), 'the Muses nine' (7.6), Bellerophon and the Aleian field where he fell when unseated from Pegasus, Bacchus, and Orpheus, here called 'the Thracian Bard' (7.34). The fourth invocation (Book 9) mentions Achilles, Turnus and Lavinia, Neptune, Juno, the Muse Urania under the sobriquet of his 'Celestial Patroness' (21), and, under the title 'Cytherea's Son' (9.19), Aenaeas. These references weight the poem overwhelmingly towards the classical, pagan world. Yet the purpose of each of these invocations is to plead for Christian enlightenment. In each case, Milton's overt theme is that the Christian world is superior even to the greatest expressions of the pagan classical era; but it is not entirely clear that the poet's heart is singing the same tune as his brain, for there is great fondness in these classical references. Embodying this tension between different worlds, Milton represents his age. His poem stands self-consciously at the end of a rich history of Christian and pagan culture, encompassing both. The Christian message must, however, apply to all men, not just some of them. Milton's epic seeks to embrace all history, not just one or even a few strands.

In sum, Milton uses these proper nouns to generate resonances with elements of the history of the world and its myths, and he thus enhances the universality of his poem. The use of names, as we have seen, adds melody to the poem: but it also adds a harmonic element to the subject matter: it enables Milton to gesture towards events outside the chronology of the strict subject matter, and thus to tell several stories at once. As we shall see in Chapter 2 of this study, the counterpoint between the main lines of the story and the harmony that supports it is not a simple one.

Other kinds of allusiveness create related effects. Milton habitually generalises the specific source of his script – the Bible. We have already noticed, for example, that Moses becomes 'That Shepherd';

his people, the Israelites, become 'the chosen Seed'; thus Moses
stands for any shepherd as well as the enlightened prophet, and his
people stand for all people of later times. These generalisations can
be very significant. When, in the first lines of the first invocation,
Milton speaks of 'Mans First Disobedience', we notice that he avoids
speaking specifically of Eve's disobedience: the effect is to point out
the relevance to his audience of that disobedience; it may have been
Eve's once, but it is now yours and mine. A little later he refers to
'one greater Man' (5) instead of Christ; again, he strives to show
the human dimension of the poem, and immediately establishes a
link between Adam, the implied lesser man, and Christ, the greater.
Similarly, when he refers to the Tree of Knowledge, he calls it pointedly 'that Forbidden Tree', elliptically including God's prohibition
and the Fall in a single phrase. Its 'mortal tast' hinges on the dual
meaning of 'mortal' – it means variously human and deadly – suggesting both its being tasted by Eve and Adam who thereby became
the first of mortals, and the idea that tasting the fruit was what
brought death into the world.

Another kind of allusiveness is quotation. We have already noticed
that line 16 quotes Ariosto ironically, and we have noted that the calling upon the muse is a convention of epic poetry. Let us notice also
that line 9 quotes the biblical 'In the beginning', supporting the insistent repetition of 'first' in these opening lines: the quotation stresses
the radical nature of Milton's project in the poem. It is perhaps not
surprising, given the subject, that there should be countless echoes (as
distinct from direct quotation) of biblical language throughout the
poem. We will have occasion to speak further about these allusions as
we explore other aspects of the poem. Suffice to say, for the present,
that the allusions are both interesting in themselves, and important in
the development of ideas in the poem.

Imagery and Symbolism

We will look now at another, equally rich aspect of Milton's verse:
his use of imagery. Here I wish to pick out three strands of imagery
that define the mood of this first invocation. These are, in effect, the
strands of imagery that choose themselves by their prominence.

The first of these strands relates directly to the subject of the whole poem: the 'Fruit of that Forbidden Tree' appears in the opening line. The reference is, of course, to the fruit of the Tree of Knowledge of Good and Evil. Conventionally in western art this fruit is depicted as an apple, and so it is sometimes called in *Paradise Lost*. The Hebrew word, however, means only 'fruit' in general, and has thus allowed Hebrew commentators to think of it as, for example, a fig or grape. From our point of view of interpretation of the poem, the general word 'fruit' is a better choice than anything more precise because of its diversity of meaning. The word 'fruit' means, in addition to its immediate denotation, a result or effect: we may think of our efforts on some project as either fruitful or fruitless. In the context of the poem, the fruit of the forbidden tree is not so much apple, as the dismal outcome of sin, death, and expulsion from the Garden of Eden – all that results from the disobedience of eating it. Thus the image of the fruit plays its role in the sequence of consequences with which the poem opens: prohibition, disobedience, mortality, trouble, loss – all to be redeemed by 'one greater Man'. The word 'fruit' reverberates through the poem with various force. After the eating of the fruit, Adam and Eve end Book 9 in 'fruitless hours' (9.1188) of mutual recrimination. Later, Adam speaks to Eve of the human race as 'the fruit of thy womb' (10.1053), echoing the wording of the Gospel of St Luke (1:42) in relation to Mary as the mother of Christ.

More broadly, the image of the fruit grows and spreads into a pervasive strand of imagery – even an environment. A few lines after the beginning, Milton refers metaphorically to the 'chosen seed' (8) of Israel, and a little later (and rather more tangentially) to the kind of fruit that might emerge from the 'oracle of God' beside the life-giving waters of 'Siloa's brook' (11–12). A few lines later still, and we find Milton beginning to speak of the 'abyss [made] pregnant' (22–3), as if the created world were the fruit of the womb of the abyss. In Book 4, of course, there is a detailed description of the Garden of Eden, the plants of which are named by Eve. The garden is fecund with fruits of all kinds, yet also bears the fruit of the forbidden tree and brings evil into the world.

How conscious was Milton of the layers of meaning in the word 'fruit', or indeed in other equally rich words? We can with a large degree of confidence answer, fully. *Paradise Lost* if full of puns. His perception of the complex meaning of 'fruit' is glaringly obvious in Eve's response to the serpent in Book 9, 'Serpent, we might have spared our coming hither, / Fruitless to me, though fruit be here t'excess' (9.647–8): the meeting is fruitful for Satan, but not for Eve; and the final excess will lie in the eating of the fruit. Thus the tree will truly become, in another lugubrious pun, 'the root of all our woe' (9.645). In his love of puns Milton shows himself a true son of an age that delighted in the play of language which had been expressed earlier in the plays of the Elizabethan and Jacobean periods, and in the poetry of the Metaphysical poets.

Another strand of imagery begins in the pregnant abyss: that of flight. The Holy Ghost 'dove-like' broods on the abyss, acting as a kind of divine midwife in bringing the created world to life. Equally, Milton prays for his theme to be brought to life by the inspiration of his Christian muse. The image he uses repeatedly for this idea is flight: the dove will help him to fly. He intends 'with no middle flight ... to soar' (14), borne upon the 'mighty wings outspread' (20) of his muse that will 'raise and support' (23) his 'adventrous Song'. The image of flight colours the other invocations, too. In the second, Milton speaks of his 'flight/ Through utter and through middle darkness' (3.15–16), and later compares himself with the nightingale, 'the wakeful Bird' (3.38). In the third, as we have seen, he is soaring 'Above the flight of Pegasean wing' (7.4). He concludes the final invocation with the fear that the cold (that is, not Mediterranean, like the classical poets) English climate may 'damp my intended wing' (9.45). Milton uses this strand of imagery for a dual purpose: to suggest both his imagination, divinely inspired, and the sublime style to which he aspires.

Flying, however, has another, opposed association: Satan. As an angel, Satan is a winged creature. He flies on his epic search for God's newly chosen creatures, and in the second invocation (Book 3) Milton too sees himself as flying through the regions of hell in his poetic vein, 'in my flight / Through utter and through middle darkness borne' (3.15–16). We may recall also the traditional link between soaring and pride expressed in the myth of Icarus and Daedalus; and it becomes evident that the poet, too, can be guilty of the sin of pride – hence his repeated appeals for divine inspiration.

Certainly, Milton shows every confidence in his own abilities. If his task is onerous, his ability matches it. After all, he compares himself not only with Orpheus, but also with Homer, the father of epic poetry, with the blind prophet Tiresias, and with Moses, the most authoritative of the Old Testament prophets. An implication of these comparisons is that Milton considers himself to be fit for his task – a modern Orpheus. As well, then, that he places such stress on the need for the divine inspiration which can raise his song to the required elevation.

This brings us to the third strand of imagery I wish to draw attention to, which is also associated with Milton's prayer for inspiration. He asks not only to be raised, but also to be enlightened; not only for sublime poetry, but for understanding. Realising that there is much he as a mere man cannot understand, he pleads that the Holy Ghost will 'illumine' the darkness of his understanding (23). Nothing more is said of this strand of imagery in this first invocation. But it reappears in the second invocation, beginning 'Hail, holy light' (3.1), referring to God's first command, 'Let there be light' (Genesis, 1.3), where, in the separation of darkness from light, the distinction of good and evil eventually symbolised by light and dark begins. For Milton, there is further meaning in the polarity. In the same invocation he associates 'Chaos and Eternal Night' (3.18), as if his blindness is a form of descent into hell, and later speaks of the 'ever-during dark' (3.45) to which his blindness confines him. However, darkness is ambiguous: on the one hand it symbolises Milton's state of isolation, hedged about by dangers in the new royalist dispensation; on the other, night is linked with his inspiration, for then it is that the muse 'Visit[s] my slumbers' (7.29), enlightening his spirit. In the fourth of the invocations, there is a further extension of this light/dark imagery, when Milton speaks of 'Sinne and her shadow Death' (9.12). The imagery of light and dark, and its associated symbolism, is thus especially rich, touching as it does both Milton's blindness, and the desire for spiritual enlightenment to inspire his verse; in the poem at large, of course, this imagery finds an apt application in both the heavenly and the hellish parts of the poem. It is not applied rigidly, however; as we shall see in later chapters, it is at the service of meaning.

Milton's use of imagery, among the other effects we have noted, produces a deeply sensuous poetry. It is not sensuous in the manner of, say, Keats, for whom sensuousness is as much a subject in itself. Milton's sensuousness is usually at the service of meaning. In this first invocation, in the appeal to the eye of the light/dark imagery, and the appeal to the ear of the musical element in the poetry, in the flight imagery that appeals to touch, and in the taste suggested by the fruit of the tree – in all these features, we see a poet bending his powers to bring to new and vivid life a story perhaps too well known to strike its hearers with the amazement its significance should command. Later in the poem, we find Milton in Book 4 using the sense of smell, too, to generate a felt disgust at the arrival of Satan in Eden.

An Overview of the Four Proems

Let us turn, now, to the question of the perspective Milton expresses in the proems as a coherent group. Evidently, the subject of the poem is already contained in the first few lines: it is the story of the loss of Eden because of the disobedience of Adam and Eve in eating the fruit of the tree of knowledge. At the beginning of the poem, the conclusion is already known: paradise, as the title tells us, is already lost. Thus the poem is serious and sombre in tone: there are very few moments of comedy. Yet the first invocation reveals that there is much more to the story than that bare summary.

Surprisingly, perhaps, there is a strong emphasis in this opening on hope. The disobedience of Adam and Eve unleashes sin and death into the world, which Milton views as a tragic event; in the fourth invocation, he says that he 'must now change/ These Notes to Tragic' (9.5–6). In the first invocation, however, having summarised the events leading to the Fall in three lines, he turns in the fourth to 'one greater man [who shall] Restore us, and regain the blissful Seat' (1.4–5) that is lost in Book 9. A few lines later, calling upon the Holy Ghost for inspiration, Milton creates an impression of that spirit, 'with mighty wings outspread/ Dove-like' (20–1), as a protective entity, embodied in the dove as the conventional symbol of peace. Milton makes the point literally in Book 11 when he deals with the dove that brings an olive leaf to Noah as the sign of God's appeasement:

> A Dove sent forth once and agen to spie
> Green Tree or ground whereon his foot may light;

The second time returning, in his Bill
An Olive leafe he brings, pacific signe:

(11.857–60)

Clearly the emphasis here is on reconciliation rather than sin and
punishment. The image of the dove in the first invocation has further
implications, for this is a dove 'brooding on the vast abyss' (1.21) and
thus making it 'pregnant'. This physical representation of the creation makes no biological sense. As a symbolic concept, however, it
is in keeping with Milton's monistic* idea of creation, and its effect
is to establish a mood of optimism that culminates in the final lines
of the first invocation, where Milton asks that he may be inspired to
the degree necessary to be able to 'assert th' Eternal Providence/ And
justifie the wayes of God to men'.

Such an affirmation indicates how much has changed since the
opening lines of the poem, and it is a change wrought by Milton's
faith. He believes in the divine plan, and that it reserves a place for
mankind. When he speaks of justifying the ways of God, he seems to
mean only that: there is no argument about it; there is no question in
his mind whether God's ways are justifiable or not; Milton is simply
explaining and exploring something known. In traditional epic style,
the poem recounts and explains events familiar to the audience, and
long past. The whole of the story coexists in human consciousness:
the fall of Lucifer, the Fall of Man, the expulsion and redemption are,
in a sense, all one; each element contains all the others; and from this
point at the end of the first invocation, Milton will plunge almost
immediately into the story of Satan. Only as the poem develops do
we become aware that Milton's theme may be a little less clear than
he first states.

The tone of the opening springs from Milton's religious ideas.
His need to explain is peculiarly Protestant* in tone. For the older
Roman Catholic* doctrine, biblical analysis and exegesis were not
matters for the individual: rather, they were expressed in the doctrines of the Church. The absolute authority in matters of faith of
the Church of Rome, pe-eminent in Dante's day – the fifteenth century – had been shattered beyond salvaging in Milton's. Only in the
more individualistic world of the Reformation* could *Paradise Lost*,
with its tone of exploration, examination and discussion, have been

written. Dante's *Divina Commedia*, the Catholic counterpart of Milton's work, inhabits a different world altogether. (Part 2 of this book contains further discussion of the religious context of Milton's time.)

With this in mind, look again at the overall pattern of the opening paragraph, and notice how it encompasses the older and newer perspectives. Notice that the final two words, 'to men', reflect the opening phrase, 'Of man's'. Milton deliberately makes the end mirror the beginning, as if the first paragraph comes full circle. But the differences are important. The opening phrase is a remote abstraction, referring to the sin of Eve or Adam or, to the extent that we are all entangled in the original sin of the fathers which is visited on the children even to the last generation – all of us; and it focuses on the conduct of man, that Latinate 'Disobedience', towards God. The final phrase, in contrast, uses the plural 'men', and addresses us in a more concrete, monosyllabic and therefore more direct way; thus it focuses on the conduct of God towards the human race. The opening paragraph, we may say, begins in the mediaeval perspective and ends in the Renaissance. In this respect the opening paragraph prefigures some important aspects of the whole poem.

We can see a further expression of the gap between the old and new religious worlds a little earlier when Milton asserts that the Holy Spirit prefers 'Before all temples th'upright heart and pure' (1.18). Here we can perceive the Protestant's distrust of the gaudier practices and cathedrals of Catholicism, and his preference for the simpler environments in which the individual Protestant can commune with his own conscience. A further implication of this phrase is that for Milton, conscience is a matter of the individual, rather than an expression of general religious doctrine: in his eyes, where Catholicism inhabits a cathedral, Protestantism – at least Milton's version of it – inhabits the individual heart and mind.

Paradise Lost, hence, though it deals with a universal theme, is also an expression of personal conviction. This poem, so long revolved and started late, is very dear to Milton's heart and mind. As much as it is a public celebration of sin punished and redeemed, it is a personal *apologia* – a defence of his convictions.

Autobiographical Elements and Narrative Method

Paradise Lost has a complex narrative structure. Parts of the poem are narrated by Raphael, Michael, Adam and Eve, and parts are perceived by Satan. Sometimes we have two or three different views of the same event – of the creation of Eve, for example. Some parts are directly narrated by Milton, or at least by the projection of Milton that speaks as the 'I' of the poem.

The 'I' – or narrative eye – of a poem or novel is not identical with the author: it is part of the structure the author creates. In the case of Milton, however, it is very clear that Milton the man has much in common with the 'I' of the poem. *Paradise Lost* shares with the prose writings Milton's habit of mingling objective and subjective writing. For one among many instances, in *Areopagitica*, a polemical tract against censorship, Milton takes time to tell us about his visit to Europe. Equally, in *Paradise Lost*, Milton has many digressions concerning his own life and opinions. For the most part, therefore, we are reasonably safe in thinking of Milton and the 'I' as occupying one and the same ground. Even so, we should be wary, and remember that the 'I' is part of the total construct of the poem, and therefore part of the author's conception and perception. Milton the narrator becomes an actor in the drama, and also stands in for the reader. We see the action, as it were, over the narrator's shoulder: he represents our fallen state, and strives with us to understand the pre-lapsarian* events he describes; but he also constantly draws our attention to his own story and thus Milton and his life become part of the dramatic totality of the poem.

In one respect, the poem has, as we have noticed, a very specific autobiographical emphasis. Repeatedly in these invocations, Milton alludes to his blindness. In this first invocation, the reference might be overlooked as simply a part of a general plea for inspiration, for the spiritual insight and sublime style his great subject demands:

> ...what in me is dark
> Illumine....

(22–3)

The primary meaning of this pithy plea is that Milton is asking for spiritual enlightenment so that he will be able to speak about matters of which mankind generally has only a limited understanding. In the second invocation, however, Milton amplifies the personal theme. The poets with whom he compares himself, Thamyris and Maeonides (Homer), were blind, as were the 'prophets old', Tiresias and Phineus (3.35–6); thus he can speak of these poets as 'equal'd with me in Fate' (3.33). Milton speaks touchingly of his own situation in feeling the warmth of the sun while unable to see it:

> [I] feel thy sovran vital Lamp; but thou
> Revisit'st not these eyes that rowle in vain
> To find they piercing ray and find no dawn
> So thick a drop serene hath quencht thir Orbs
> Or dim suffusion veild.
>
> (3.22–6)

It is as if Milton has a mental image of how he must appear to others, eyes rolling in a hopeless effort to find the light. He is unsure of the cause of his blindness – whether it is the effect of a 'drop serene' or a 'dim suffusion' – but knows only that no matter how 'piercing' the light, it is absent from him: the cause would appear to be what we think of as cataracts. Later, his plaint becomes more emphatic and more mournful. He cannot rejoice in the turning of the seasons or the alternation of night and day, nor perceive the everyday pleasures of the natural world, nor recognise 'human face divine' (3.44), but must resign himself to 'ever-during dark' (3.45). The brief catalogue of his disadvantages reaches a climax when he mourns 'wisdom at one entrance quite shut out' (3.50). Then, suddenly turning to a more optimistic theme, Milton pleads for compensation in the form of spiritual vision:

> Shine inward, and the mind through all her powers
> Irradiate, there plant eyes, all mist from thence
> Purge and disperse, that I may see and tell
> Of things invisible to mortal sight.
>
> (3.52–5)

From this insistent demand, it appears that the earlier parallels with Tiresias and Phineus were not accidental. Clearly, Milton views himself as having prophetic powers, his spiritual vision intensified and enhanced by his physical loss. He wishes to have the insight to speak of matters which are invisible to the eyes of mere men ('mortal' sight), to speak with the tongue perhaps of a demi-god.

In the third of the invocations, Milton refers only in passing to his blindness. He spends more time there on a different autobiographical feature of the poem, when he speaks about his political plight. As a committed republican, he found himself at odds with the social structure that pertained after the restoration of the monarchy, and paints an anxious picture of his precarious situation:

> ... I Sing with mortal voice, unchang'd
> To hoarce or mute, though fall'n on evil dayes,
> On evil dayes though fall'n, and evil tongues,
> In darkness, and with dangers compast round,
> And solitude.
>
> (7.24–7)

The intensity of Milton's fears stands out in the repetition and reversal of the second and third lines here: 'fall'n ... evil ... evil ... fall'n ... evil', and in the alliteration of 'days ... days ... darkness ... dangers'. The darkness Milton mentions here is not only the darkness of blindness, but also the darkness of prison, and the dangers were the real dangers of intimidation and perhaps even execution. He presents himself as 'unchang'd': he has remained true to his convictions despite political change: his response to the defeat of his principles is neither to complain with excessive stridency ('hoarce') nor to retreat into a fearful silence ('mute'); he will continue to 'Sing with mortal voice' what he believes to be true.

The independence of spirit this passage expresses finds an echo in the structure of the poem as a whole. Milton, as a political revolutionary, anti-monarchist and anti-episcopalian*, chose a revolutionary form for his work, rejecting the bondage of rhyme, much as he rejected the authority of both church and state over men. The verse he writes is a political statement. The voice with which he speaks is utterly individual. In *Paradise Lost*, he writes, in a sense, his own life.

This passage is the strongest indication in the poem that Milton thinks of his work as being his own epos* as well as that of Adam and

Eve. His subject is heroic, and one of the heroes in Milton's mind is himself. In the fourth of the invocations, he belittles the conventional heroic poetry of his own times – the 'long and tedious havoc [of] fabl'd Knights/In Battels feign'd' (9.30–1) – and upholds instead 'Patience and Heroic Martyrdom' (9.32) as the proper subject for epic. He writes of matter that 'justly gives Heroic name/ To Person or to Poem' (9.40–1). His task in *Paradise Lost* is the greatest imaginable. Only by preserving his own heart upright and pure, and calling on divine inspiration, can he hope to do justice to the epic story. Only so can he, blind and isolated, become another Orpheus, another Homer, another Moses.

Conclusions

It is time to summarise what we have discovered of the features that mark the distinctive rhetoric of the poem.[7] Milton was fully conscious of the seriousness of his subject and of its demands, and strove to devise a style that would suit its gravity: the result is far from what Wordsworth would have described as 'the real language of men'[8] for the subject matter of angels and demons, principalities and powers, demands much more. What Milton invents he refers to in the fourth of the invocations as 'answerable style' (9.20), which is to say an appropriate style, befitting his great subject, which he pleads to develop with the help of his 'Celestial Patroness'. The expression of matters no man has yet attempted demands a style that 'with no middle flight [will] soar' (1.14), a 'Heroic Song' to celebrate a 'higher Argument' (9.42). There is, indeed, a conscious tone of oratorio, if not grand opera about *Paradise Lost*, and the features of style that we have noticed support it.

Thematic Features

- Milton's purpose is clear and precise: to show that God's treatment of Adam and Eve, and of humanity in general, is just.
- Milton follows the epic models of classical writers, especially Homer and Virgil, but hopes to exceed their achievements.

- The poem contains autobiographical elements, referring to Milton's blindness, and to the political and religious issues of his own time.
- The poem mingles pagan and Christian elements: its subject comprehends the whole of human history.
- Milton uses rich imagery, often sustained imagery.
- Sound is important in the poem, both as a subject and as a stylistic feature.
- Some motifs run throughout the whole poem, such as the multiple meaning of 'fruit'.
- Milton controls the pace of the verse by manipulating the pattern of the decasyllabic line and its caesura to produce a measured, ceremonial tone in keeping with his serious subject.
- Milton's choice of verse form reveals independence of thought and reflects his anti-authoritarian attitudes to church and state.

Stylistic Features

- Absence of formal rhyme.
- Decasyllabic verse, metrically strict, basically iambic but often distorted.
- Variable caesura, creating incremental breaths and paragraphs of verse.
- Lines sometimes but by no means habitually end-stopped.
- Latinate syntax* and vocabulary intermixed with Anglo-Saxon words.
- Quotations and echoes of the Bible and other sources.
- Many musical effects, including alliteration and assonance.
- Use of exotic place names and personal names from biblical and classical sources, partly for their melodic effect and partly for their historical resonance.
- Subtle use of imagery and symbolism.
- Play on words, particularly puns and ambiguities.
- Sensuousness.
- Use of conventions such as the appeal to the muse.
- Allusion to a wide range of sources and periods, classical, biblical and Renaissance.
- Generalisation.

Other features will emerge from discussions in later chapters, but
those listed will provide a starting point for your analysis of the other
invocations suggested in the section at the end of this chapter on suggestions for 'Further Work'.

Methods of Analysis

- The first requirement is to read carefully and repeatedly to ensure
  full understanding of the extract. We tested out the rhythms of the
  verse, following the natural phrasing of the voice, and listening to
  the sound of the verse, as a first guide to its meaning. We tried to
  see the extract as a performance.
- Then we checked on the meanings of unfamiliar words or references. For you, this means consulting the notes in a good scholarly
  edition. (For me, it meant consulting the notes in several!)
- Moving on to closer analysis, we looked at the versification: metrical effects such as inversions* of metrical feet, rhyme (or lack of it)
  and caesura, particularly.
- We considered the syntactical structure of the extract. Ignoring
  the verse structure, we looked for the natural phrasing and
  sentence-structure.
- We then considered the stylistic elements in the extract, such as
  allusions, imagery, sensuousness, rhetorical* effects, ambiguities,
  alliteration and generalisation.
- Finally, we tried to sum up the thematic effect of the invocations in
  general, including the autobiographical features.

Further Work

Select one of the other invocations, and analyse its style and meaning.
Explore the impression Milton creates, what he reveals of his purpose,
and what emerges about Milton himself, and his religious and political ideas. There are several pointers in the discussion in this chapter,
but there is much more to be discovered in each of the invocations.
Here are some of the topics you may wish to consider (including some
features not present in the first invocation):

Among the stylistic characteristics you might look out for:

- Classical and biblical references: look at their meaning in the context.
- Sound effects such as alliteration, assonance: show how they support the meaning.
- Imagery: the use of simile, metaphor, metonymy to generate vivid ideas.
- Rhythmic effects, including repetition, apposition*, elision.
- Appeal to the senses: colour, sound, taste, touch, smell.
- Vocabulary – Latin and Old English.
- Syntax – often periodic*.
- Play on words through puns and ambiguities.

Among the thematic features:

- How does Milton view the figures in the drama?
- How does he see the relationships among them?
- What does he say about sin, the Fall, and redemption?
- What is the significance of these ideas for Milton's own time?
- Consider the harmonic effect of Milton's references.

Among the personal features of the poem:

- Consider the autobiographical content of the invocation.
- Explore the religious ideas that emerge from the invocation.
- Look for political implications in the invocation you have chosen.

You should not treat these suggestions as limiting. Follow up any additional ideas that occur to you.

2

The Epic Structure
of *Paradise Lost*

Book 6. 296–315 ('They ended parle ... thir jarring Sphears confound')
Book 1. 192–213 ('Thus Satan talking ... his own dark designs')
Book 1. 283–313 ('He scarce had ceas't ... amazement of their hideous change')

In this chapter we look at some of the features that define the epic nature of Milton's poem. The general characteristics of classical epic have been widely documented, and you can find them listed in Appendix A. Here, beginning with Book 6, which deals with the war in heaven, we will focus on only a few of the general characteristics: Milton's approach to the scale of his subject, including his use of epithets; his treatment of the chronology of his subject; and his use of devices such as the epic simile*.

The key to epic is grandeur. Broad vision, power, and awe are essential. Epic is typically large in scale, important in subject, heroic in incident, and weighty in style. The subject is often the fate of whole nations; the protagonists are heroic, often with god-like or semi-god-like qualities; their struggles demand superhuman endurance or talent; their journeys are arduous; their battles are marked by dazzling bravery; the language is generally solemnly ceremonial; lofty comparisons abound. Everything is larger than life.

Epic Language and the Use of Epithets

Nothing could be grander than Milton's subject: the ultimate fate of mankind. The protagonists of the war in heaven are the archangels

Michael, Gabriel and Lucifer, the champions of good and evil, whose heroic exploits have an appropriate epic scale. Though Book 6 opens with a lesser figure, Abdiel, he too has epic status as 'the dreadless angel unpursu'd' (6.1) who journeys 'All night' (6.1) to reach heaven, and finds preparations for war already in progress. God's voice emerges from a 'Golden Cloud' (28) to despatch his generals in these terms:

> Goe Michael of Celestial Armies Prince,
> And thou in Military prowess next
> Gabriel, lead forth to Battel these my Sons
> Invincible.
>
> (6.44–7)

Here the characteristic use of apposition (Michael/prince, thou/next/Gabriel) enhances the angels' status; so does the insistence on power and greatness in the sequence 'celestial ... prowess ... invincible'. A little later, Satan confronts Abdiel with comparable power and grandeur:

> Satan with vast and haughtie strides advanc't,
> Came towring, armd in Adamant and Gold.
>
> (109–10)

Notice how Milton combines physical and psychological qualities in these lines: 'Vast and haughty' impresses us with the conviction of power, but reminds us also of Satan's flaw: his pride. The next adjective, 'towring', conveys both his monstrous size and his monstrous sin.

Often the epithets occupy the foreground. Milton dispenses with characters' names and refers to them by their distinctive qualities. Thus God is 'the Sovran voice' (56) and Satan 'the grand foe' (149). Notice too how the epic scale of the verse is strengthened by Milton's preference for inversions* of noun and adjective. 'Abdiel stern' is more impressive than 'stern Abdiel'; compare 'sons / Invincible' above, 'fight / Unspeakable' below, and countless other instances.

The epic purpose defines the style of the dialogue, too. When the characters speak, they speak formally. Every important action is matched by speech as well as narrative, and both forms are serious. Speech is ceremonial in style as well as content, so that each speech is introduced, and more often than not concluded, with a formal flourish. This, for example, is how Milton frames Abdiel's address to Satan:

> To whom in brief thus Abdiel stern repli'd:
> 'Apostat, still thou errst nor end wilt find
> Of erring ...
> This greeting on thy impious Crest receive.'
> So saying, a noble stroke he lifted high.
>
> (171–90)

Every detail here is designed to enhance the solemnity and impressiveness of the confrontation. Abdiel is 'stern' because he is on the side of right, and castigates Satan as the 'Apostat', 'impious', while he prepares an attack 'noble' in both its power and its justice; it is 'lifted high' morally as well as physically. The use of 'Crest' for helmet reminds us again, with its suggestion of flamboyant decoration, of Satan's essential flaw. All this is enhanced by the formal structure that encloses the speech in the emphatic 'thus ... repli'd' and 'So saying'. Adam and Eve, too, though human, share something of the same ceremonial style in their conversation.

The structure of these exchanges, like the frequent use of epithets, comes to Milton from his classical models. In Homer too, we find the formal speeches formally introduced. There too, the war of words is a conventional prelude to armed battle.

Milton's methods of presenting the protagonists of the drama are among many characteristics that *Paradise Lost* shares with the classical models. So also are his methods of representing battle; but as his subject exceeds the classical subjects in significance, so does his language. The syntax of *Paradise Lost* is characterised also by other kinds of inversions than the simple noun/adjective inversion that we looked at above. These stem from the classical languages, and add solemnity to the narrative. For example, the word order of 'a noble stroke he lifted high' (instead of 'he lifted a noble stroke high') focuses attention on 'noble' and 'high' and slows our reading. In the poem as a whole, Milton cultivates a deliberate awkwardness (in terms of modern English) of word order that he has learnt from Latin and Greek, and that suits his purpose by adding stateliness, and thus epic power, to his language.

We saw in Chapter 1 that the opening paragraph of the poem establishes a solemnity of style and subject that marks the whole. As the events of Book 6 unfold, Milton uses that portentous style to create a powerful impression of awe where cataclysmic conflicts shake the foundations of the universe. Book 6 is full of passages of arms in which the scale of events outdoes the classical models. In describing the early stages of the war in heaven, Milton piles epithet upon epithet in a strenuous endeavour to establish the terror of the conflict with its violence and clangorous noise: the 'ruinous assault' (216) and 'dire attack' (248) of the battling armies, the 'inextinguishable rage' (217) of the contestants; the heavens are filled with the sound of trumpets, the 'horrible discord' (210) of arms clashing on armour, 'the dismal hiss Of fiery Darts' (211–12). Then, as in the classical models, there is a pause to allow the protagonists, Michael and Satan, to exchange warlike taunts (262–95); Michael sneers at Satan as hitherto 'unknown ... unnamed' (262, 263); Satan dismisses Michael's challenge as empty boasting, as 'wind /Of airie threats' (282–3).

And now, what new drama can possibly follow? Far from attempting to redouble the vividness of his description of 'grim war' (236), Milton gives us this interesting passage:

> They ended parle, and both addrest for fight
> Unspeakable; for who, though with the tongue
> Of Angels, can relate, or to what things
> Liken on Earth conspicuous, that may lift
> Human imagination to such highth   300
> Of Godlike Power: for likest Gods they seemd,
> Stood they or mov'd, in stature, motion, arms
> Fit to decide the Empire of great Heav'n.
> Now wav'd thir fierie Swords, and in the Aire
> Made horrid Circles; two broad Suns thir Shields
> Blaz'd opposite, while expectation stood
> In horror; from each hand with speed retir'd
> Where erst was thickest fight, th' Angelic throng,
> And left large field, unsafe within the wind
> Of such commotion, such as to set forth   310
> Great things by small, If Natures concord broke,
> Among the Constellations warr were sprung,
> Two Planets rushing from aspect maligne

Of fiercest opposition in mid Skie,
Should combat, and thir jarring Sphears confound.

(6.297–315)

Here the clashing of vast armies gives way to the conflict of two individual angels. As in the classical epics, single duel can determine the
outcome of great struggles. The angels are rendered, however, in epic
perspective: they are huge and powerful.

How does Milton create the epic effect in this passage?

First, he communicates the sense of scale by means of simple
hyperbole*: the angels seemed 'likest gods' (302); their shields are
'Two broad suns' (305), while their 'fierie Swords' describe, with
their savage cuts, 'horrid Circles' (305) in the air – 'horrid' not as
a substitute for 'horrible', but because Milton, using the word in its
original Latin sense, wishes to suggest how the flames stand out from
the edges of the sword. The conflict is stupendous. Such the angelic
powers must be if the fate of the war in heaven is to depend on their
prowess; they must be seen to be 'Fit to decide the Empire of great
Heav'n' (303).

Next, Milton employs the personification* of 'expectation' (306)
to dramatise the emotional power of the battle. The use of the word
'stood' (306) suggests immobility – a paralysis with fear – and the emotive 'horror' (307) picks up the earlier 'horrid' with a new meaning.

Milton concludes the passage with a simile that compares the duel
of the angels with the collision and confounding of the crystalline
spheres in which, in mediaeval cosmology, the planets were fixed.[1]
The collision brings a physical, muscular shock – a 'jarring' of the
structure of the universe – but also has a metaphysical meaning: it
suggests a cosmic breaking of the natural order, a wounding of the
essence of nature.

In addition to his efforts to communicate the scale of the conflict,
then, Milton thinks on a deeper, moral level. The collision of planetary spheres can not happen: for such an event, the essential order of
the universe, 'Natures concord' (311) would first have to be broken.
But that, of course, is exactly what has happened in the angels' rebellion, which is contrary to every principle of nature as it is contrary to
every law of God. It is a 'maligne' event, something not only evil in
itself, but tending to generate evil.

A similar moral judgement is implied ironically earlier in the passage, when Milton questions who, even one blessed with 'the tongue of Angels' (297–8), can find a way to describe the nature of the cataclysm, for the choice of language here clearly reflects the biblical warning about charity:

> Though I speak with the tongues of men and of angels, and have not charity, I am become as sounding brass, or a tinkling cymbal.
>
> (1 Corinthians 13:1)

But here, Milton applies the words to a conflict instigated by Lucifer out of resentment, envy, and insolent ambition. *Caritas* (the word 'charity' in the King James version of the Bible that Milton would have known) does not mean charity in the current sense, but rather 'love', as more modern translations of the Bible tend to have it. Of course, Milton is also reminding us that these lines are spoken not by any human voice, but by the actual angelic voice of Raphael. But, more significantly, Milton here alters the stress of his narrative from its superficial features of grandeur and terror to its inner meaning; he focuses now on the moral enormity of the war in heaven rather than its physical dimension.

The other element that communicates the awe of the battle in these lines is Milton's acknowledgement of inadequacy. If even the tongue of an angel must fail to render the battle, what can a mere poet hope to achieve? The fight is 'unspeakable' (297) in more than one sense. Thus he must resort to the planetary simile, and even then admit that even this fails to capture actuality – is to compare 'Great things [with] small' (311). The human imagination, Milton tells us, cannot comprehend the stupendous nature of the event – to do so would be god-like.

In effect, Milton's final weapon is to give in. Here he pretends (in Raphael's voice) to throw down his tools. He has done all he can to describe the war in heaven, and realises that he has failed. The rest must be left to the imagination and empathy of his audience. (Inevitably, the confession of failure is yet another familiar convention in the epic writers' armoury.)

Though descriptively mere words must fail, yet on the conceptual level Milton maintains absolute control, touching here the springs of the whole poem. He presents the war in heaven as an offence against nature. In this context, the references to 'god-like' men and angels 'likest gods' remind us of the motive that Lucifer is moved by, and attempts to move Eve by. He wished to compete with God; and he tempts Eve by telling her that if she eats the fruit of the tree of knowledge of good and evil, she will become as a god herself; that, he suggests, is the real reason for God's prohibition.

The self-allusive feature of the language of this extract comes as close as a sequential medium can to a harmonic effect. Milton keeps before our imagination Satan's rebellion, his temptation of Eve, and Eve's Fall, while describing the war in heaven. The collation of disparate elements in this extract is no isolated instance. Throughout in the poem, Milton balances all the essential elements of the narrative against each other, constantly cross-referencing among events and times. The poem began in this way, as we saw in chapter 1. We shall see a similar effect when we come to discuss epic similes. Since all the events are contained in the casket of history, they may be seen as one. Chronology, it seems, is almost irrelevant when each event contains all the others.

Chronology

The chronology of the classical epics is conventional, but it is well recognised as one of their common features that they begin *in medias res* – that is, in the middle of things, when the action has already reached a critical point. *Paradise Lost*, in keeping with the general observation, begins after the fall of Lucifer, and plunges us in Book 1 into hell. But Milton goes much further than his classical models in rearranging the events of his basic story. Consider the following summary of the books of the poem in the light of their chronological order of their contents:

1. Satan in hell with his angels, immediately after their expulsion from heaven.
2. The council in hell; Satan makes across Chaos towards the new-created world.
3. God prophesies the Fall of Man, and the Son offers himself as man's salvation; Satan makes his way towards Eden.

4. Satan enters Eden, finds Adam and Eve, but is discovered and banished from Paradise.
5. Raphael warns Adam and Eve of their danger, and recounts to them the war in heaven.
6. Continuation and conclusion of Raphael's account of the war in heaven.
7. Raphael tells Adam about the Creation.
8. More about the Creation, and the origin of Adam and Eve.
9. Satan's return to Eden, and the Fall.
10. God's judgement; Adam and Eve recognise their new condition.
11. Michael comes to expel Adam and Eve from Paradise, and shows them the future of the human race.
12. Michael's revelations about the future continue, reaching the life of Jesus; he expels Adam and Eve from the Garden.

Thus the earliest events chronologically appear in books 5 and 6 and not at the beginning. Adam and Eve, the main focus of the epic, are not introduced until Book 4.

Looking at the organisation of the poem from a different point of view, we may record the rough chronology of events, and find a structure something like this:

The council in heaven	Book 6
The war in heaven	Books 5–6
The expulsion of Lucifer and the rebel angels from heaven	Book 6
Satan and the rebel angels in hell	Book 1
The creation of the world	Book 7
The creation of Adam and Eve	Book 8
The council in hell	Books 2–3
Satan enters Paradise	Book 4
The Fall	Book 9
God's judgement	Book 10
Expulsion from the Garden	Book 12
The future of the human race	Book 11

Clearly Milton's intention is not to stress the sequence of events. Instead, using flashbacks and reported events, Milton focuses attention on the meaning of the events, on their pattern. In particular, he succeeds in containing all the events of the poem within two parallel expulsions: the expulsion of Satan from heaven, and the expulsion of Adam and Eve from the Garden of Eden.

If we consider the chronology in more detail, still more dislocation becomes speedily apparent. For example, the subject of the creation of Adam and Eve appears in books 4 and 8, interspersed with other material; Satan's first incursions into Paradise appear in books 2, 3 and 4 interspersed with other material.

If we look at references to events (as distinct from descriptions of events), we reach a yet deeper level of chronological confusion. We noticed in chapter 1 that the opening paragraph of the poem already looks forward beyond the fall of Lucifer, beyond the Fall of Adam and Eve, beyond the prophets and beyond the life of Christ to the promise of redemption in death and resurrection of the Saviour, which does not actually occur until *Paradise Regained*.

This anti-chronological sequence is typical of Milton's epic structure. Epic does not offer surprising twists, or intriguing mysteries, or psychological analysis: it gives us the sweep of great events already known, a celebration of a familiar pattern. Thus Milton has no secrets to keep at the beginning of the poem. His intention is to offer an interpretation of events thoroughly known, commented on, and analysed. His poem opens not merely *in medias res*, but *sub specie aeternitatis* (from the perspective of eternity): all the events of the poem are already known as they have been known in the inclusive consciousness of the Creator, from the beginning of time. The Fall of Man was already known to God before Lucifer rebelled. It is as if time is short-circuited. In this poem Milton offers us as it were a God's eye-view of the history of the world in which all events are eternally present.

Epic Similes

All the features of *Paradise Lost* that we have considered in this chapter fall together in our next topic: Milton's epic similes. The epic simile is so called because it is inherited from the classical epics of Homer; it also has epic proportions. Essentially, an epic simile is distinguished by its formal structure – it usually begins with a phrase like 'as when' to introduce the comparisons, and concludes equally formally with a 'so' to return to the main subject; it is extended, often to many lines; and the comparisons are elaborated, temporarily occupying the foreground of our attention. In the hands of Milton the epic simile flowers into something extraordinary. In *Paradise Lost*, most of the epic similes occur in the earlier books, especially in Book 1; most frequently, they relate to Satan. We will consider two examples, beginning with this, the first of the epic similes:

> Thus Satan talking to his neerest Mate
> With Head up-lift above the wave, and Eyes
> That sparkling blaz'd, his other Parts besides
> Prone on the Flood, extended long and large
> Lay floating many a rood, in bulk as huge
> As whom the Fables name of monstrous size,
> Titanian, or Earth-born, that warr'd on Jove,
> Briarios or Typhon, whom the Den
> By ancient Tarsus held, or that Sea-beast   200
> Leviathan, which God of all his works
> Created hugest that swim th' Ocean stream:
> Him haply slumbring on the Norway foam
> The Pilot of some small night-founder'd Skiff,
> Deeming some Island, oft, as Sea-men tell,
> With fixed Anchor in his skaly rind
> Moors by his side under the Lee, while Night
> Invests the Sea, and wished Morn delayes:
> So stretcht out huge in length the Arch-fiend lay
> Chain'd on the burning Lake, nor ever thence   210
> Had ris'n or heav'd his head, but that the will
> And high permission of all-ruling Heaven
> Left him at large to his own dark designs,
> That with reiterated crimes he might
> Heap on himself damnation, while he sought
> Evil to others, and enrag'd might see
> How all his malice serv'd but to bring forth
> Infinite goodness, grace and mercy shewn
> On Man by him seduc't, but on himself
> Treble confusion, wrath and vengeance pour'd.   220
>   (1.192–220)

The passage occurs immediately after the first dialogue in the poem, when Beelzebub and Satan, driven out of heaven and cast down upon the lake formed from the thunderous storm that followed them, consider their desperate plight. Though vanquished, Satan remains defiant, and will soon rear himself up from the waters to rally his cohorts and begin the work of reconstruction. Here, however, Milton pauses to consider the awesome state to which he has been reduced.

Let us begin by analysing the structure of the passage as simply as possible:

1. The first sentence (192–5) acts as an end-stop to Satan's speech to Beelzebub, his 'neerest' companion – whether in physical proximity or in likeness of character is unclear – and establishes, in the 'Head up-lift' and the blazing eye, that Satan's defeat has rendered him angry and rebellious rather than disheartened.
2. There follows a statement of Satan's vastness: his 'other parts' sprawl over the waters larger than the famous monsters of legend (194–7).
3. Then Milton deploys (198–202) two comparisons that form the content of the epic simile: the war of the Titans (including Briareos and the giant Typhon) against Jove; and the sea monster, Leviathan – the whale.
4. While the first comparison goes undeveloped, the second is amplified over the next six lines in which Milton alludes to stories of seamen of small craft anchoring at the side of a whale that they mistake for an island (203–8).
5. The simile concludes (209–10) by reaffirming the subject in the sentence beginning 'So'.
6. Finally, I have appended for the sake of the context, Milton's warning that it is only with the permission of God that Satan is able to restore his powers.

The complexity of the simile is already apparent from this brief summary. We can now go on to explore its purpose and effect.

Clearly, much of the point of the simile is to deepen our impression of its root topic, Satan himself. The direct description focuses on three features of Satan. It insists on his bulk, alliteratively in 'extended long and large', and repetitively in 'huge...hugest...stretched out huge in length' (196, 202, 209) and 'monstrous'. The extremity to which he is reduced appears in the paradoxical* identity of water and fire: Satan, 'Chain'd on the burning lake', has eyes blazing defiance. Finally, the enormous effort of rallying his crushed followers after their defeat – all the more dreadful because of his greatness – is symbolised in another alliterative phrase, 'heaved his head' which suggests that only with a great, even heroic, effort of his own will, can he raise even his head from the burning lake.

Part of the effect of these comparisons is to emphasise the sheer magnitude of Satan. Size is part of the conventional power of the heroic figures of epic; Satan, fittingly, is preternaturally huge. He exceeds in size the Titans, represented by Briareos, and their allies the Giants, represented by Typhon; and, of course, he is greater than the Leviathan. Part of the purpose of the extension of the simile of the sea-pilot who mistakenly anchors for the night at the side of a whale in Norwegian waters is to stress the extraordinary size of the monster, and therefore the yet greater magnitude of Satan.

There is, however, much more to this simile than the obvious point of Satan's physical impressiveness. Milton also stresses the moral significance of Satan by placing him in a multiple historical perspective, referring to classical mythology, the Hebraic tradition, and Renaissance experience. Specifically, the rebellion of the Titans and Giants against the Olympian gods is a clear parallel in classical mythology for Satan's rebellion against God; the reference to the Leviathan recalls references in the Old Testament books of Job and Isaiah; and the digression on the Norwegian whales brings us forward to the Renaissance world of exploration and trade. Thus, in this epic simile Milton reflects the anti-chronological organisation of the whole poem: the story of Satan and his rebellion absorbs human experience up to Milton's own era.

The Leviathan has a further significance. Though Milton moves on to speak of whales in the Norwegian seas, the adjective 'monstrous' and the reference to the Leviathan as a 'sea-beast' point to a much less prosaic significance. The description of the Leviathan in Job, Chapter 41 suggests a mythical beast of gigantic proportions, and no mere whale. Isaiah is more pointed:

> ... the Lord with his sore and great and strong sword shall punish leviathan the piercing serpent, even leviathan that crooked serpent; and he shall slay the dragon that is in the sea.
>
> (Isaiah 27.1)

We may see this as a hint of the future embodiment of Satan as a serpent or dragon, one of 'crooked' intent. This image is a foretaste of the insistent themes of deceitfulness or straying represented in a sustained imagery of serpentine sinuousness, twisting, error, meandering and wandering that dominates much of the poem.

For some readers this simile, in depicting a relatively peaceful episode of seafaring life, contrasts dramatically with the description of the physical and metaphysical horrors of hell that immediately precedes it. The reader is permitted, as it were, to take a breath of fresh air before submerging once again in the infernal element. At the same time, Milton underlines the drama and significance of his transcendental theme by contrasting it with the mundane life of the seafarer going about his ordinary business, who to this extent stands for all of us, unaware of the turmoil of preternatural history. For others, anxiety is the keynote. The night is a time of tension and uncertainty, drawn out psychologically by longing for the break of day. From this point of view, the seafarer's safe harbour is a dangerous delusion; at any moment, his apparently secure island anchorage my capsize him with a casual flick of its tail and smash him and his vessel to pieces. We may see in it a precursor of Eve's innocence in trusting the superficial attractiveness of Satan when he appears before her in the Garden of Eden (Book 9). Neither seaman nor Eve has any inkling of the fragility of their position: for both of them, a calm surface conceals undreamt depths of peril.

Evidently, Milton's use of the extended simile has a range of purposes. Taking the device from his classical models, Milton inhabits it with a wealth of meaning. In the example we have discussed, the components of the simile add dramatic power and vivid image to the narrative, making it more readily comprehensible, and at the same time deepen the historical, moral and thematic significance of the events. There is a similar depth in many other examples of the epic simile, and indeed similar kinds of imagery recur in them frequently.

Let us turn to our second example of the epic simile, which occurs a little later in Book 1 after Beelzebub speaks of the task of reviving the stunned company of the fallen angels. The setting is the same as in the first example, but there are more similarities than that between the two examples:

> He scarce had ceas't when the superiour Fiend
> Was moving toward the shore; his ponderous shield

Ethereal temper, massy, large and round,
Behind him cast; the broad circumference
Hung on his shoulders like the Moon, whose Orb
Through Optic Glass the Tuscan Artist views
At Ev'ning from the top of Fesole,
Or in Valdarno, to descry new Lands,   290
Rivers or Mountains in her spotty Globe.
His Spear, to equal which the tallest Pine
Hewn on Norwegian hills, to be the Mast
Of some great Ammiral, were but a wand,
He walkt with to support uneasie steps
Over the burning Marle, not like those steps
On Heavens Azure, and the torrid Clime
Smote on him sore besides, vaulted with Fire;
Knotholes he so endur'd, till on the Beach
Of that inflamed Sea, he stood and call'd   300
His Legions, Angel Forms, who lay intrans't
Thick as Autumnal Leaves that strow the Brooks
In Vallombrosa, where th' Etrurian shades
High overarch't imbowr; or scatterd sedge
Afloat, when with fierce Winds Orion arm'd
Hath vext the Red-Sea Coast, whose waves orethrew
Busiris and his Memphian Chivalrie,
While with perfidious hatred they pursu'd
The Sojourners of Goshen, who beheld
From the safe shore their floating Carkases   310
And broken Chariot Wheels, so thick bestrown
Abject and lost lay these, covering the Flood,
Under amazement of their hideous change.

                                        (1.283–313)

Since the context is almost the same as in the first example, we will proceed at once to the second part of the analytical process and summarise the components of the passage. This passage contains three epic similes. In the first, Milton compares of Satan's shield with the moon (286-91); next, he compares Satan's spear with the mast of an admiral's flagship (292–4); finally, he compares the fallen angels with the fallen leaves of autumn or uprooted reeds floating on a river or fallen soldiers (301-11).

All three of the similes support the heroic theme. The first emphasises the size of Satan's moon-like shield, which is of supernatural strength ('Ethereal temper') and great weight ('ponderous' and 'massy'); the second stresses the length of his spear, infinitely greater than the tallest Norwegian pine; and the third shows the numberless infinity of the defeated army of rebel angels, fallen physically like leaves, but also fallen morally. The setting, as in the first example, is vivid: there is a brilliant brassy yellow in the shield/moon, contrasting with the dull reds, browns and yellows of dead leaves, the burning of the dark waters 'inflamed' and their shore of 'burning Marle', the dramatic shadows ('Vallombrosa' describes a shaded valley), the whole canopied by a searing vault of fire. The scene suggests the aftermath of violent conflict: Satan's shield is on his back for retreat, and the angels are like the carcases of those slain in war. Satan, having gathered himself by force of will from the lake, makes his way, enduring the pain of the fiery environment, with 'uneasie steps' to the shore, where he stands and summons his followers. Endurance, indeed, is the key to Satan's state at this point: in pain, with the wreckage of his ambitions around him, he is defeated but as yet unbowed. Reference is made to the 'hideous change' in his state and that of his followers – how different his steps here are from those he strode in 'Heavens Azure' – yet he is already bent on continuing the struggle. Though he is carefully introduced here with oxymoronic* humour as 'the superiour Fiend', Satan's bravado nevertheless strikes a chord with readers.

In aggrandising Satan, and in other ways, too, this example matches the first. (The repetition of the references to Norway/Norwegian is incidental, and there are no other such references in *Paradise Lost*.) As in the first example, Milton suggests the imperfection of Satan. Here his shield resembles the moon: the romantic perfection associated with the moon in the songs of poets is revealed by Galileo's telescope to be illusion; it is now a 'spotty Globe', symbolising the flaws in Satan. Similarly, Satan, supporting himself on his spear, may suggest to us the frailty of age as easily as the grandeur of his scale.

As in the first example, too, and as frequently elsewhere in the poem, Milton alludes to different eras and different cultures.

The earliest of these cultures is classical: the pre-Roman Etruscan culture based in Etruria. The symbolism of leaves came directly from classical sources, being familiar to Milton from the *Iliad* and the *Aeneid*, whence Dante had borrowed it for the *Inferno*. The image of the shield also appears in the *Iliad* (wherein the shield of Achilles is compared with the moon) and in the *Aeneid*. The range of reference in the passage from *Paradise Lost* is, however, much wider and more varied, partly for necessary historical reasons, than in its classical and Renaissance precursors, who had a less extensive perspective to draw on.

The Hebraic tradition appears here, too, with the reference to Exodus 21–31. Busiris was the tyrannical Pharaoh whose Egyptian armies pursued the Israelites from their homeland in Goshen until they made their escape across the Red Sea which, its waters having parted to allow their passage, closed again to swallow up the 'Memphian Chivalrie'. (The oddly anachronistic-sounding 'Chivalrie' may be taken to mean the Egyptian cavalry or chariots.) Here, fittingly, Milton chooses to remind us of the real nature of the Satanic order by associating it with a nation of oppressors led by a tyrant – a useful corrective to the powerful impression Satan gives.

Both these traditions – the Etruscan and the Hebraic – are associated with the figure of the giant Orion. In classical mythology, he is usually represented as a hunter armed with a sword. The constellation named after him also appears in the Bible.

Milton's reference to the Renaissance world is much broader here than in our first example. As we have just noted, Dante is one of the sources for the symbolism of dead leaves. Much more significant, however, is the discussion of the 'optic glass', the telescope developed by Galileo, the 'Tuscan artist' who lived in Fiesole above the valley of the Arno ('Valdarno') near Florence. It is hard to see Galileo as a parallel for Satan, despite – or perhaps, in view of Milton's Puritan sympathies, because of – his dispute with the Catholic authorities. Rather, Galileo represents the freedom of thought that was an essential element of the Renaissance world. Thus we can sense delight in the principle of discovery when Milton speaks of the technology that enables us to 'descry new lands'.

In contrast with that mood of intellectual excitement, the images associated with Satan and his crew are either of destructive power (fire and armaments), or death. The fallen angels are compared with dead leaves, or with the uprooted vegetation floating on the Red Sea; there is a sense here of Satan as the harbinger of the death of the natural world.

The ideas that emerge in these examples of the epic simile recur elsewhere in the poem, and you will meet them in your study of some of the other similes suggested in the Further Work section of this chapter. The sea and sailors reappear in 2.288, 4.159, and 9.513. Fire recurs frequently associated with Satan, whose turbulent nature finds expression in the imagery of a volcano (1.233) or gunpowder (4.815). Even the Tuscan artist, Galileo, appears again, in 5.262. Another interesting strand of imagery is the sequence Milton uses in the course of the narrative to describe rebel angels, who are variously leaves, dead soldiers, locusts, barbarians, engineers, bees and pygmies among other things.

We have spent a great deal of time discussing the thematic ideas that emerge from these epic similes. Equally important, however, is Milton's dramatic realisation of the events. Satan is no mere idea. We see his eyes blazing with defeated fury; we are made to feel the torpor of his long limbs as he lies 'chain'd on the burning Lake' (210); we feel with him as he heaves his huge head from the water, draws himself up, and, gathering up his massive shield, the symbol of his will to fight on, strides over the burning marl to reach the shore. We hear him discussing his plight with Beelzebub and calling his legions to defiance. We feel the weight of his shield in the incremental vowel sounds in 'massy, large, and round' (285) and in the tactile way it 'Hung on his shoulders' (287). The painfulness of his situation is stressed: the intolerable heat of his fiery new home 'Smote on him sore besides' (298), striking us more powerfully because of the reversal of the opening foot of the line. Another reversal stresses the number of fallen angels 'Thick as autumnal leaves' (302). The fires of hell seem harsher because of the dramatic contrast with 'th' Etrurian shades' of Vallombrosa (303) – and they shortly give way to the violent storms of Orion.

Milton's effort then, is not merely to argue a case – to justify the ways of God to men – but to make us feel the emotional and moral power of the conflict he envisages in a dramatic realisation. His approach to epic brings all human experience – Classical, Hebraic, Christian, and Renaissance – to bear upon his subject. The result is language used in a style comparable to harmony in music. At any given moment, Milton constantly reminds us of what came before and after the events he describes, of the undertones and parallels that give the events depth and significance. Sometimes this harmonisation takes the form of epithets that recall the meaning of a character or situation – so that Satan is the 'Apostat' (6.172 and elsewhere) or 'the Arch-fiend' (1.156, 209), for example – and sometimes it takes the form of an epic simile such as those we have discussed.

The Dissimile

The harmonic tone of the epic simile sometimes takes the form of a dissimile* – that is, a negative simile. There is a brief example above, where Milton compares Satan's experience in hell with his experience in heaven, saying that his steps on the burning lake were 'not like those steps / On Heavens Azure' (1.296–7). Sometimes, however, the dissimile can approach epic form, for instance in Milton's hymn to wedded love. When Adam and Eve retire to their bower, Milton stresses the purity of their love in these negative terms:

> Here Love his golden shafts imploies, here lights
> His constant Lamp, and waves his purple wings,
> Reigns here and revels; not in the bought smile
> Of Harlots, loveless, joyless, unindeard,
> Casual fruition, nor in Court Amours
> Mixt Dance, or wanton Mask, or Midnight Bal,
> Or Serenate, which the starv'd Lover sings
> To his proud fair, best quitted with disdain.   770
> These lulld by Nightingales imbraceing slept,
> And on thir naked limbs the flourie roof
> Showrd Roses, which the Morn repair'd.
>
> (4.763–73)

Here Milton brings out the ideal nature of the relationship between Adam and Eve positively with the personification of love in the first line recalling the image of Cupid and his arrows ('shafts'), with the image of light from a 'constant' (that is, undying, not faithless) lamp, and with the rich colour and implication of value in the imagery of gold and purple. Repeated liquid consonants ('Love ... imploies ... lights ... Lamp ... purple ... Reigns ... revels') help to suggest ease and pleasure. At the end of the extract, we move towards

morning with the song of the nightingale, the implied scent and colour of roses, and the ever-renewed 'flourie roof' beneath which the
lovers shelter. Milton does not, of course, show us the sexual congress of Adam and Eve. The extract we are considering forms part
of an extended ellipsis* that draws a metaphorical veil over their
love-making.

The contrasting dissimile forms the texture of that veil. Milton
takes the opportunity to revile the evils of sexual behaviour as he sees
it expressed in his own time. He condemns the forms that encourage promiscuity: dancing, serenading, masques and balls. He takes
special notice of the 'court Amours' that he thinks of as one of the
evils attending monarchy. And he focuses especially on the convention of courtly love, symbolised in the 'starv'd Lover' singing to his
'proud' mistress, and ironically ending with the recommendation of
'disdain' – a word closely associated with the manner of the mistress
in courtly love. Here Milton contrasts the corrupt music of his world
with the natural song of the nightingale, and speaks contemptuously
of the 'bought' smile of the harlot, for whom sex is contaminated by
cash. Notice, too, how the mellifluous phrasing of Milton's description of the love of Adam and Eve modulates to disjointedness and
irregularity in the rhythm of 'bought smile / Of Harlots, loveless, joy-
less, unindeard, / Casual fruition' (765–7).

In this instance, then, as in the epic similes we considered above,
Milton uses comparison not simply to illuminate the nature of his
subject, but also to place it in the perspective of his own time and
experience. At times there is an implied dissimile that has a comparable effect, as when Milton speaks of the fruit of the trees of Eden
as 'Hesperian Fables true, / If true, here onely' (4.250–1): these fruits
are not like the golden apples of the Hesperides, because those are
only legend, and could only become real here in Eden. The dissimile,
like the epic simile, contributes to the harmonic nature of Milton's
language; he uses it to draw parallels or contrasts with the classical and
Renaissance worlds.

The dissimile is crucial to the descriptions of Adam, Eve, and
Paradise. Since Milton is there describing perfection, the only parallels he can conveniently make with the world of actual human experience must be by way of contrast: he can only describe the ideal by
saying what it is *not* like.

The Pun and the Anti-pun

A related feature of the poem is Milton's use of the pun and, more pertinently, the negative pun. The best example of the pun is the most obvious – the pun on 'Eve' and 'evil'. We can find it when Eve reaches out 'in evil hour' (9.780) for the forbidden fruit, and Adam stresses it when he bewails her error in 'O Eve, in evil hour didst thou give care / To that false Worm' (9.1068-9).

However, it is the anti-pun – those cases where Milton excludes alternative meanings – that shows the harmonic nature of the poem. We may illustrate the device by reference to the extract above, which refers to the fashion for the 'wanton Mask' (4.678) – those entertainments in which the dancers wore masks to conceal their identity and so get away with behaviour that would otherwise be considered, at the least, unbecoming. There 'wanton' means promiscuous. However, the word has more than one meaning. Eve's hair also is described as falling 'in wanton ringlets' (4.306), and part of Adam's job is to control the 'wanton growth' (4.629) of the trees of Paradise. In these examples, 'wanton' means 'naturally abundant' rather than 'promiscuous'; nevertheless, in our fallen minds, the word retains its negative associations. Later, in Book 9, wanton regains its negative meaning of corrupt disorder when Satan appears before Eve curling 'many a wanton wreath' (9.517), and after the Fall, the relationship of Adam and Eve changes so that 'hee on Eve / Began to cast lascivious Eyes, she him / As wantonly repaid' (9.1013-15).

Similar complexities of meaning attend language associated with wandering, meandering, and erring. Milton often uses in a specific sense a word that resonates for us with contrary senses. Thus the language of the poem has in itself an epic dimension, embracing contraries, and containing both the ideal and fallen worlds in one harmonic structure.

Conclusions

- The epic structure of *Paradise Lost* is based on classical models: the *Iliad* and *Odyssey* of Homer, and on Virgil's *Aeneid* in particular.
- Scale is essential to epic. Milton goes beyond the classical authors in emphasising the size, strength, and moral power of the characters.

- Milton's poem, like the classical epics, deals with known public and historical events with known outcomes.
- The narrative has large significance: Milton's subject is even greater than those of the classical writers.
- Milton follows the classical writers in applying a range of descriptive epithets to the characters, emphasising either their qualities or their role in the narrative.
- Milton uses classical syntax that enhances the ceremonial tone of the poem.
- As in the classical epics, the universal conflict depends on the individual battles of heroic protagonists.
- Epic traditionally begins when the action is already approaching the climactic point. Milton follows the tradition, but goes further by adopting an anachronological form, stressing the dramatic themes of the narrative.
- Milton's use of the epic simile embodies in miniature many of the features of epic in general, containing a wide range of reference to different times and situations.
- Other features of Milton's language, such as the dissimile and the anti-pun, enhance the range of reference of the poem.
- These features of style are not distributed evenly through the poem: Milton's 'answerable style' varies with his subject matter.
- Milton's language often plays upon the difference between contemporary and etymological meanings of words, or on other semantic ambiguities.
- The focus of *Paradise Lost* is on the eternal significance of the action: the poem is a celebration of God's providence, as the opening address claims.

Methods of Analysis

As a preliminary, let us recall the importance of reading and re-reading to ensure that we understand the meaning and rhythm of the passage for analysis, as explained in chapter 1.

- As a preliminary, in your own analysis, you really do have to read the notes the editor of your edition has provided. You may also find it necessary to consult other sources to discover the significance of the proper nouns Milton uses.

- The next step is to mark the structure of the passage, as we have done in our analysis, noting where each logical unit begins and ends, and summarising its content.

- Then we examine each unit, considering its language carefully, and paying particular attention to any elements of vocabulary, imagery, or syntax that appear in any way noteworthy. (Some of these points we will not pay attention to in the end; but we have to know what we are dealing with before we can decide to ignore it. For example, consider the word 'rood' in the first of the epic similes we discussed above. We recall or discover that it is an archaic measure of distance or size, and also that it is an archaic word for the cross on which the Saviour was crucified. However, we can conclude that the second meaning is here irrelevant, and that nothing is to be gained from discussing this element of vocabulary. Nevertheless, the decision to ignore it is a positive decision that has to be taken, and is worth taking trouble to make.)

- Remember that the sound of the language can affect meaning. Look carefully at instances of rhyme, assonance and alliteration particularly, as probably the most important among a range of auditory effects.

- The language often has different layers of meaning. Think about whether Milton speaks in a direct and simple, or a more elaborate, Latinate style. Notice examples of ellipsis, which is common in *Paradise Lost*, and consider its effect in complicating or simplifying meaning.

- Then we move on to the synthetic stage of discussion: we look for significant links, both stylistic and thematic, among the components.

- The final stage of discussion of the extract is to relate the passage to the poem as a whole together with its characters and themes to show how it reflects or contrasts with other parts of the poem. Does our analysis alter our perception of the poem as a whole?

- Remember that it is not essential to find something of note in every word and phrase, and that there is not necessarily anything there to be found: you have to use your own judgement.

Further Work

Select one or two other epic similes for close analysis. Below are some suggestions.

In the case of each example below, treat the comparisons in turn, and then think about the impression Milton is creating. Take into account the imagery employed, the sound of the language, and the meanings (possibly more than one) of the words used. Then think about what the whole extract contributes to the portrait of its subject in the poem as a whole, and how the subject relates to other thematic and dramatic aspects of the poem.

- Book 1, 331–55 ('They heard, and were abasht ... Gibraltar to the Lybian sands'). This is a group of similes describing the fallen angels.
- Book 1, 759–88 ('they anon ... with joy and fear his heart rebounds'). This group also describes the fallen angels. Explore each comparison, and then consider the links among them, and the effect they create together.
- Book 2, 528–46 ('Part on the Plain ... Into th' Euboic Sea'). Milton describes the angels practising feats of arms.
- Book 4, 180–93 ('Due entrance he disdained ... into his Church lewd Hirelings climbe'). This series of comparisons describes Satan. Consider the emotional effect of each comparison, and the appeal Milton makes to the senses.
- Book 4, 264–87. ('The Birds thir quire apply ... Creatures new to sight and strange'). Consider the implication of the comparisons, and comment on the point of view that dominates in this passage. There is a fine example of the dissimile here, too.

As an alternative, consider a number of briefer examples taken from the following list. One of the ways you might treat them is to choose two or three that illustrate a strand of imagery such as those mentioned at the end of our discussion above.

Book 1. 235–8, 589–600, 611–15, 674–8, 705–16
Book 2. 284–94, 486–95, 587–94
Book 3. 430–41, 566–71, 540–4, 613–23

Book 4. 15–18, 497–502, 813–19, 977–89
Book 5. 15–18, 257–66
Book 6. 71–6
Book 9. 510–18, 631–45, 666–78
Book 10. 209–19, 272–81, 285–93, 293–8, 927–41
Book 11. 754–62

In each example you choose, take care to analyse the components of the simile and understand its grammatical structure. Only then go on to think about the implications of the comparison, and how (or if) it relates to the other examples you have selected. Consider the appeal it makes to the senses, what ideas it generates, how it develops the character(s) described, and how it contributes to the themes of the poem.

3

God, His Son, and the Realms of Light

Book 3. 56–79 ('Now had the Almighty Father ... foreseeing spake')
Book 6. 824–66 ('So spake the Son ... Burnt after them to the bottomless pit')
Book 7. 192–220 ('So sang the Hierarchies ... and the World unborn')
Book 5. 616–38 ('So spake th' Omnipotent ... rejoycing in thir joy')

In this chapter we begin by considering Milton's treatment of God, his Son, the good angels, and their heavenly abode. The extracts we choose will touch on all these aspects of the celestial world Milton describes and will raise questions about the relationship between God and his Son, between God and Satan, between the Son and Satan, and, most pointedly, between God and his first created human beings. In presenting these elements in the poem, Milton faced a variety of difficulties, literary, moral, and theological.

Almighty, eternal, omniscient, Creator, Author ... God's attributes are reverentially addressed by the Son in these lines from Book 6:

> O Father, O Supream of heav'nly Thrones,
> First, Highest, Holiest, Best ...
>
> (6.723-4)

How can a mere mortal such as John Milton hope to represent an entity definable only by absolutes and capital letters? Leaving aside the sheer audacity of the attempt to represent the infinite, the problems that confront the artist are both ideological and practical. Put at its simplest: how can he hope to get the picture right, and are the tools of his mortal's mind adequate to the task?

As we saw in Chapter 1, Milton, all too aware of his practical deficiencies, seeks at the outset of his project the help of divine inspiration. Thereafter, he delays his attempt to represent God directly until Book 3 of the poem, after the description of the fall of Satan and the other rebel angels. Thus God's power and supremacy are already established before we meet him. Milton delays the meeting still further by opening Book 3, like the first, with an invocation in which he again asks for inspiration, for divine light to illuminate his darkness.

Milton's ideological problems are of his time. The Renaissance names a period marked by the development of new learning and, with it, new beliefs and moral perspectives: but it did not forget the older perspectives. Thus Milton inherits the bones of the heavenly environment from an earlier era. His vision of the actuality of God and the angels and heaven derives from a Mediterranean, mediaeval theology; the mediaeval theologians in particular concerned themselves greatly with, as it were, the natural history of the divine world.[1] Milton's moral vision, however, derives from a much later era, from the northern, Lutheran ideology. From this contradiction there grows an interesting variety and complexity in Milton's vision.

God

When at last God appears in person, it is with direct simplicity. Milton solves his problem, as a Renaissance man, a humanist, must: he recreates God in the image of Man. Milton gives him a location and a throne, a voice, eyes and opinions; he also gives him emotions. Let us explore how Milton first depicts God towards the beginning of Book 3:

> Now had the Almighty Father from above,
> From the pure Empyrean where he sits
> High Thron'd above all highth, bent down his eye,
> His own works and their works at once to view:
> About him all the Sanctities of Heaven   60

> Stood thick as Starrs, and from his sight receiv'd
> Beatitude past utterance; on his right
> The radiant image of his Glory sat,
> His onely Son; On Earth he first beheld
> Our two first Parents, yet the onely two
> Of mankind, in the happie Garden plac't,
> Reaping immortal fruits of joy and love,
> Uninterrupted joy, unrivald love
> In blissful solitude; he then survey'd
> Hell and the Gulf between, and Satan there   70
> Coasting the wall of Heav'n on this side Night
> In the dun Air sublime, and ready now
> To stoop with wearied wings, and willing feet
> On the bare outside of this World, that seem'd
> Firm land imbosom'd without Firmament,
> Uncertain which, in Ocean or in Air.
> Him God beholding from his prospect high,
> Wherein past, present, future he beholds,
> Thus to his onely Son foreseeing spake.
>
> (3.56–79)

This passage, which immediately follows the invocation in which Milton asks for spiritual enlightenment to tell of things 'invisible to mortal sight' (56), at once establishes God's authority as he considers the whole of his creation in its various forms. It is God's perceptions that determine the form of the extract, and it is with its form that our analysis should begin.

The passage divides structurally into four logical sections each containing distinctive material:

1. Milton describes God enthroned in his ethereal realm. The 'pure Empyrean' is a classical conception of the rarefied atmosphere of a superhuman layer of reality. At his right hand sits the Son, according to biblical authority. About him are the angels and other heavenly entities, collated as 'all the Sanctities of Heaven'. 'Sanctities' is variously interpreted in details, but generally refers to holy entities (56–64).
2. God looks upon Adam and Eve, happy in their innocent state, immortal and blissful in the Garden of Eden (64–9).

3. God sees hell, and sees Satan, having made the journey through chaos from hell, about to alight on the half-lit outer margin of heaven, before setting off on his journey towards Paradise (69–76).
4. The all-inclusiveness of God's vision, both spatial and temporal, is established immediately before he addresses the Son (77–9).

There is no attempt here to describe God: all the material inhabits God's point of view, reporting his world, what he sees, and what he is about to say. What Milton focuses on is not a physical reality, but a quality of existence and faculty of vision.

Let us try to define the quality of existence Milton brings before us. The region is the 'pure Empyrean' – quite simply, the most exalted and refined stratum of the heavenly world, often thought of as a realm of pure light. This aspect of God's abode is reflected, fittingly, in the reference to the Son as the 'radiant image of [God's] Glory' (63). No more is directly said at this stage of the light of heaven, but what there is gains by contrast with the gloom of Satan's journey, dominated as it is by the references to the 'dun [dark or murky] air' (72) and night. The dominant quality of heaven, however, rather than light, is height. God is the 'Almighty Father from *above*' (56) who '*High* Thron'd above all *highth*...bent *down* his eye' (58) and at the end of the extract speaks to the Son 'from his prospect *high*' (77). Such emphasis points to more than cosmological height: God is the superior being in every sense. Beyond these non-specific indications, there is very little other description. We have impressions of numbers of other heavenly beings, 'Sanctities...thick as Starrs' (60–1) that 'Stood' (61) as if thronging the throne of God, from seeing whom they receive 'Beatitude' (62) – a general word betokening blessings. (With characteristic economy, Milton uses the phrase 'His sight' here to mean the angels' sight of God; you may like to consider, by the way, why 'seeing him' would not do, even if it fitted in metrically.) None of this is specific, and for the very good reason that the actuality of the bliss of heaven is literally 'past utterance' (62) – not susceptible to description. Thus, although Milton treats God as if he were any character in the drama, he does so by means of general impression. He avoids impropriety or bathos* by inviting the reader's imagination to work on hints: the reader is allowed to create God in his own image.

The Son, likewise, is not described. We know that he sits at the right hand of his Father, but beyond that we are again given only impressions: the power and authority of his position, and his radiance, the reflection of God's own radiance.

In the second part of the extract Milton offers a parallel vision of bliss in a vignette of Adam and Eve in the garden of Eden. Their solitude is 'blissful' (69), their garden is 'happy' (66). ('Happy', incidentally, is a transferred* epithet, and illustrates Milton's freedom with language: it is actually Adam and Eve who are happy, not the garden.) Milton elides their physical work, their immortality and their emotional state when he speaks of their 'Reaping immortal fruits of joy and love' (67): the tilling of the soil to eat its fruits mirrors their mutual love and respect. But this is a lesser ideal than heaven. Their 'solitude', joyous though it is, can hardly match the angel-crowded fields of heaven. More significantly, their joy already exhibits warnings of its end. Milton's introduction of Adam and Eve as 'Our two first parents' (65) stresses their importance but also reminds us of the history of mankind fallen – including them and their offspring. Furthermore, the seemingly intensive repetition in '*joy* and *love* / Uninterrupted *joy*, unrivalled *love*' (67–8) with its emphatic repeated negatives presents the pair as enjoying unalloyed happiness; yet also implies the possibility of interruption and rivalry; specifically, the line looks forward to the termination of their joyful immortality by sin, and the interpolation of Satan into their mutual regard. From God's standpoint, as from ours, the end of the story is already known.

It is a natural progression to move from Eden to Satan. The mood of the verse changes: from light to dark, from delight to pain, from society to solitude; from the happy host of angels to the tortured foe of mankind on his solitary quest. Satan does not stride majestically here: he slinks, 'Coasting' (71) the border of heaven. Associated with darkness – 'Night' and 'dun' (71, 72) – Satan shows none of the confidence of the angels and the human characters. The alliteration of 'wearied wings and willing feet' (73) emphasises his desperate condition, and the use of the word 'stoop' (73) to describe his movement suggests his menacing behaviour and evil intent: the word means the swooping of a bird of prey to capture its kill, but it also suggests moral inferiority and the doing of evil. The archetypal outcast, he is restricted to the 'bare outside' (74) of heaven, and is destined never to regain his place there. Indeed, he finds himself in a region without clear identity, 'Uncertain which, in Ocean or in Air' (76), that matches his moral confusion.

The vignette of Satan, like that of Adam and Eve, contains past and future as a single history. Satan is exhausted from his defeat in the war in heaven, but looks forward to the possibility of finding new opportunities in the new world. And this vignette appears alongside the other components of the epic, held within the encompassing vision of God, who has at his right hand his Son, man's hope in the distant future. Thus it is that Milton can confidently assure us that God's vision comprehends 'past, present, future' (78) and that his words to the Son are 'foreseeing' (79), that is to say, spoken in full knowledge of the whole history of his creation. When Milton tells us that God is omniscient, his manner of recounting God's vision has already enacted that truth.

Structurally, therefore, this passage is another instance of the harmonic nature of Milton's language that we explored in discussing his use of epic similes. The whole of the epic history is contained in skeletal form within these twenty lines, looking forward as they do beyond the loss of paradise to its recovery through the sacrifice of the Son in his future role as Jesus of Nazareth.

Let us now draw together our analysis of these lines and consider their emotional and thematic effect. Since this is the first time that Milton has focused his attention on God, the initial impression is very important. As we have seen, Milton uses simple contrasts to stress God's power. He contrasts light against dark, divine radiance against the darkness of evil, the angels shining 'thick as starrs' against the night. Then he opposes the exaltation of heaven in its moral and geographical height against the stooping of Satan, and contrasts the richness of the heavenly world with the outer darkness to which Satan is restricted by the protecting 'wall of Heav'n' (71). Less tangible contrasts occur too: the happiness and holiness of heaven with 'all the sanctities' and its 'Beatitude past utterance' match the earthly paradise, 'the happy garden' and the 'blissful solitude' of its inhabitants as they sow and reap 'joy and love', and both contrast dramatically with Satan in his unhappy isolation 'coasting' the scene of happiness with 'wearied wings and willing feet'. (Note that here 'willing' may imply not enthusiasm, nor a sense of anticipation, but a forcing of his exhausted form to complete his task from a misguided sense of duty, or from desperation.)

One further contrast between the light and dark aspects of this passage, and an important one, is dynamic. The visions we are offered of heaven and of paradise are images of stasis: the heavenly host reflecting God's radiance reflected in his Son; Adam and Eve blissfully reaping joy and love. There are, of course, implications of change to come, but at this stage we see only a completed delight. Satan's portrait is very different. Him we see wearied with recent struggle, edging along the wall of heaven and in the process of making a heroic sortie from his new home through the void to the new world that God has created. Satan, in short, is the only dynamic figure in this extract, as he is the source of dynamism in the whole epic; he it is who, having failed in his effort to overturn heaven, will disrupt Paradise; desperate and defeated, he is nevertheless the energy source.

How then does Milton wish us to envision God Himself? This first introduction to Milton's God in person is likely to be of some significance. First, let us consider what we do not know, a much larger field that what we do know. We know nothing from his own mouth at this stage of his relationship with his Son, nor of his attitude towards Adam and Eve; nothing in this extract reveals his perspective on the other major characters. We have only the two words Milton uses to specify his topic: 'Almighty Father' (56). But these two words are carefully chosen. The first focuses attention on God's absolute power: 'Almighty' means precisely that God's might is total, including everything; nothing is, without God's will and permission. The second word has a double meaning. God is 'Father' in that he is the author of all creation; it also suggests his protectiveness of what he has created; as fathers tend to, he may be expected to love what he has created. If we choose for a moment to see the poem as a courtroom drama in which God stands in the dock, awaiting the outcome of his trial, then in this opening phase of the defence we hear Milton as his advocate suggesting equally his power and his love.

We will leave our detailed analysis of the extract at this point, and explore briefly the dialogue that follows. In the dialogue between God and the Son, there is a curious double vision at work. On the one hand we see God, embodying both accuser and judge, inveighing against and making judgements about Adam; on the other we hear Milton working out his thesis that God's treatment of man is reasonable, or, in his word, 'justifiable'. God discusses Adam's failure to withstand the temptations of Satan, referring to his creature with all too human intemperance as an 'Ingrate!' (97) destined to father 'faithless Progenie' (96). Then, moving on from accusation, he expresses a sense of personal injury ('He had of mee / All he could have', 97–8), and later asserts his own innocence in that '[Adam and Eve] themselves decreed / Thir own revolt, not I' (116–17). This God, alternating between raging and whining, is not attractive. But this personal perspective leads to a more abstract, philosophical passage in which God explains that his foreknowledge does not imply predestination:

> If I foreknew
> Foreknowledge had no influence on their fault
> Which had no less prov'd certain unforeknown.
>
> (117–19)

The economy of this statement is astonishing, given the tortuousness of the argument, which had troubled theologians and philosophers from the beginning, and which remains unresolved.[2] Note in this connection that the idea of predestination in general links with the specific question of Calvinist election[3] that Milton raises in the following passage:

> Some I have chosen of peculiar grace
> Elect above the rest
>
> (183–4)

Here it seems that Milton may be endorsing the Calvinist notion that some men are singled out by God from the beginning for salvation. These issues about predestination and free will arise frequently in *Paradise Lost*, and deserve to be considered when you are looking at passages from the poem for yourself. (See Chapter 8 for further discussion of Milton's views.)

At its conclusion, God's statement distinguishes the sin of Man from that of Satan, which is devoid of justification because Satan himself invented it; in contrast, man shall, because he succumbed to temptation rather than wilfully and voluntarily rejecting God, find mercy. But it is a limited mercy, perhaps even a little grudging. The Son's response is to reflect and enhance the promise of mercy, re-emphasising the folly of

harshness with a flood of rhetorical questions (cf. 149–64). Eventually
Father and Son speak with one voice, as God states in his response:

> Son of my bosom, Son who art alone
> My word, my wisdom, and effectual might,
> All has thou spok'n as my thoughts are, all
> As my Eternal purpose hath decreed.

(169–72)

This mutual reflection recurs when, in answer to God's demand for
reparation for the crime that will have been committed, the Son offers
Himself as the ransom for man's sin, and is lauded for this selflessness
and love first by the Father, and then by the choir of the heavenly host,
with much touching of perfectly tuned harps and universal raising of
voices in gratitude and triumph. All is as has been foreseen from the
beginning. Satan will remain outcast. But man will find redemption
through the agency of the Son in his incarnation as Jesus of Nazareth.

In these exchanges, Milton treats the Father and the Son as separate entities: only so can they converse, only so can Milton dramatise
his theses, and thus arises the question of his orthodoxy. According to
orthodox belief, the Father and the Son are one and indivisible, and
coterminous. Milton, in contrast, treats the Son as a secondary being.
The Son, in *Paradise Lost*, does not share God's omnipotence, but functions as the agent (God's 'effectual might') through whom the creation
of the world comes about. Here in Book 3, however, in the dialogue
between the Father and the Son, the Son's point of view differs significantly from that of the Father, in being more generous and less rigorous.
Even though all is 'As my Eternal purpose hath decreed', it seems to us
from the dramatic sequence of speeches as if God relents in response to
the Son's words. Finally, when God, still demanding reparation for the
fault that is yet to be committed, asks for a sacrifice to cancel the debt
that the sin of Adam and Eve will generate, the Son volunteers himself
as if he is a separate entity. In doctrinal terms, Milton's treatment of the
dialogue, among other elements in the poem as a whole, implies that
he is not a Trinitarian, but inclines towards Unitarianism, or Arianism.[4]
This anomaly runs through the dialogue, and is one of the subjects that
you are likely to need to address in discussing some of the passages suggested in the Further Work section at the end of this chapter.

The Son

The Son has a complex role in the poem. Though one with the Father according to orthodox ideas, the Son in Milton's drama is not only secondary to, but is separate from the Father. Unlike God, he is neither omnipotent nor omniscient. According to the orthodox view it is chiefly through the Son that God's love towards man is manifested. At this stage in the story, however, the Son is not Jesus, nor Christ (the anointed one) nor the Messiah (the deliverer): he is simply the Son of God. As we have seen, when the Son engages in conversation with the Father, the words 'Son' and 'Father' constantly echo back and forth, so that we are bound to see them as two distinct characters. Further, the Son refers to Adam as 'Thy youngest Son' (151) – metaphorically, since in reality the Son is God's 'Onely begotten Son' (80). Although the Son here speaks metaphorically, his words nevertheless serve to stress his own separateness from the Father.

Functionally, the Son has at least four distinct roles:

- He is, first, at once the expression and the reflection of the Father's glory, as we have seen in the foregoing discussion of the extract from Book 3; dramatically, his function is to enhance the impression of magnificence and power that Milton strives to build in the parts of the poem dealing with the heavenly forces.
- Secondly he is the agent of creation, as Abdiel succinctly expresses it when he remonstrates with Satan in Book 5:

> Thy self though great & glorious dost thou count,   830
> Or all Angelic Nature joind in one,
> Equal to him begotten Son, by whom
> As by his Word the mighty Father made
> All things, ev'n thee, and all the Spirits of Heav'n
> By him created in thir bright degrees
>
> (5.833–8)

That 'by whom' begs many questions, not least the role of the third person of the Trinity, the Holy Spirit, which in the opening statement of the poem is described as a dove bringing the world to birth. In the event, the Spirit receives remarkably little attention in the poem: it is the Son who is instrumental in the creation as it is described in Book 7.

- Thirdly, the Son completes the rout of the fallen angels in Book 6 – part of which we shall discuss in detail shortly; as Abdiel's words quoted above imply, the poem suggests a rivalry between the Son and Satan, who was accounted 'great and glorious … Equal to him, begotten Son'.
- The Son's fourth role extends beyond the immediate focus of *Paradise Lost*, when he becomes, as he promises in Book 3, Jesus Christ, the Messiah, the saviour of mankind in *Paradise Regained*.

We may wish to add a fifth role – that of exemplar, the model of human life to which Adam's progeny should aspire. All these functions point to a seemingly inescapable conclusion: the hero of this epic poem is the Son.

For our final analyses we will look at two of these aspects of the Son. Both present him in heroic style, riding out on his chariot to do the bidding of the Father. Here, in Book 6, after addressing the loyal angels and acknowledge his own responsibility as leader, the Son prepares to confront the rebel angels:

> So spake the Son, and into terrour chang'd
> His count'nance too severe to be beheld
> And full of wrauth bent on his Enemies.
> At once the Four spred out thir Starrie wings
> With dreadful shade contiguous, and the Orbes
> Of his fierce Chariot rowld, as with the sound
> Of torrent Floods, or of a numerous Host.   830
> Hee on his impious Foes right onward drove,
> Gloomie as Night; under his burning Wheeles
> The stedfast Empyrean shook throughout,
> All but the Throne it self of God. Full soon
> Among them he arriv'd; in his right hand
> Grasping ten thousand Thunders, which he sent
> Before him, such as in thir Soules infix'd
> Plagues; they astonisht all resistance lost,
> All courage; down thir idle weapons drop'd;
> O're Shields and Helmes, and helmed heads he rode   840

Of Thrones and mighty Seraphim prostrate,
That wish'd the Mountains now might be again
Thrown on them as a shelter from his ire.
Nor less on either side tempestuous fell
His arrows, from the fourfold-visag'd Foure,
Distinct with eyes, and from the living Wheels,
Distinct alike with multitude of eyes,
One Spirit in them rul'd, and every eye
Glar'd lightning, and shot forth pernicious fire
Among th' accurst, that witherd all thir strength,   850
And of thir wonted vigour left them draind,
Exhausted, spiritless, afflicted, fall'n.
Yet half his strength he put not forth, but check'd
His Thunder in mid Volie, for he meant
Not to destroy, but root them out of Heav'n:
The overthrown he rais'd, and as a Heard
Of Goats or timerous flock together throngd
Drove them before him Thunder-struck, pursu'd
With terrors and with furies to the bounds
And Chrystall wall of Heav'n, which op'ning wide,   860
Rowld inward, and a spacious Gap disclos'd
Into the wastful Deep; the monstrous sight
Strook them with horror backward, but far worse
Urg'd them behind; headlong themselvs they threw
Down from the verge of Heav'n, Eternal wrauth
Burnt after them to the bottomless pit.

                                 (6.824–66)

The structure of this passage is marked by a rapid change of focus, consistent with the fast-moving narrative:

1. The Son turns a stern countenance on his foes (824–7).
2. His chariot of winged cherubs is briefly described as it begins the assault (827–30).
3. The Son drives his chariot into the rebel forces (831–7).
4. The rebel angels are struck with terror (837–43).
5. Volleys of arrows rain from the cherubim down upon the rebels, leaving them exhausted (844–52).
6. The Son drives the rebels before him, intent not on their destruction but on their expulsion from heaven (853–60).

7. A gap opens in the walls of heaven, through which the rebels throw themselves towards hell (860–6).

We will not analyse this passage piece by piece. Its general meaning and structure are sufficiently apparent from our short summary. Before we move on to discuss its thematic significance, however, perhaps a word needs to be said about the monstrous machine, the Son's chariot, which is described in this passage.

The Son's chariot, a living, sentient structure, comprises four cherubim, with their wings closely interlocked ('contiguous', 828) so that they resemble the night sky – vast in extent, 'Starrie' (827) but blotting out light with their 'dreadful shade' (828) – dreadful not in a general sense, but in the root sense of striking fear into the heart. The thunderous wheels of the chariot, described as 'Orbes' (828), add to the sense of terror. If 'Orbes' seems an odd choice of word at this point, it makes sense later when Milton describes the wheels as full of eyes from each of which fire and lightning shoot forth (846–9). (The chariot and several details of the passage echo the first chapter of the biblical Book of Ezekiel, which is worth reading in this connection.)

In the context of the whole passage, the chariot has the primary function of giving focus to the mood of violence, terror and vengeance that Milton strives to generate. The 'fierce' (829) chariot matches the countenance of the Son, 'too severe to be beheld' (825). While the chariot's myriad eyes 'Glar'd lightning' (849), the Son's hand clutches 'ten thousand Thunders' (836). The chariot 'shot forth pernicious [causing injury] fire' (849); the Son's thunders 'in thir souls infix'd / Plagues' (837–8) – 'Plagues', emphatically placed at the beginning of the line where it disrupts the metre, is used metaphorically to suggest continuing tortures. Here the Son has the character of the traditional epic hero, defeating and punishing his enemies by force of arms. Fearless and determined, he 'right onward drove' (831) with such overwhelming power and terror that the rebel angels, disparagingly referred to as 'impious Foes' (831), give up without a fight, throwing down their 'idle' (useless, 839) weapons in instantaneous recognition that struggle would be pointless. The emphasis is on excitement, noise, wonder and terror. The violent lighting of the episode, with its starry darkness, lightning, burning wheels and 'pernicious fire'. its thunderous sound, and its physical shocks great enough to shake the 'stedfast Empyrean' (833), the foundation of heaven itself, suggest a scene of chaos that might come from a newly-created hell.

However, there is more to this episode than violent spectacle. The superficial impression of the Son as an agent of vengeance in the conventional epic style gives way to a more considered vision of an agent of divine providence.

First, from the beginning of the passage, Milton associates the Son's vengeance repeatedly with natural forces. Thus the wings of the cherubs that form the chariot are like the starry night sky, and the terrifying sound of the wheels is like 'torrent Floods' (830); the Son's arrows fall 'tempestuous' (844). In contrast, the rebellion of the fallen angels appears unnatural.

Secondly, the Son's vengeance is moderated. Fearsome though the armoury of the Son and his chariot seems, they do not destroy. The Son rides, in conventional destructive epic fashion, 'O're Shields and Helmes, and helmed heads' (840). Yet the Son 'check'd / His Thunder in mid Volie, for he meant / Not to destroy, but to root them out of Heav'n' (853–5). Note here the emphatic position of 'Not' at the beginning of the line, reversing the normal metre of the verse: Milton forcefully contradicts the impression of vengeance. Far from destroying his enemies, the Son 'The overthrown ... rais'd' (856), to herd them together like sheep ('timerous flock', 857) or goats. The simile is familiar from the biblical idea of the Last Judgement, at which the souls of the dead are divided into those loyal (the sheep) and those incapable of accepting God's grace (the goats) and then consigned to their appropriate destination in heaven or hell. Milton's idea here is clearly different from that. Here sheep and goats alike are evil. The simile at once diminishes the rebel angels as creatures no better than beasts of the field, with nothing heroic or epic about them. More significantly, perhaps, it shows that even at this point, dealing with his foes, the Son reveals a hint of his later role as the shepherd who cares for his flock. Thus, though the primary theme of this extract is punishment of the rebel angels, the overtones invite us to think of the Son's gentler attributes.

In the last section of the extract, the focus falls on the rebel angels. Confronted by the fierce chariot, they are not ultimately destroyed. They are reduced ironically to 'Thrones and mighty Seraphim prostrate' (841); they could now wish for the recurrence of their earlier punishment, when mountains were heaped upon them (cf. 6.637–66), for dire as it would be, it would afford some protection from the fury now visited upon them. Their strength is 'witherd all' (850), and leaves them, in a line emphatic in its heavily rhythmic repetitiveness, 'draind, / Exhausted, spiritless, afflicted, fall'n' (851–2). They are 'Thunder-struck' (858) literally, 'pursu'd / With terrors and with furies' (859) and finally trapped between 'the monstrous sight' of the 'wastful Deep' (862) on one side and horrors 'far worse' (863) on the other. In the event, it is not the Son who pushes the rebels into hell. Rather, 'headlong themselves they threw' (863); they choose hell now, as they chose Satan earlier. Thus it is their will as much as God's that they go to hell. Milton orchestrates the scene in the style of an epic battle of uncertain outcome. In actuality, of course, the decision is already made, but at this point dramatic effect is more important than theological precision.

The episode closes in violent and majestic mood. Consider the violent disruption of the metre in the final lines. I use underlining for the base metre, bold type for the natural emphasis:

> ... the **mon**strous <u>**sight**</u>
> **Strook** <u>them</u> with **horr**or **back**ward, <u>but</u> **far** <u>**worse**</u>
> **Urg'd** <u>them</u> be**hind**; **head**<u>long</u> them<u>selves</u> they **threw**
> **Down** <u>from</u> the <u>verge</u> of <u>Heav'n</u>, <u>Eter</u>nal **wrauth**
> **Burnt** <u>af</u>ter <u>them</u> to <u>the</u> **bott**om<u>less</u> **pit**.
>
> (862–6)

Here, as we can see from the irregular emphases, Milton represents rhythmically the violent paroxysms of the outcome. The impression of violence is reinforced by active verbs: strook, urged, threw, burnt. In the last line Milton uses plosives* (**B**urnt, **b**ottomless, **p**it) to point the finality of the closing, absolute, emphatic monosyllable, which we should hear spat out with all the delicious disgust of finest melodrama

In these lines we can hear Milton revelling in description of the brutal and macabre vision. But that should not blind us to the ambivalent portrait of the Son that is presented here. In summary: though he acts as the agent of God's vengeance against the rebel angels, the Son metes out a measured punishment with something of the care of the shepherd. In the end, the rebels consign themselves to their destiny.

There are unorthodox elements in Milton's presentation of the Son and the rout of the angels. We noted that the image of the Son as a herdsman driving the rebel angels as sheep and goats before him implies care as well as control. This is an idea foreign to the moral world of the poem, and foreign to orthodox theology, too. Then the image of the rebel angels pursued 'With terrors and with furies' (859) recalls the classical function of the Furies, who, originally considered to be the agents of retribution for great evil, later came to express also grief at harsh punishment. In effect, Milton picks out from the broad canvas of crime and vengeance some hints of a less than absolute condemnation, even of mercy and regeneration.

In our next extract, which is from Book 7, it is the creative aspect of the Son that emerges most strongly. Here, the Son appears as the agent of creation, when he enacts the Father's will to generate a new world out of chaos. He is above all active. Milton succinctly explains the Son's function immediately after God's announcement of his intention to create a new world:

> So spake th' Almightie, to what he spake
> His Word, the Filial Godhead, gave effect
>
> (7.174–5)

The heavenly host lift up their harmonious voices in rejoicing at God's beneficent purpose ('Good out of evil to create', 7.188). Heaven is filled with 'Great triumph and rejoycing' (180) and 'Glorie they sung' (182), but there is no action: that is left to the Son. While the countless heavenly hierarchies are engrossed in their paeans, it is the Son who enacts the word of God:

> ...Mean while the Son
> On his great Expedition now appeer'd,
> Girt with Omnipotence, with Radiance crown'd
> Of Majestie Divine, Sapience and Love
> Immense, and all his Father in him shon.
> About his Chariot numberless were pour'd
> Cherub and Seraph, Potentates and Thrones,
> And Vertues, winged Spirits, and Chariots wing'd,
> From the Armoury of God, where stand of old   200
> Myriads between two brazen Mountains lodg'd

> Against a solemn day, harnest at hand,
> Celestial Equipage; and now came forth
> Spontaneous, for within them Spirit livd,
> Attendant on thir Lord: Heav'n op'nd wide
> Her ever during Gates, Harmonious sound
> On golden Hinges moving, to let forth
> The King of Glorie in his powerful Word
> And Spirit coming to create new Worlds.
> On heav'nly ground they stood, and from the shore   210
> They view'd the vast immeasurable Abyss
> Outrageous as a Sea, dark, wasteful, wilde,
> Up from the bottom turn'd by furious windes
> And surging waves, as Mountains to assault
> Heav'ns highth, and with the Center mix the Pole.
> Silence, ye troubl'd waves, and thou Deep, peace,
> Said then th' Omnific Word, your discord end:
> Nor staid, but on the Wings of Cherubim
> Uplifted, in Paternal Glorie rode
> Farr into Chaos, and the World unborn...   220
>   (7.192–220)

This extract is easy to analyse structurally:

1. In the opening section, the Son emerges from the confines of heaven (198–209).
2. There follow six lines in which the Son and his entourage survey the region of chaos from which the new world is to take shape (210–15).
3. At the end of the extract, the Son commands the calming of disorder (216–17).
4. Finally, he issues into chaos to do the Father's bidding (218–20).

Evidently this is a passage of strong contrasts. The magnificent order of heaven is balanced against the external disorder; description is balanced by sharp command and sudden action; the expansiveness of the earlier part of the extract gives way to abruptness in the final phase.

The lines describing the issuing forth of the Son are marked by abundance, light, and magnificence. The Son appears 'with Radiance crown'd' and clothed ('Girt') in omnipotence. The entities, more or less abstract (from 'Potentates' to 'Virtues'), that crowd about him are 'numberless'. The chariots are winged, part of a 'myriad'. Milton enhances the images with grandiloquent language: he describes the harnessed horses as 'Celestial Equipage'; heaven's gates as 'ever during' (everlasting) and 'op'nd wide' as befits the grandeur of the occasion. Golden hinges in heaven do not squeal: they move in stately fashion with a 'harmonious sound'.

In the early lines of the extract, the sense of expansiveness depends largely on repetition and parallelism. Thus the population of heaven is categorised: cherub, seraph, potentates, thrones, virtues, winged spirits, chariots. ('Winged' is repeated albeit with slightly different emphasis – wingéd and wing'd – in a single line, emphasising the sense of airiness or perhaps freedom or spontaneity that heaven expresses.) The phrase 'Girt with omnipotence' develops in reversed structure to 'with Radiance crown'd / Of Majestie Divine'. References to the Son form the spine of these lines, developing the impression of power incrementally from 'the Son' (192) and 'thir Lord' (205) to 'The King of Glorie in his powerful Word / And Spirit' (208–9).

Milton's sound world matches the sense with a range of different effects contributing to the sense of harmony. Alliteration appears in 'harnessed at hand', for example, and there is an informal rhyming pattern in 'omnipotence ... radiance ... sapience'. Most important in contributing to the effect of spaciousness, however, is the assonantal long 'a' sound that dominates the passage: 'Radiance ... Sapience ... Potentates ... brazen ... day ... came ... Spontaneous ... Gates ... create'. (Follow the pattern of a different vowel sound for yourself: try the long 'o', for example.)

Contrast emphasises these effects when we come to the spectacle of chaos (211–15) that the Son looks out upon: instead of infinite heaven with its 'numberless' entities, we confront the 'immeasurable Abyss'. Instead of harmony we confront an 'Outrageous' realm, 'wilde ... furious ... surging'. Instead of population, we have 'wasteful' emptiness (that is, chaos is, in the literal meaning of 'wasteful', full of waste). Instead of radiance we have a 'dark' outlook. Instead of order we have a mad region in which the bottom of the sea is turned up, and 'Center' and 'Pole' are mixed: confusion reigns. Compare the effect of the alliteration here in 'wasteful, wilde' with the example we noticed above in the earlier part of the passage: here it stresses disorder. Chaos is, it goes without saying, indescribable. Milton uses the image of a tempestuous sea to represent the idea of disorder; incidentally, he echoes the idea of Satan's disorderly behaviour when he speaks of the waves behaving like mountains 'To assault / Heav'ns highth'; comparably, Satan behaves like a greater than himself to aspire to God's place. This is a curious example of a simile nested inside a simile: chaos is like a sea which in turn is like a mountain – and this too is an instance of the kind of convolution associated in the poem with the ungodly.

The Son's reaction to the chaotic vision that faces him is decisive, brief, and full of authority. He speaks three commands: 'Silence ... peace ... your discord end' (216–17). Milton describes him with characteristic magniloquence as 'th' Omnific Word'. 'Omnific', meaning all-creating, is a word invented by Milton by analogy with 'omniscient', and it represents what the Son is about to do in executing God's will. The Word is shown here in action, commanding order out of chaos: this is the language of an inspiring leader – of a hero.

These words find their match in action elliptically described (118–19), giving the impression of speed and decision: 'Nor staid' – meaning 'he did not wait any longer' – suggests decisiveness, almost impatience. Referencing two ideas from the beginning of the passage, Milton describes the Son winged by the cherubim, and expressing 'Paternal Glorie' as he flies 'Farr into chaos' (220). This reversal of the first foot in line 220 suggests the energy of the traditional hero undaunted by potential difficulty, and looking forward to the promise of the 'World unborn' which he is about to bring into being.

It is thus the Son who stands forth as the most vivid and persuasive representative of the forces for good in the poem. He is God's champion, with many of the characteristics of the traditional epic hero, yet with also a measure of control and compassion that the conventional hero lacks, and a deeper awareness of the pattern of which he is a part.

The Angels and Other Heavenly Entities

The Son is by far the most powerful of the elements associated with God and heaven. Aside from the Father, indeed, there are very few individuals differentiated among the heavenly forces. They are, specifically, Abdiel, Gabriel, Ithuriel, Michael, Raphael, Uriel, Uzziel, Zephon and Zophiel. Most of these have names ending with the syllable '-el', an abbreviation of the name of God in Hebrew.[5]

The differentiated angels have varied functions. Michael commands God's armies in the battle against the rebel angels, and is the only individual who wounds Satan himself. He is also God's emissary in expelling Adam and Eve from the Garden of Eden. Gabriel commands the angels assigned to defence of Eden, a task in which he has assistance from Uzziel, and he confronts Satan there. Zephon and Ithuriel co-operate in capturing Satan in Book 4 and bringing him before Gabriel. Raphael dominates in Books 5–7, where he is sent by God to warn Adam and Eve against Satan, and recounts for them the history of Satan's rebellion, and gives an account of the Creation. Abdiel opposes Satan's plans and rebukes Satan for his rebelliousness. Zophiel is the angel who in Book 6 warns the angels of the approach of Satan's rebels. Uriel is the angel who in Book 2 unwittingly directs Satan to the Garden of Eden.

Beyond these few outstanding individuals, the angels are generalised as a 'multitude of angels' (3.145) as indistinct as the 'ambrosial fragrance' (3.135) that fills their harmonious realm of 'Jubilee and loud Hosanna's' (3.348). This lack of differentiation seems an essential element of the celestial realm. In this 'charming symphony' (3.168) there is 'No voice exempt, no voice but well could join / Melodious part, such concord is in Heav'n' (3.370–1). There is, in other words, no room for dissent. All are united in universal hymn of praise. In contrast, there are more sharply distinguished individuals among the rebel angels.

Not only undifferentiated, angels are also pan-organic: that is, their senses are distributed throughout their substance (cf. 6.350). Further, they are invulnerable: the war in heaven dramatises an essentially moral conflict; the specific details Milton offers are there to make us feel vividly the power of a non-material struggle.

The angelic world, though undifferentiated, acts as a vivid backdrop for the individualised characters. It is defined by radiant light, harmonious music, and intricate dance. Brightness, radiance, light are essential to the heavenly world, and we have seen above how the Son's radiance reflects that of God himself. In contrast, Satan's corruption is marked by loss of his original brightness, as Zephon points out:

> Think not, revolted Spirit, thy shape the same,
> Or undiminisht brightness

(4.836–7)

Satan retains something of his former glory, however, and still appears to Eve 'shap'd and wing'd like one of those from Heav'n' (5.55).

Music appears throughout the poem, both in the heavenly world and in the earthly. However, the heavenly harmony represents peace, in contrast with the silence or more raucous noises of hell. The Son's response to God's decision to show mercy to Adam and Eve is to promise hymns of thanksgiving:

> ... both Heav'n and Earth shall high extol
> Thy praises, with th' innumerable sound
> Of Hymns and sacred Songs, wherewith thy Throne
> Encompass'd shall resound thee ever blest.'
>
> (3.146–9)

Adam speaks to Eve of 'Celestial voices ... Sole, or responsive each to others note ... With Heav'nly touch of instrumental sounds / In full harmonic number joind' that 'Divide the night' (4.682–8). Satan, defeated and condemned, takes a negative view of the angelic music. In Book 2 he voices his scorn for the rent-a-mob angels who are bound by 'Strict Laws impos'd, to celebrate his Throne / With warbl'd Hymns, and to his Godhead sing / Forc't Halleluiah's' (2.241–3); he scorns, it seems, not only their behaviour but also, in 'Warbl'd', their questionable pitch! Later, in his confrontation with Gabriel in Book 4, he sneers at the servile angels whose only task is 'with songs to hymne his Throne, / And practis'd distances to cringe' (4.944–5).

The imagery of dance is particularly interesting. Milton associates it with the 'Starry dance' (5.180) of the cosmos, but links it with the activities of hell as much as with those of heaven, dismisses it as scandalous in his diatribe against 'Mixt Dance, and wanton Mask' (4.768). The following passage – our final, brief extract – comes from Book 5 immediately after God's proclamation of his unity with his 'onely Son' and his warning against disobedience:

> So spake th' Omnipotent, and with his words
> All seemd well pleas'd, all seem'd, but were not all.
> That day, as other solem dayes, they spent

In song and dance about the sacred Hill,
Mystical dance, which yonder starrie Spheare   620
Of Planets and of fixt in all her Wheeles
Resembles nearest, mazes intricate,
Eccentric, intervolv'd, yet regular
Then most, when most irregular they seem:
And in thir motions harmonie Divine
So smooths her charming tones, that Gods own ear
Listens delighted.

(5.617–27)

Here Milton shows us the angels celebrating – soon, as evening
approaches, tables of food and drink will be brought forth for
feasting. First, however, the angels express their joy in singing and
dancing. Milton's vision here is essentially Pythagorean. The music
and movement reflect the music of the spheres according to the
Pythagorean theory that each planet, set in its crystalline sphere,
emits a note, which together with the notes of the other planets, creates 'harmonie Divine' (625); the pitch of the notes is defined by the
distances between the planets or the spheres in which they are fixed,
as a guitar string, for example, will give a different note depending
on where the finger presses it against the fingerboard. A little later,
when they turn to eating, the angels are grouped 'in Circles' (631) –
appropriately, since the circle is geometrically perfect according to
Pythagoras.

However, the image of perfection Milton presents here contains
the seeds of imperfection. The angels' dance is of great intricacy, like a
maze, 'Eccentric, intervolv'd' (623) – that is, not exactly circular, and
intertwined, so that the angels mingle in patterns that though not
circular, occur within a controlled perfection; thus, they are most regular 'when most irregular they seem' (624). This consonance of simplicity and complexity mirrors the stars and planets, mingling those
fixed in their spheres with those unfixed and wandering. The effect is
smooth and 'charming' (626, with the sense of spell-binding rather
than merely agreeable), so that God Himself listens with delight, but
Milton insists on the irregularity of the dance: intricate mazes suggests the possibility of corruption here and elsewhere in the poem;
'Eccentric' may mean unorthodox as well as simply not circular, and
'intervolv'd' may carry the meaning of devious.

These ambiguities support the hint in the second line of the extract, where Milton describes the response of the angels to God's pronouncement with an ominous echo: 'All seemd well pleas'd, all seem'd, but were not all.' In the mind of Satan, as Milton describes a little later, God's proclamation and the adoration of the Son awaken only envy. As Lucifer, the light-bringer, he is considered to have been pre-eminent among the angels – though Milton does not go quite so far, describing him as 'of the first, / If not the first Arch-Angel' (656–7). Hitherto, the Son has been only his rival. Now he feels overlooked and thus diminished: he 'thought himself impaird' (662). Thus Milton dramatises Satan's rebellion against God, depicting him here almost as the pantomime villain, slinking off to the wings muttering 'Curses!' to conspire with his closest cronies.

There is, too, a less crude point to this portrayal. If Satan can rebel against God, there must be in the seeming perfection of heaven the possibility of disobedience. In this extract, Milton illustrates that possibility in the deceptive eccentricity of the angels' dance. The worm of evil lurks in heaven, then, as well as in the Garden of Eden.

The correspondences we have noted between the Heavenly and earthly worlds – the dance reflecting the planets, and the common presence of evil – take material form in the second part of the extract:

> (For we have also our Eevning and our Morn,
> We ours for change delectable, not need)
> Forthwith from dance to sweet repast they turn   630
> Desirous, all in Circles as they stood,
> Tables are set, and on a sudden pil'd
> With Angels Food, and rubied Nectar flows:
> In Pearl, in Diamond, and massie Gold,
> Fruit of delicious Vines, the growth of Heav'n.
> They eat, they drink, and with refection sweet
> Are fill'd, before th' all bounteous King, who showrd
> With copious hand, rejoycing in thir joy.
>
>   (5.628–38)

This describes the glorious feast, the 'refection sweet' that follows the dancing and singing. Milton's view of heaven hardly accords with the orthodox notion of a spiritual realm. Here there is food, and 'rubied Nectar' (633) is drunk as in classical epic by Homer's gods, but there may also be wine, 'Fruit of delicious Vines' (635), rather than grapes; the appearance of the food in its dishes is represented in material terms as 'In Pearl, in Diamond, and massie Gold' (634).

To accord with this material aspect of heaven, Milton modifies the portrait of God, who now turns into something like a feudal chieftain, bestowing his bounty 'With copious hand' (638) on his loyal followers. He acknowledges this change of focus when he calls God not 'th' Omnipotent' as at the beginning of the extract, but now 'th' all bounteous King' (637). We may wonder quite how 'Angels Food' (623) differs from the fruits of the Garden of Eden, if at all.

The materialistic view of heavenly life that Milton presents here is no aberration. Later in the poem, Raphael visits the Garden of Eden to eat with Adam and Eve, and then, when questioned about angelic life, explains that angels experience sex, or at least something related to it, just like humans:

> Whatever pure thou in the body enjoy'st
> (And pure thou wert created) we enjoy
> In eminence, and obstacle find none
> Of membrane, joynt, or limb, exclusive barrs:
> Easier then Air with Air, if Spirits embrace,
> Total they mix, Union of Pure with Pure
> Desiring; nor restrain'd conveyance need
> As Flesh to mix with Flesh, or Soul with Soul.
>
> (8.622–9)

Of course, what Raphael and his ilk experience is refined even beyond the 'pure' (622) of Adam and Eve, so that no physical barriers exist. Angels, it seems, merely melt into each other to experience the love 'without [which there is] no happiness' (621).

Without needlessly going into the details and implications of whether angels are of one sex, or both, or neither, and whether they can procreate, and how religious and biblical authorities differ.[6] we can see that Milton has a vision of angels that is highly unorthodox, and perhaps peculiar to him alone. For him, the angelic world reflects the material world, both in its constellations and in its sexuality, and is essentially of the same substance. The angelic world is simply more refined, less materially confined, than the human world. Indeed, angels share something of human embarrassment at open discussion of sexuality, for when Raphael answers Adam's direct question, he blushes deeply, speaking 'with a smile that glow'd / Celestial rosie red' (8.618–19). (The related question of Milton's monistic beliefs is addressed in Chapters 7 and 8 of this book.)

With the delights of singing, dancing, feasting, drinking and loving all available, it appears that the world of the angels lacks nothing as compared with human experience. The angels experience all these pleasures in a more rarefied, more refined way than humans can, and they do so with the added privilege of the presence of God. Thus Milton is able to give the spiritual realm a dramatised reality that would be impossible if he were to attempt to present it in abstract terms. He achieves this, too, within the boundaries of a consistent, if unorthodox, theological vision.

Conclusions

Milton's problems in dealing with God, the Son, heaven and its other inhabitants are essentially twofold:

1. To represent perfection through the imperfect medium of human language.
2. To represent the abstract with words which relate to a material world.

These are the features that emerged from our analysis:

- Milton dramatises the relationship between God and the Son. This gives immediacy to his poem, but it also raises questions of theological orthodoxy.
- God is often referred to indirectly by circumlocutions that enhance his majesty and distance his identity ('th' omnipotent', 'a voice').
- The poem proposes a dramatic rivalry between Satan and the Son.
- The Son is presented as a heroic figure: as a possible protagonist for the epic history.
- The Son is subordinate to the Father, created by him and not coterminous with him, and is less powerful.

- Milton describes heaven metonymically. It has gates, a throne for God to sit on, and mountains, for example. The Son rides on chariots. The angels and other heavenly entities have voices. God and the Son engage in conversation.
- Milton's theology is unorthodox. In particular, he adheres to the Arian heresy, according to which God created the Son as a secondary entity.
- Heaven is associated with a variety of more or less abstract attractive qualities: brightness, harmony, height, gold, joy. It also includes singing, dancing, feasting, drinking, and love.
- When he describes heaven and its inhabitants, he also refers to the differing worlds of Satan, whose world conflicts with heaven, and of Adam and Eve, whose world both reflects and contrasts with heaven.
- Milton is concerned about the problem of reconciling the notion of human free will with the omniscience of the Deity. He tends sometimes towards Arminianism (as opposed to the Calvinist view of predestination). Furthermore, he raises questions about the fairness or harshness of God's disposition.
- Milton makes use of non-specific language in his description of heaven (for example, 'radiance') and makes much use of abstractions ('sanctities', 'joy').
- The Son, like God, is frequently referred to by his attributes such as 'the Word'.
- The eye of God sees present and past, all history gathered up in an instant's perception.
- The heavenly world is seen as a reflection and continuation of the human world, of essentially the same substance, in a less material form.
- Milton makes much use of rhetorical devices such as ellipsis, repetition, patterned phrasing, and reversal to underline his meaning.

Methods of Analysis

- In each piece of analysis, we began with a structural analysis of the passage, looking as simply as possible at what was being said and splitting into logical sections.

- Then we took each section of an extract in turn, exploring the kind of language employed in it. This involved analysing:
  o Semantics: the meanings of the words, especially unusual words or words used in an unusual way ('omnific', for example)
  o The connotations of the language – its associations, echoes and implications (discord, for example)
  o Imagery: the similes and metaphors, particularly
  o Versification effects such as rhyme, alliteration, and assonance
  o Syntax: the linguistic structure of the section
  o Patterned language: formal repetitions and reversals in phrasing
  o Functional grammatical usage, such as ellipsis
- Then we considered the relationship among the sections, looking for similarities and contrasts.
- Finally, we considered the overall effect of the passage and its function in the poem as a whole. For example, we considered the presentation of the Son as a heroic figure, and the nature of the angelic world as presented in the poem as a whole.

Further Work

I offer here other passages taken from Books 3, 6 and 7 for you to analyse in your own way. You do not have to follow the sequence outlined above in Methods of Analysis, but you should try to find something to say about each of the topics mentioned there.

1. God talks to the Son about Satan, Man, and the question of free will:

   Book 3. 80–134 ('Onely begotten Son ... But Mercy first and last shall brightest shine').
   Your main task in discussing this extract is to trace the argument God uses to distinguish the trespasses of Satan and of the human characters, and the path by which he comes to his final judgement.
   How persuasive is God's logic?
   What is your impression of the nature of God as presented by Milton?

Remember to think about the language Milton uses: look at the dramatic contrasts in the extract, at the patterning of phrasing by repetition and reversal, and at the use of rhetorical questions.

2. Raphael's description of the Son's chariot:

Book 6. 746–68 ('So said, he o're his Scepter bowing, rose ... He onward came').

Your main focus here is likely to be Milton's descriptive techniques. Show how Milton applies his poetic resources to developing a sense of power and wonder.

It would be interesting to look at the biblical source of this passage, Ezekiel 10: 9–10, and consider how Milton adapts ideas from it and builds upon it.

3. God prepares to create the world:

Book 7. 221–42 ('For Chaos heard his voice .... Sojourn'd the while').

In discussing this passage, you should consider particularly how Milton represents the power of God, using physical details such as the golden compasses; at the imagery of light and dark, order and disorder.

Think about the meaning of the role played by the Spirit of God.

Look closely at Milton's use of language in this passage, especially words like *fervid, vertue, conglob'd, Disparted,* and *quintessence.* You will probably need to consult the editor's notes in your edition.

4

Satan, the Rebel Angels, and their World of Darkness

Book 1. 27–75 ('Say first... unlike the place from whence they fell!')
Book 1. 314–30 ('He call'd so loud... arise, or be for ever fall'n')
Book 2. 1–10 ('High on a throne... proud imaginations thus displaid')
Book 4. 1–30 ('O For that warning voice... sat high in his Meridian Towre')
Book 4. 172–204 ('Now to th' ascent... or to thir meanest use')

In this chapter our subject is Satan and other rebel angels in *Paradise Lost*. We will focus on Milton's portrayal of Satan, the angels' rebellion, their situation and their expectations, but will defer discussion of Satan's temptation of Eve until Chapter 6.

Milton devotes much time and energy to portraying Satan and his supporters. Many more rebel angels than good angels are named in the poem, and they are more strongly characterised. Satan himself is by general agreement the most vivid character in *Paradise Lost*; indeed, for some readers he is also the de facto hero of the poem. So marked is his dominance as to lead to doubts in the minds of some critics, notably William Blake, about the success of Milton's essential enterprise – to justify the ways of God to men. We defer discussion of this question until Chapter 9.

We will cautiously sidestep the issue for the present, and move on to look at the actuality of the presentation of Satan. He appears early in the poem – immediately after the first invocation, in fact. This is the point at which we may expect Milton to set out the essentials of Satan's part in the epic, and in it we find an interesting change of direction:

Say first, for Heav'n hides nothing from thy view
Nor the deep Tract of Hell, say first what cause
Mov'd our Grand Parents in that happy State,
Favour'd of Heav'n so highly, to fall off   30
From their Creator, and transgress his Will
For one restraint, Lords of the World besides?
Who first seduc'd them to that fowl revolt?
Th' infernal Serpent; he it was, whose guile
Stird up with Envy and Revenge, deceiv'd
The Mother of Mankinde, what time his Pride
Had cast him out from Heav'n, with all his Host
Of Rebel Angels, by whose aid aspiring
To set himself in Glory above his Peers,
He trusted to have equal'd the most High,   40
If he oppos'd; and with ambitious aim
Against the Throne and Monarchy of God
Rais'd impious War in Heav'n and Battel proud
With vain attempt. Him the Almighty Power
Hurld headlong flaming from th' Ethereal Skie
With hideous ruine and combustion down
To bottomless perdition, there to dwell
In Adamantine Chains and penal Fire,
Who durst defie th' Omnipotent to Arms.
Nine times the Space that measures Day and Night   50
To mortal men, he with his horrid crew
Lay vanquisht, rowling in the fiery Gulfe
Confounded though immortal: But his doom
Reserv'd him to more wrath; for now the thought
Both of lost happiness and lasting pain
Torments him; round he throws his baleful eyes
That witness'd huge affliction and dismay
Mixt with obdurate pride and stedfast hate:
At once as far as Angels kenn he views
The dismal Situation waste and wilde,   60
A Dungeon horrible, on all sides round
As one great Furnace flam'd, yet from those flames

No light, but rather darkness visible
Serv'd only to discover sights of woe,
Regions of sorrow, doleful shades, where peace
And rest can never dwell, hope never comes
That comes to all; but torture without end
Still urges, and a fiery Deluge, fed
With ever-burning Sulphur unconsum'd:
Such place Eternal Justice had prepar'd   70
For those rebellious, here their Prison ordain'd
In utter darkness, and their portion set
As far remov'd from God and light of Heav'n
As from the Center thrice to th' utmost Pole.
O how unlike the place from whence they fell!

(1.27–75)

This passage contains three sharply defined sections, beginning with the narrator's request of his muse for enlightenment, and ending with a vision of hell. The passage is particularly sonorous, and will repay repeated readings with attentive ears. We will follow our regular practice of looking at the literal content of the verse to ensure our understanding:

1. The poet asks the muse to enlighten him about the reason for the transgression of Adam and Eve, 'our Grand Parents' (29) in disobeying God's single restriction, when they were otherwise lords of their world. A second question asks who was to blame (27–33).
2. The response is immediate: it was the serpent. The poem proceeds to amplify the nature of the serpent, who was cast out from heaven with his rebel followers for seeking to set himself above the other angels ('his Peers', 39) and even to place himself equal with God (44).
3. The remainder of the extract recounts the dreadful punishment for Satan's defiance, beginning with the fall of the angels into hell and their lengthy (nine days and nights) state of helpless confusion immediately afterwards (44–53).
4. The poet turns to Satan's individual circumstances: he suffers more severe punishment for having aspired to rule in heaven, because the

contrast with his dismal circumstances makes him more sharply aware of the loss he has suffered (53–75).

We will look at each section in turn before proceeding to a more general discussion.

The opening seven lines begin with an urgent insistence ('Say first') addressed to the muse on whom Milton is relying to reveal to him the deepest secrets of heaven and hell to speak about the origin of the Fall. The word 'first' reappears twice (28, 33), stressing the need to know the absolute source of evil, and also picking up the repetitions of the same word in the opening invocation of Book 1: thus it is the Milton returns to the fall of Satan as the initiating event in this poem dealing with the God's dispositions for mankind. The mood of these lines is argumentative, even legalistic, in tone. There is an edge of formal interrogation, as if in a courtroom, in the repeated questions, and a pleading note of counter-accusation against the arbiter of their fate in the reference to Adam and Eve as 'For [except for] one restraint, lords of the world besides' (32).

Milton's language, however, is also highly emotional. He refers repeatedly to the delights of innocence that have been lost: 'that happy State' (29) that those 'Favour'd of Heav'n so highly' (30) enjoyed. Mournfully, or perhaps with a sense of outrage, he refers with equal emphasis to the Fall (30), to the transgression of Adam and Eve, and in the emphatic final line to their 'fowl revolt' (33). That last vivid phrase is preceded by the strongest word in these opening seven lines: 'seduc'd'. In it is contained all that Milton later describes of the evil trickery by which first Eve, and then Adam, are betrayed by the insidious cleverness of their foe.

Structurally these lines are dominated by the contrast established at the beginning between 'Heav'n' and 'the deep Tract of Hell'. The repeated contrast between our progenitors' happy state and their fall all develop from that. Milton's writing is dense, using resonant language, speaking of Adam and Eve as 'Mov'd' (inspired in both action and emotion) to 'fall off' and 'transgress' and finally and most emotively as 'seduc'd'. The passage contains typical Miltonic ellipses: 'For' means 'Except for', and 'besides' means 'apart from that single restriction' in line 32, and 'what time' (36) means 'at that time when'. Everything leads rapidly to the concluding questions. These questions differ from each other in a significant way. The first demands 'say first what cause' (28) resulted in the Fall; the second, however, asks 'Who first seduc'd them...?' (33). The first question ironically echoes the nature of God as the first cause of all that is; the second personalises the specific source of evil.

This change of perspective from *what* to *who* leads at once to the answer to Milton's questions in the second section of the extract, which establishes the way in which we should see Satan with absolute clarity. The enemy of mankind is introduced in a single emphatic phrase, as 'Th' infernal Serpent' (34), that answers flatly and unambiguously the double question. Here 'infernal' has, of course, its literal Latin sense of 'of hell', and Milton follows Christian tradition in identifying the serpent of Eden with Satan. Milton immediately develops this answer with a torrent of accusations: Satan is guilty of 'guile...Envy and Revenge...Pride' (34–6); he 'deceiv'd' Eve (35). There follows a brief account of Satan's history that stresses his hateful qualities, above all his pride: he rose up 'with ambitious aim' (41) to confront God, 'aspiring / To set himself in Glory above his Peers' (38–9); he expected to place himself equal with God (40), and to this end raised 'impious War...Battel proud' (43). In contrast with these accusations, Milton stresses the rightful supremacy of God, 'the most High' (40): thus Satan's uprising is grandly described in epic terms as a revolt 'Against the Throne and Monarchy of God' (42). Inevitably, Satan fails – he is eternally doomed to failure: his pride itself 'cast him out from Heav'n' (37), as we saw in the last chapter; and the section ends with a half-line, 'With vain attempt' (44) that dismisses all Satan's ambitions as worthless, 'vain' having a double meaning for us here of both 'empty' or 'futile', and 'self-loving'.

In the third section of the passage, Milton describes the punishment to which 'the Almighty Power' (44) subjects Satan. Milton seems to relish the vividness of this moment, inverting the syntax for dramatic effect and huffing and puffing alliteration to the final emphatic monosyllable:

> Him the Almighty Power
> Hurld headlong flaming from th' Ethereal Skie
> With hideous ruine and combustion down

(44–6)

In hell, dire punishments await. In 'bottomless perdition' (48), chained with adamant – the hardest of all materials according to legend – and consumed with 'penal Fire' (48), Satan seems doomed forever. Utterly defeated despite his previous eminence ('vanquisht ... Confounded though immortal', 52–3), he is powerless at this point to do anything but drift at the mercy of the fiery waves of hell.

Thus far, Milton has moved from questioning the cause of the Fall, to accusing Satan, and to briefly describing his rebellion and punishment. Now, in the final phase of the extract (53–75), he considers Satan's situation in more detail.

Milton begins this final phase by singling Satan out from the rest of the angels who fell with him, for Satan is tormented by the thought not only of 'lasting [everlasting] pain' but also of 'lost happiness' (55) – that is, the foiling of his aspirations. This is the 'more wrath' that he is condemned to suffer. More remarkable than the fact, however, is that Milton reveals Satan's thoughts to us at all. Satan has in this poem, after all, merely a functional role as the agent of the Fall of man. Yet in this phase of the extract we think with Satan's mind, and we see with Satan's eyes: 'Round he throws his baleful eyes' (56), 'as far as Angels kenn he views' his surroundings; the final exclamation of the extract (75), though cast in the third person, adopts Satan's point of view as he bemoans all that he has lost.

Once again, Milton appears to relish the delightful horrors of hell in sonorous verse, using all the rhetorical resources at his command to bring to vivid life the 'dismal Situation' of the fallen angels. Alliteration appears in the 'waste and wilde' (60) panorama and in 'Furnace flam'd', emphatic reversal in the metaphor of the 'Dungeon horrible' (61), parallelisms of several kinds in 'Regions of sorrow, doleful shades' (65) and 'rest can never dwell, hope never comes' (66), effects of paradox and oxymoron in 'hope never comes / That comes to all' (66–7), in 'ever-burning Sulphur unconsum'd' (69), in burning waves, and in 'darkness visible' (63); ellipsis occurs in 'No light' (63; 'shone' is understood) and 'those rebellious' (71; 'angels' is understood)); the metaphor of the dungeon reappears a few lines later in the 'Prison ordain'd' (71), and the metaphor of fire for pain runs throughout; an odd simile (discussed below) occurs in the final lines of the extract. The opposition of light and dark is central to the section: the rebel angels are imprisoned in 'utter darkness' (72), for ever exiled from the 'light of Heav'n' (73). These technical features create a powerfully emotive effect. The darkness of the angels' damned world mirrors the extinction of their hope. The physical tortures of the horrid crew reflect the psychological torments of Satan, and both are represented by the burning of the 'fiery Deluge' (68), whose unnatural flames cast 'No light' (63). The phrase 'darkness visible', famous for its imaginative inspiration, encapsulates this shadowy realm of suffering, all the more terrifying for being formless. In sum, Milton finds in Satan and in hell apt subjects on which to exercise his most vivid poetic powers.

In the light of this exploration, let us now review the extract as a whole.

The picture Milton paints is beyond human conception, but he communicates it, necessarily, by using the human scale of perception. In fact, Milton succeeds in making the events very vivid. He makes them live for us. Thus he describes the period of time Satan spends enervated in mystical terms as 'Nine times the Space that measures Day and Night' (50) – the same period of time that the angels spent falling from heaven. The scale is both epic and comprehensible. Equally, Satan's tortures, epic in their severity and range, take a material form that we can easily understand: he is chained, burned in darkness in a lake of fire as hot as a furnace, imprisoned as if in a dark dungeon. Milton represents the distance of his removal from God in the most extreme physical, geographical terms imaginable: 'As from the Center thrice to th' utmost Pole' (74). There can be little doubt that this extract is poetically very effective. The question is whether this vividness works in favour of the message Milton wishes to deliver.

As far as overt intent goes, Milton clearly defines the opposition between good and evil. God is described always as the defining power of the universe: 'Creator', 'the Throne and Monarchy of God', th' Omipotent', 'Eternal Justice' (70). Satan, on the other hand, is consistently defined by negative epithets: 'Th' infernal Serpent', 'aspiring'. 'ambitious'; his qualities are 'Envy', 'Revenge', 'guile', 'obdurate pride and steadfast hate' (58). Adam and Eve are always referred to with respect as 'our Grand Parents' (29), and Eve is called 'The Mother of Mankinde' (36); by implication they are the victims, 'seduc'd' by the wiles of the serpent. Conceptually speaking, therefore, Milton delineates his message clearly.

The poetic qualities of the verse tell a different story, however. The only character we can identify with here is Satan. In the whole of this extract, which refers to God, Adam and Eve as well as Satan, we find only one specific physical feature mentioned, and it is Satan's:

> ... Round he throws his baleful eyes
> That witness'd huge affliction and dismay
>
> (56–7)

This reference maintains the epic scale – fixing on a detail of Satan's physical form has the effect of applying a microscope and thus enhancing the magnitude of the whole – but it also gives Satan a quasi-human aspect. What his eyes perceive – the ruin of all his expectations – invites, almost astonishingly, our sympathy. Here, then, is the hinge that that changes the perspective of the extract. Despite his obdurate pride and steadfast hate, it is with Satan's baleful eyes that we view, with horror, the dark tortures of hell. Despite his presumptuous and vain attempt, it is his tortured feelings that we are invited to share.

To sum up: our initial review of the extract showed that the focus of this writing changes. Each phase has its own topic, and each takes a step closer to Satan. As we have seen, radical changes of perspective are essential to the effect of the extract. Beginning with the idea of transgression, Milton proceeds to consider the cause of the transgression, then the punishment for it, and finally the transgressor. This is logical, and orthodox. However, the poetic effect of these lines is not orthodox at all. From that point of view, the change of perspective in this extract invites us to sympathise not with God or Adam and Eve, but rather with Satan: not to admire him, but to see events from his point of view.

The remainder of Book 1 strengthens the power of Satan in our minds. As the fallen angels discuss their situation, drag themselves from the burning lake and gather on a solid promontory, it is Satan who assumes command, inspires the other angels with new purpose and resolves to establish a nether kingdom in hell. This is how he calls upon the angels:

> He call'd so loud, that all the hollow Deep
> Of Hell resounded. Princes, Potentates,
> Warriors, the Flowr of Heav'n, once yours, now lost,

If such astonishment as this can sieze
Eternal spirits; or have ye chos'n this place
After the toyl of Battel to repose
Your wearied vertue, for the ease you find   320
To slumber here, as in the Vales of Heav'n?
Or in this abject posture have ye sworn
To adore the Conquerour? who now beholds
Cherube and Seraph rowling in the Flood
With scatter'd Arms and Ensigns, till anon
His swift pursuers from Heav'n Gates discern
Th' advantage, and descending tread us down
Thus drooping, or with linked Thunderbolts
Transfix us to the bottom of this Gulfe.
Awake, arise, or be for ever fall'n.   330
                                                    (1.314–30)

This call to arms, Satan's first speech in the poem, reveals qualities that will appear later in very different contexts. Satan is an orator. Adept at using language to stir the heart and mind, he here alternately flatters, castigates and seeks to inspire his followers to renewed struggle.

Milton likewise bends his poetic powers to enhance the force of this speech. Notice the repeated, bell-like ululation of consonants alternating with drumming *d* sounds, and the sonorous vowel sounds at the beginning of the extract:

He call'd so loud, that all the hollow Deep
Of Hell resounded

                                                          (314–15)

Internal rhymes and assonances enhance the effect (called, all; loud, resounded). Milton tells us that the voice of the fallen angel resounded throughout hell: his poetry makes us hear it, too. Notice now the power of the repeated plosives in the exclamations with which Satan's speech begins:

Princes! Potentates! (315)

The sounds of the words generate explosions in keeping with the violence of Satan's theme.

The structure of Satan's argument falls into four stages. He begins by reminding the angels of their status as princes, potentates, and lastly warriors: it is as warriors that he now wishes them to see themselves. Later in his speech, he continues to flatter them as 'the Flowr of Heav'n' and 'eternal Spirits'. At that stage, however, he is introducing a new element into his theme, reminding the angels of the change in their circumstances, their loss of heaven. At the same time, he offers hope: lines 316–17 take a little effort to understand properly, and their meaning is important. Heaven was once theirs, he says, but is 'now lost, / If such astonishment as this can seize / Eternal Spirits'. A rough paraphrase will need to expand Milton's elliptical lines thus: you may consider heaven finally lost, if you can respond to this one defeat only with shocked weakness, despair and enervation (all implied in 'astonishment'). It is already clear at this point that Satan wishes his followers not to accept final defeat, but to stir themselves to continued proud resistance.

In the second part of his speech Satan turns to scorn to stimulate a response from his followers, suggesting caustically that they need to rest after the stress of battle, and that perhaps they would prefer in their laziness to 'slumber here' than to renew the fight. Further, he questions their loyalty: perhaps they have chosen 'To adore the Conquerour' (313) – it is unclear whether this epithet refers to God or to the Son, or both, and perhaps it does not matter. Satan's point is to sneer at submission as an acceptance of humiliation, an 'abject posture' (322).

Thirdly, Satan instils fear of further punishment when he suggests that the powers of heaven will send 'swift pursuers' (326) to drive home the victory against a demoralised enemy. He dramatises the threat with the image of 'linked Thunderbolts / Transfix[ing]' (328–9) the rebel angels in the depths of hell. Again, he implies hope in the idea that the enemy 'descending [will only] tread us down / Thus drooping'; notice how the repeated *d* underlines the meaning.

This picture of ultimate defeat leads on to the clarion call of the final line of the speech, the fourth stage of Satan's appeal. Instead of the defeated dullness of drooping despair, he offers action with a rising inflection of hope: 'Awake, Arise'. There is no alternative than to 'be forever fall'n' (330).

This is a stirring speech. That it is completely dishonest does nothing to diminish its power. There is no hope. The defeat is complete.

The rebels' damnation is eternal. But Satan will invent a mirage of false hope where none exists because his inordinate pride will not allow him to admit that he has no way to pursue his original goal. In the end, he will settle for the loss of heaven, if he can reign in hell; indeed, for his vanity, it is the better option, as it is 'Better to reign in Hell, then serve in Heav'n' (1.263). After the angels emerge from the lake and those of highest status come forward singly, Satan reaffirms his posture of defiance:

> ... Peace is despaird
> For who can think Submission? Warr, then, warr
> Open or understood, must be resolv'd.
>
> (1.660–2)

The remainder of Book 1 is largely devoted to a description of the building of the magnificent infernal palace of Pandemonium, henceforth the dwelling-place of all the demons. It closes with preparation for the council in hell at which the fallen angels discuss how they may continue their fight against God. Milton's verse rings with demonic energy and power. That this renewed spirit of defiance has grown from lies is almost forgotten. In his role as orator and prince of angels, Satan's rhetorical skills have won the day. He is the prince of lies as well as of angels.

Immediately before the council of the fallen angels, however, Book 2 begins with a portrait of Satan enthroned that combines superficial grandeur with ironic ambiguity. In paradoxical language, Milton underlines the deceitful reality underlying the spectacular show of renewed confidence we witnessed in the latter part of Book 1:

> High on a Throne of Royal State, which far
> Outshon the wealth of Ormus and of Ind,
> Or where the gorgeous East with richest hand
> Showrs on her Kings Barbaric Pearl & Gold,
> Satan exalted sat, by merit rais'd
> To that bad eminence; and from despair
> Thus high uplifted beyond hope, aspires
> Beyond thus high, insatiate to pursue
> Vain Warr with Heav'n, and by success untaught
> His proud imaginations thus displaid.   10
>
> (2.1–10)

We do not need to analyse this short extract in the systematic way we normally employ. Its content is simple. Instead we will proceed straight to analysis of its effect, which is not simple at all.

This grandiose opening gives a superficial impression of extravagant wealth and power. Milton deploys an extraordinary range of rhetorical tricks to create the effect: there is a miniature epic simile comparing Satan with oriental potentates, there is vivid imagery, and there is the personification of the 'gorgeous East' that 'Showrs' her kings with untold riches. The first word in the extract, 'High', sets the tone of what follows. Satan's enthronement, his 'Royal' environment, the comparison with the kings of the orient, the introduction of the exotic place-names, Ormus and Ind, the brilliant lighting of the scene, richer than the 'gorgeous East' with its 'Barbaric Pearl and Gold', all contribute to support the theme of majestic grandeur that characterised the scene of the building of Pandemonium.

That opening word, however, also picks out Satan's flaw. The idea of his high ambition is picked up again in line 5, where he 'exalted sat'; the word 'high' is repeated, indeed, three times in these ten lines (1, 7, 8), each time with greater irony; he is 'rais'd' (5), 'uplifted' (7). Thus Satan has the kind of eminence in hell that God has in heaven. Milton's language makes it clear, however, that Satan's eminence is a delusion, the fruit of 'proud imaginations' (10) without real substance; 'high uplifted beyond hope'; carried away by what he has achieved, he has lost his sense of reality. If we recall the description of God on his throne that we looked at in Chapter 3, is, we will notice the simplicity of real power and authority:

> Now had the Almighty Father from above,
> From the pure Empyrean where he sits
> High Thron'd above all highth, bent down his eye,
> His own works and their works at once to view
>
> (3.56–9)

Contrast the exotic tone of Satan's enthronement! However, the description of God towards the beginning of Book 3 occurs after the description of Satan; the effect is that Satan is allowed to make his impact unopposed. It is only later that we see where true power lies, and where moral height, as opposed to overweening ambition, resides.

Multiple ambiguities illustrate the illusory nature of Satan's power. The 'merit' (5) by which he is raised is something different from what we normally mean by the word: here it means rather evil achievements than good, and it leads not to worthy exaltation, but to a 'bad' (6) eminence. Satan is 'insatiate' (8) to pursue war with heaven: the word implies both greed and his failure to understand his impotence against God; he can achieve only 'Vain Warr' (9), the spondee* (two long syllables in a foot) underpinning the significance of the phrase. 'Success', like 'merit', has an unusual meaning, depending on its Latin origin. Milton regularly uses the word in its modern sense, but here it means the outcome of Satan's rebellion, a failure from which he has learned, seemingly, nothing.

The whole passage is evidently overblown. Full of ironies, it exposes Satan's speciousness as it relishes his vividness. An oxymoron acts as a key to the whole: 'bad eminence'. In that ironic coupling Milton summarises both Satan's greatness and his emptiness.

The folly of the Satanic enterprise emerges more practically from what follows. At the council in hell, the fallen angels resolve that rather than attempt a direct confrontation with God, they will be better advised to explore the new world that God has created. They know that any direct confrontation with God is doomed to failure. Satan knows this too. But true to his indomitable nature, he refuses to acknowledge the fact. Instead, Satan volunteers, in a heroic style appropriate to his royal enthronement, to make the epic journey across Chaos to Eden.

Satan on the Border of the Garden of Eden

We will consider two passages from Book 4, in which Satan explores Eden, discovers Adam and Eve, and is eventually confronted by Gabriel, who banishes him from Paradise. Before turning to Satan's reaction to the sight of Eden, we will review the introductory section of Book 4, before Satan's address to the Sun:

> O For that warning voice, which he who saw
> Th' Apocalyps, heard cry in Heaven aloud,
> Then when the Dragon, put to second rout,

Came furious down to be reveng'd on men,
Wo To The Inhabitants On Earth! that now,
While time was, our first Parents had bin warnd
The coming of thir secret foe, and scap'd
Haply so scap'd his mortal snare; for now
Satan, now first inflam'd with rage, came down,
The Tempter ere th' Accuser of man-kind, 10
To wreck on innocent frail man his loss
Of that first Battel, and his flight to Hell:
Yet not rejoycing in his speed, though bold,
Far off and fearless, nor with cause to boast,
Begins his dire attempt, which nigh the birth
Now rowling, boiles in his tumultuous brest,
And like a devillish Engine back recoiles
Upon himself; horror and doubt distract
His troubl'd thoughts, and from the bottom stirr
The Hell within him, for within him Hell 20
He brings, and round about him, nor from Hell
One step no more then from himself can fly
By change of place: Now conscience wakes despair
That slumberd, wakes the bitter memorie
Of what he was, what is, and what must be
Worse; of worse deeds worse sufferings must ensue.
Sometimes towards Eden which now in his view
Lay pleasant, his grievd look he fixes sad,
Sometimes towards Heav'n and the full-blazing Sun,
Which now sat high in his Meridian Towre. 30
(4.1–30)

This opening paragraph contains a mixture of direct comment, narrative, and psychological insight. This is my basic structural analysis:

1. A miniature proem in which the narrator bewails the unpreparedness of Adam and Eve for the test that awaits them when Satan invades Paradise (1–8).
2. A statement of Satan's arrival, together with his purpose in brief (8–12).
3. A description of the violent emotions that trouble Satan's mind (13–26).
4. Satan's indecision reflected in his physical behaviour (27–30).

Though the meaning of the passage is not hard to grasp, we still need to explore it to ensure that we fully understand the nuances of the ideas Milton expresses, and the implications of his portrait of Satan.

The first section of this extract is much less extensive than the proems we discussed in Chapter 1, but is no less powerful. It contains no appeal to the Muse, but instead refers to the 'warning voice' that John envisioned in the Book of Revelation:

> And I beheld, and heard an angel flying through the midst of heaven, saying with a loud voice, Woe, woe, woe, to the inhabiters of the earth, by reason of the other voices of the trumpet of the three angels, which are yet to sound! ...
>
> Woe to the inhabiters of the earth and of the sea! For the devil is come down unto you, having great wrath, because he knoweth that he hath but a short time. (Book of Revelation, 8:13, 12:12)

Other material in the extract derives from the same part of the Bible. 'Apocalypse' is simply the Greek name for the Book of Revelation, and the reference to Satan as a dragon is perhaps from that source, which refers to 'the dragon, that old serpent, which is the Devil, and Satan' (Book of Revelation, 20:2). These direct biblical references create an atmosphere of seriousness appropriate to this eventful part of the poem.

The emotional intensity of this section matches the seriousness of the subject. No other book of the poem begins with an ominous exclamation: Book 4 establishes a mood of foreboding from the beginning. The source of this mood is the conviction that the possibility of avoiding sin can be no more than an illusory hope. Adam and Eve might have escaped the menace of Satan 'haply': the word means 'perchance' and suggests also 'with a happy result'. But no warning voice speaks, and thus they will be caught in the fatal plot ('mortal snare') of Satan's 'secret' wiles. The repetition of 'scap'd' implies longing for a deliverance already known, in fact, to be vain.

Next, in the second section of the extract, the narrator turns his attention to Satan, but the focus remains on the human effect of Satan's incursion. Man is 'innocent frail', here the guiltless victim of a vengeful enemy. Satan, 'inflam'd with rage', intent on assuaging the pain and fury of his loss of heaven by first tempting Adam and Eve to disobey God's will, and then accusing them before God.

The concentration of these lines is extraordinary. Consider the wealth of meaning contained in brief phrases. For example, 'While time was' means 'Before it was too late'. Later, in one incisive phrase, 'innocent frail man' reminds us that man has not yet fallen, but is frail in that he *will* fall. Satan's whole campaign, as 'The Tempter ere th' Accuser' of mankind, is summed up in two words.

In the third section of the passage, we inhabit the turmoil of Satan's thoughts. He is absorbed in his 'dire attempt' – his plan to bring about the Fall of man. He is 'bold', yet full of 'horror and doubt'. He is himself the embodiment of hell (20–1), and we experience something of its pains in the tortured conflict of emotions that Satan here suffers. It seems odd to see the word 'conscience' (23) used of Satan's thought: but here it means 'consciousness' rather than the voice of God, and 'memorie' means rather 'awareness' than merely recollection of the past: Satan thinks over his situation, recalling the diminishment he has suffered, and the harsher punishment he can look forward to in the future. These ideas are communicated in forceful, incisive language. When Satan feels 'what he was, what is, and what must be' (25) the spare repetition and metre reinforce the meaning. In the following line, the triple repetition of 'worse' reverberates from its emphatic position at the beginning of the line to confirm Satan's absolute despair.

After this intense insight, the final part of the extract returns to action. Satan, turning his gaze from Eden that 'Lay pleasant' before him, towards the Sun, 'full-blazing' at noon ('in his meridian Towre') constitutes, 'sad' and 'grievd' as he is, a blot of darkness between two glories. Here, as at the end of the first extract in this chapter, we adopt Satan's position: we see with him what is 'in his view'. At the same time, we watch him 'fix...his look' on the sun and Eden. Thus this concluding section invites us both to share his perspective and to perceive his pain and envy.

When we review this passage as a whole, we are struck by its extraordinary combination of ellipsis and repetition. We have already noted above the repetition of ''scap'd' and 'worse'. However, the 'Worse' that occurs at the beginning of line 26 reduces to the absolute minimum the idea that what is to follow for Satan after the successful temptation of Eve must inevitably be further pain. We also noted above phrases with concentrated meaning such as 'innocent frail', 'mortal snare' and 'what he was, what is, and what must be'. A further instance focuses on an essential idea about the nature of Satan. The threefold repetition of 'Hell' (21–2) develops the reference to Satan's 'flight to Hell' (12), and an inversion of phrase stresses the identity of Satan with hell:

> The Hell within him ... within him Hell.

This repetition of words supports a reduplication of meaning in lines 20–3, where Milton tells us that Satan has hell 'within him', that he carries hell not only with him but also 'round about him', and that he can no more escape hell that he can himself. Here the repetition enacts the sense of absolute impotence, of hopeless entrapment, lying at the heart of Satan's actions. Satan knows that he can ultimately achieve nothing but further punishment. He knows that his 'dire attempt' – which Milton with ironic metaphor describes as 'nigh the birth – will inevitably be stillborn. Thus, then, the violent emotions that trouble his 'tumultuous breast': 'Horror and doubt', 'conscience', 'despair', 'bitter memory'.

This concentrated repetition creates intense dramatic power. We share Satan's violent passions even as we recognise his powerlessness. Milton uses vivid language to represent his feelings. His plan is 'rowling' towards its fulfilment, his passion 'boiles', his anxious emotions 'distract' and 'stir' him. Simile and personification bring these abstract feelings to life: in his contradictory state and his self-destructiveness, Satan is like a firing cannon, a 'devillish Engine [that] back recoiles';[1] his knowledge of the vanity of his enterprise 'wakes despair / That slumberd'. It is perhaps no accident that Milton's lines about Satan embodying hell echo a theatrical predecessor. It is Mephostophilis in Marlowe's *Doctor Faustus* who says in answer to Faustus questioning why he is out of hell:

> Why this is hell, nor am I out of it.[2]

Milton's Satan equally embodies hell, and the word itself dominates the extract with an ominous warning. Like Marlowe's Mephostophilis, however, Milton's Satan is a dramatic figure, and when we see him at the end of this extract, grieving and saddened in his dark nowhere between heaven and Eden, it is hard not to feel some compassion for him in his predicament.

When we look at the overall shape of this extract, moving from a dire warning of impending disaster towards a portrait of Satan as a tragic figure, we witness a change of focus parallel to that which occurred in the first extract we discussed in this chapter. There the narrator asks about the cause of the Fall, moves on to talk about Satan's expulsion from heaven for the sin of pride, and then portrays him looking about him in hell. Here in Book 4 the narrator focuses much more strongly on Satan's essential part in the downfall of mankind; the narrator begins by bewailing the absence of any warning of what is to befall, and proceeds to discuss Satan's plan, and its source in pain and envy. Satan is therefore depicted as the ultimate enemy, yet he is depicted from within, and thus inevitably may attract sympathy.

In the passage immediately following, Satan addresses the sun 'in sighs' (4.31) and, recalling his rebellion with its motives and results, falls to self-recrimination and thence to self-pity in the phrase 'Me miserable!' (4.73). A little later, however, having accepted that there is for him no route to repentance and pardon, he puts doubts aside ('Farewell remorse!' 4.109) and resolves on his future path: 'Evil, be thou my good' (4.110). This declaration, which echoes a biblical warning, 'Woe unto them that call evil good, and good evil' (Isaiah, 5:20), reveals the depth of Satan's iniquity. Yet even here, it is possible to find a modicum of sympathy for him because of the force of his will, and because he takes the only course open to him.

Thus far, then, our response to Satan is almost inevitably ambiguous. In his active energy and his indomitable refusal to submit, he impresses, even as his nature appals us.

Satan Enters the Garden of Eden

The change of scene to Eden marks a significant change in Milton's portrayal of Satan. When he finds Adam and Eve and considers how he can turn them to his purpose, Satan's evil nature becomes more defined. This is partly an effect of his actions: as he seeks to corrupt, his own corruption becomes more evident. However, the process of Satan's diminishment begins as he enters Eden, before he sees the human characters:

> Now to th' ascent of that steep savage Hill
> Satan had journied on, pensive and slow;
> But further way found none, so thick entwin'd,
> As one continu'd brake, the undergrowth
> Of shrubs and tangling bushes had perplext
> All path of Man or Beast that past that way:
> One Gate there onely was, and that look'd East
> On th' other side: which when th' arch-fellon saw
> Due entrance he disdaind, and in contempt,   180
> At one slight bound high overleap'd all bound
> Of Hill or highest Wall, and sheer within
> Lights on his feet. As when a prowling Wolfe,
> Whom hunger drives to seek new haunt for prey,
> Watching where Shepherds pen thir Flocks at eeve
> In hurdl'd Cotes amid the field secure,
> Leaps o're the fence with ease into the Fould:
> Or as a Thief bent to unhoord the cash
> Of some rich Burgher, whose substantial dores,
> Cross-barrd and bolted fast, fear no assault,   190
> In at the window climbes, or o're the tiles;
> So clomb this first grand Thief into Gods Fould:
> So since into his Church lewd Hirelings climbe.
> Thence up he flew, and on the Tree of Life,
> The middle Tree and highest there that grew,
> Sat like a Cormorant; yet not true Life
> Thereby regaind, but sat devising Death
> To them who liv'd; nor on the vertue thought
> Of that life-giving Plant, but only us'd
> For prospect, what well us'd had bin the pledge   200
> Of immortalitie. So little knows
> Any, but God alone, to value right
> The good before him, but perverts best things
> To worst abuse, or to thir meanest use.
>
> (4.172–203)

This extract splits naturally into three sections and a postscript thus:

1. Satan makes his way towards Eden but finds the way blocked by thick undergrowth. Approaching from the west, he sees that the only gate is on the far side of Eden. Ignoring the gate, Satan leaps over the boundary into Eden. (172–83).
2. A series of similes. Satan's invasion of Eden is compared with a wolf preying on sheep, with a thief stealing from a wealthy town-dweller, and with paid clergy entering the church. (183–93).
3. Taking the shape of a cormorant, Satan flies up to the crown of the Tree of Life, not for its virtuous qualities, but to obtain a better view of Eden. (196–201).
4. The narrator muses on Satan's behaviour, which reminds him that only God is capable of complete understanding (201–4).

Though the extract is evidently dominated by the vivid similes Milton applies to Satan, the introductory lines are important. Like the previous extract, the first section of this passage reveals Satan's thoughts. Absorbed in the thoughts we have discussed briefly in relation to aftermath of the previous extract Satan has made a 'pensive and slow' (173) journey to the borders of Eden, its laboriousness suggested in the phrase 'journeyed on' (173). Now, confronted by a barrier of intertwined thickets, he changes in mood and behaviour. Faced with practical difficulty, he abandons fruitless introspection and becomes active. Scorning the wall of undergrowth as insignificant, and eschewing the formal entrance of the gate to the east of Eden, he leaps with 'one slight bound' (181) into the garden. Now that the time for action has come, Satan is decisive, energetic, and poised: he 'Lights on his feet' (183). This moment dramatically transforms the troubled introspection that characterised Satan's travelling across the void. The transformation is moral as well as physical. The repetition of 'bound' (181) expresses Satan's power: an easy leap can carry him over any material boundary, and, of course, no moral boundary means anything to Satan. The setting supports the moral meaning with symbolic detail: the wild hillside, with its 'thick entwin'd' vegetation, the 'tangling' branches that would have 'perplext' the way of men or beasts suggests the idea of a moral maze to which the close of the extract reverts.

The theme of Satan's evil and predatory nature links the epic similes in the second section of the extract. The first, comparing Satan with 'a prowling wolf', refers to 'hunger' as the source of his seeking 'new haunt for prey'. This is a close parallel with Satan, whose envy first leads him to explore Eden where Adam and Eve become his prey, and Satan leaps into Eden with the same ease that the wolf leaps over the fence that protects the sheep. The use of the word 'hurdl'd' to describe the fence matches the intertwined vegetation that guards Eden. The flocks in their pen are 'secure': the word suggests 'safe', but Milton is using it primarily in its Latin sense, 'free from care'; in this respect, the sheep reflect the innocence of Adam and Eve. However, the context may also imply foolishly careless or overconfident. As a whole, the simile of wolf and sheep presents Adam and Eve as innocent victims of a monstrous enemy. It recalls also several biblical references to sheep as symbols of innocence, and to Christ as a good shepherd.[3]

The second simile changes the focus from country to town. Here the victim is no sheep, but a 'rich burgher'; instead of a hurdled pen, he is protected by 'substantial dores / Cross-barrd and bolted fast'. He has, however, something in common with the sheep of the previous simile: as they are 'secure', he, like his doors, 'fear[s] no assault'; also like them, he has no safety from a predator that can find a devious route past his defences. We are here invited to see Satan as a thief who finds out and steals ('unhoord[s]') a wealthy man's money. The idea of the hoard, further, suggests something hidden or protected, and may thus recall the prize of immortality that belongs to Adam and Eve. All are equally threatened by the evil unleashed by this 'first grand Thief'.

Milton's purpose here appears to be to universalise the threat of Satan. In the first two similes he moves from an agricultural environment to a commercial one. In the third and final simile, he brings the parallel up to date in a religious environment. Now Satan is like one of the 'lewd Hirelings' who climb into God's church. We may interpret this as a general criticism of clergy who are motivated by greed instead of faith, though in actuality, Milton is here voicing a more personal view.[4] The odd use of the archaic 'clomb' here instead of 'climbed' avoids the threefold repetition of forms of 'climbes ... [climbed] ... clim be'; it also looks back down history, enhancing the universality of the pattern of moral predation Milton describes here.

After that triple simile, the narrative reverts to Satan in Eden. The fourth section of the extract focuses on the perversion of good. Satan is compared with a cormorant, a symbol of greed and thus a link with the wolf and thief of the epic similes.[5] In this form, he sits like a dark harbinger of death on the crown of the Tree of Life in the centre of the Garden of Eden.[6] Milton emphasises the irony of his perch where he 'devis[es] Death' to Adam and Eve – 'Them who liv'd' in the sense that they have immortality. The irony deepens as Satan, giving no thought to the 'vertue' (that is, the beneficial properties) of the tree that bestows immortality, uses it as a vantage point to spy on the garden. This idea is stressed by the alliterative conflict between 'prospect' and 'pledge', when he uses the Tree of Life merely as a vantage point.

The final sentence of the extract picks up the idea of Satan's negligence or ignorance of the meaning of the Tree of Life, using it to express a sententious criticism of the general foolishness of humankind. To God alone is it given to value good; mere humans will always turn good into evil ('pervert ... / To worst abuse') or to some trivial purpose. The extract fittingly closes with a strong emphasis on the idea of perversion, abuse and 'meanest use'. This is the idea that colours our interpretation of what follows, when Satan surveys the beauties of the garden: we know from the beginning that he does not value it.

Reviewing the extract as a whole, we can see a radical difference in perspective from the extracts we discussed earlier. In each of the earlier extracts, we may find it possible to think of Satan in a sympathetic light: as he lies on the burning lake, and as he thinks over his desperate state, we can feel his pain with him. In this third extract, in contrast, the Satan who enters the Garden of Eden prefigures and authors evil down the ages. He is the wolf in the sheepfold, the thief in the night, the corrupt clergyman. From this point on, Milton treats Satan in increasingly negative terms.

The World of the Fallen Angels

Of course, the world of the demons is always presented as evil. The demons themselves are spoken of disparagingly as henchmen of a petty criminal. Milton uses unpleasant metaphors and similes to describe them, as in the 'a pitchy cloud / Of Locusts' (1.340–1) that hovers at the rim of hell. He refers to them contemptuously as 'the Godless crew / Rebellious' (6.49–50)[7] or a 'revolted Rout / Heav'n-fall'n' (10.534–5). Their palace, Pandemonium, has all the pomp and splendour of the greatest palaces and temples, yet remains a sulphurous realm dominated by 'a hill ... whose griesly top / Belch'd fire and rowling smoak' (1.670–1).

In several points, the world of the angels contrasts diametrically with the heavenly world. Where heaven is dominated by radiant light, hell is murky, pitchy, dark, dun, or gloomy. The light of fiery tortures serves only to emphasise the blackness of the environment – this demonic home 'on all sides round / As one great Furnace flam'd, yet from those flames / No light, but rather darkness visible' (1.61–3). Where heavenly celebration is marked by the intricate dancing of the angels, hell is heavy, burdened, sluggish, and weary: it takes supreme effort for Satan to lift his head from the burning lake where he is thrown, and when eventually 'upright he rears from off the Pool / His mighty Stature' (1.221–2) and takes wing, 'the dusky Air ... felt unusual weight (1.228–9). He carries a 'ponderous' (1.284) shield, and uses his tall spear 'to support uneasie steps ... not like those steps / On Heavens Azure' (1.295–7). His followers, demoralised, have to be cajoled into activity. And where heaven resounds to the angels' singing, hell has, until Belezebub begins to speak, only 'horrid silence' (1.83). Hell, clearly, is the antithesis of Heaven; the region of the damned consists of utter desolation, realised as darkness, torpor, and silence. Raphael affirms their ultimate fate in Book 7: 'Canceld from Heav'n and sacred memorie, / Nameless in dark oblivion let them dwell ... Eternal silence be thir doome' (6.379–85).

The condemned angels, however, introduce energy into the emptiness and, with energy, sound. In contrast with the heavenly music of the loyal angels, however, the fallen demons create less harmonious sounds, with 'Trumpets loud and Clarions ... Sonorous mettal blowing Martial sounds' (1.532–40). When the demons raise their voices, they do so with 'A shout that tore Hells Concave, and beyond / Frighted the Reign of Chaos and old Night' (1.542–3). Not all the sounds of hell are unpleasant. Indeed, when the fallen angels gather to hear Satan they move 'in silence to soft Pipes that charm'd / Thir painful steps o're the burnt soyle' (1.561–2), and when Pandemonium takes shape, we hear 'the sound / Of Dulcet Symphonies and voices sweet'

(1.711–12). However, at other points Milton uses sound to assist in opposing heaven from hell. We can focus the contrasts Milton intends with comparative analysis of contrasting extracts. Here, for example, Milton describes the acclamation of the angels for God's announcement of the Son's redemptive purpose with the demons' acclamation of Satan's war policy:

> No sooner had th' Almighty ceas't, but all
> The multitude of Angels with a shout
> Loud as from numbers without number, sweet
> As from blest voices, uttering joy, Heav'n rung
> With Jubilee, and loud Hosanna's fill'd
> Th' eternal Regions.
>
> (3.344–9)

> He spake: and to confirm his words, out-flew
> Millions of flaming swords, drawn from the thighs
> Of mighty Cherubim; the sudden blaze
> Far round illumin'd hell: highly they rag'd
> Against the Highest, and fierce with grasped arm's
> Clash'd on their sounding shields the din of war,
> Hurling defiance toward the vault of Heav'n.
>
> (1.663–9)

Here we can see simple parallels: the 'multitude' of the angels matches the 'Millions' of swords of the devils; both extracts are 'Loud' or full of 'din'. But the differences are more evident. Where the heavenly shout is 'sweet', 'din' suggests unpleasant noise and the swords 'Clash'd on their sounding shields'. Where heaven is filled with 'blest voices', Hell's demons 'rag'd'; where we hear the angels 'uttering joy [and] Jubilee', we hear the demons 'hurling defiance'. We notice, too, that in heaven there are no weapons. In hell, there are swords and shields. These are important, for it is the 'sudden blaze' from the unanimous brandishing of 'flaming swords' that 'Far round illumin'd hell'. The effect, however, is inevitably temporary. In heaven, light, which goes unmentioned here, is the constant medium the angels inhabit.

Let us look briefly at two further extracts to confirm Milton's careful notation of the different environments. In the first, heaven's gates open to allow the Son forth to do battle with the rebels, and in the

second, the doors of hell are opened to allow Satan egress to journey
to the new world:

> Heav'n op'nd wide
> Her ever during Gates, Harmonious sound
> On golden Hinges moving, to let forth
> The King of Glorie in his powerful Word

(7.205–8)

> ... on a sudden op'n flie
> With impetuous recoile and jarring sound
> Th' infernal dores, and on thir hinges great
> Harsh Thunder, that the lowest bottom shook
> Of Erebus.

(2.879–83)

There is an obvious contrast here between the 'Harmonious sound'
of heavenly gates and the 'jarring sound' of their infernal counterpart.
Other contrasts are only slightly less direct: 'golden Hinges' match with
'hinges great'; the majestic 'op'nd wide' of the heavenly gates matches
the violent 'on a sudden op'n flie' of the infernal doors. Violence,
indeed, is thematic in the extract from Book 2: 'op'n flie ... impetuous
recoil ... Harsh Thunder ... shook'.

Hell has nothing to recommend it. In itself, as the domain of evil,
it is simply the negation of all the felicities of heaven. The features that
the demons bring to it are almost entirely horrific or unpleasant. Only
when we come to Satan do we find a problem of insidious attraction.

The Transformation of Satan

Among the rebel angels, Satan stands pre-eminent physically as well as
morally. He calls his followers to arms, he undertakes the journey to
Eden, and he himself brings his demonic plan to its climax. In Book
1 his stature reflects his status:

> ... He above the rest
> In shape and gesture proudly eminent
> Stood like a Towr

(1.589–91)

Satan is damned, yet he is proud. As the 'dread Commander' (1.589) of the rebel angels, he commands also a measure of respect. At this stage, he appears impressive, not only towering tall, but still also retaining something of his beauty as the brightest of the angels in heaven ('Lucifer', his heavenly name, means 'light-bringer'), for 'His form had yet not lost / All her Original brightness' (1.591–2). However, in the course of time, he loses his beauty. When Uriel catches sight of him on Mount Niphates, he recognises him as 'disfigur'd more then could befall / Spirit of happie sort' (4.127–8). Then, when Zephon disovers Satan in the garden, he taunts him that 'thou resembl'st now / Thy sin and place of doom obscure and foule' (4.839–40). At the end of Book 4 Gabriel castigates Satan as a 'sly hypocrite' (4.957), and sends him from the garden. The final line of Book 4 describes Satan's flight from the prospect of a losing battle as a retreating of darkness, for 'with him fled the shades of night' (4.1015).

The moral darkening of Satan finds expression in metaphorical devices. At the beginning of Book 4, immediately before an extract we analysed earlier, Satan is associated with the stink of rotting fish (see 4.166–71). Images of animals chart Satan's gradual degradation. In Book 4 he is initially associated with the Dragon, later takes the form of a wolf and a cormorant in the extract we discussed above, and elsewhere appears as a lion 'with fiery glare' and as a tiger (4.402–3). All these are predatory beasts. Later, however, Satan takes the loathsome form of a toad as he squats at the ear of Eve (4.800) hoping to pervert her dreams. Finally he possesses the serpent, creeping 'like a black mist low' to inhabit its 'labyrinth of…suttle wiles' (9.180–4). The serpent is a perfect vehicle for Satan, expressing in its folds Satan's convoluted rhetoric, in its forked tongue his duplicity, and in its hissing voice the threat underlying the superficial attractiveness of his speech; its lowliness, ultimately, reflects Satan's moral baseness. The last view we have of Satan in the serpent after it has completed its task shows the arch enemy, the fiend, the wolf, leaving the scene of his bitter victory in anything but heroic style:

> …Back to the Thicket
> Slunk the guiltie Serpent.

> (9.784–5)

This shameful flight sets Satan at his true value. Once the brightest of the angels, he now hides from the light, choosing the obscurity of the thicket to conceal his perfidy.

Conclusions

- Satan is a vivid character in the poem, and has qualities with which we find it possible to associate ourselves. He feels quasi-human emotions after his expulsion from heaven, and we may perhaps sympathise with his desire to regain something of what he has lost.
- Milton appears to enjoy writing about Satan. His violence, passion and decisiveness, and the horror of his plight lend themselves to powerful poetic expression.
- Satan is the most dynamic character in the poem. It is a narrative because of what he does, what he achieves, and what he fails to achieve.
- Satan refuses to accept defeat, even when he knows that his defeat is final.
- Satan shows no pity for Adam and Eve.
- None of the other demons has the attractive power of Satan.
- Milton touches constantly on the reality of Satan's viciousness, using imagery (such as the animal imagery we have considered, or the symbolism of light and dark), pointed epithets ('the tempter ere the accuser of mankind', for example), exclamations ('O for that warning voice') and action (such as the confrontation between Satan and Gabriel).
- We are consistently reminded of the effects of damnation by the contrasting of what Satan once was, and the hopelessness of his damnation.
- The narrator's perspective changes significantly, showing us Satan's thoughts and feelings at some points, and at others treating him merely as the author of the Fall of mankind.
- Satan's presentation changes in the course of the poem, so that he appears more powerful and attractive at the beginning, and more despicable at the end.
- Milton draws sharp contrasts between heaven and hell, using light, sound, and dance.

Methods of Analysis

- As in previous chapters, we have normally begun each discussion with a simple structural analysis, following up with an attempt to reach a full understanding of the content of the passage.
- In this chapter we have then focused especially on the changes of focus that occur in all three of the extracts, exploring the way in which we are drawn from Satan's function in the narrative into exploration of his mind, and then withdrawn again to see him as an evil presence.
- The use of imagery is particularly important in defining the character of Satan: the animal images, the devilish engine, the dragon, the dungeon and chains, darkness, light, and the thief among others. Milton is careful in his use of images to define aspects of Satan's character and function.
- We noted several examples of syntactical effects, in which Milton uses repetition and verbal patterning to enhance the dramatic effect of Satan's woes or to stress the thematic significance of the events.
- We contrasted Milton's description of heaven with his description of hell in order to bring out the evaluation of these two states in the poem.
- Finally, we generalised from the different images of Satan in the third extract to look briefly at the development of his character in the poem as a whole, showing how Milton endeavours to diminish him.
- There are too many aspects of Milton's technical artistry to record them all here in the form of a checklist. The important thing when you analyse other parts of his poem is to be aware of the effects of his language, and to try to see how those effects are achieved.

Further Work

Satan perhaps merits closer attention than any other topic in the poem, so I suggest a larger number of studies than in other chapters of this book.

1. In Book 1, lines 84–126 ('If thou beest he...but rackt with deep despare') Satan addresses Beelzebub and encourages him as well as

himself, to renewed struggle against God. Explore Satan's reasoning, showing how Milton implies their worthlessness. What kind of character does Satan show here? Is it in any way admirable?

2. Consider Satan's acceptance of hell as his realm in Book 1, lines 242–63 ('Is this the Region ... Better to reign in Hell, then serve in Heav'n'). Is there anything heroic in his behaviour and state of mind? From the stylistic point of view, pay special attention to Milton's use of rhetorical questions, to the variety of sentence length, and to his use of alliteration and repetition.

3. Review Book 1, lines 544–621 ('All in a moment through the gloom ... Words interwove with sighs found out their way'). This is a long passage, but lines 572–87 offer a series of parallels for the fallen angels that do not require detailed consideration: their existence is more important than the detail of their meaning, and they are devoted to enhancing the impression of number and power that Milton wishes the fallen angels to make. Use this passage to see how Milton presents the angels in a sympathetic light, using parallels from human experience, and how he develops the sense of loss by using natural imagery.

4. Discuss Satan's soliloquy in Book 4, lines 32–78 ('O thou that with surpassing Glory crownd ... the Hell I suffer seems a Heav'n') or lines 79–113 ('O then at last relent ... this new World shall know'). I call this a soliloquy because of its dramatic qualities. Consider how Milton gives Satan human qualities, treating him like a character in a drama, torturing himself over his options. Does Satan win our sympathy here? It is worth reading (or reviewing the final pages if you know the play) Marlowe's *Doctor Faustus*, which Milton may well have had in mind in writing these lines. From the stylistic point of view, consider the effect of the rhetorical questions, and of the paradoxical statements in either part of this passage.

5. Analyse the concluding lines of Book 4, where Satan submits to Gabriel, lines 977–1015 ('While thus he spake ... with him fled the shades of night'). How does this event influence our perception of Satan? Compare the impression Satan makes here with the impression we have of him from the beginning of Book 4. In this passage, Milton's use of simile, metaphor and symbolism is especially rich. Consider the effect of the various parallels Milton introduces,

including classical, rural, geographical and astrological references, the symbol of the scales, and the symbolism of light and dark. Finally, what is the effect of the anticlimax (that is, the promise of a great duel fading away in flight) with which the book ends?

6. Lines 505–38 of Book 4 ('Sight hateful, sight tormenting!... o're hil, o're dale his roam') show us Satan's reaction to the happiness of Adam and Eve, and his resolution to destroy it. Here in another soliloquy he is depicted very much as the stage villain as he works out how to bring about their downfall. Can our response to him at this point be anything other than abhorrence? Consider Milton's use of rhetorical questions, and the cleverness and logic of Satan's brief rehearsal of the arguments he will use against Eve. How does Milton reveal his envy and express the deceitfulness of his arguments?

7. Drawing together Chapters 4 and 5, you could tackle a 'compare and contrast' question, such as one of the following:

   • Compare Satan's offer to explore the new world in Book 2, lines 427–66 ('Satan, whom now transcendent glory rais'd... None shall partake with me') with the Son's offer to atone for man's sin in Book 3, lines 218–65 ('And silence was in Heav'n: on mans behalf... in thy presence Joy entire'). Show how Milton brings out the character and motives of each speaker, and consider how the contrast between the extracts illuminates the poem as a whole. You should look also at the reception each speech receives in the eight or ten lines following the speeches.

   • Analyse the confrontation between Gabriel and Satan at the end of Book 4 (lines 877–976, 'To whom with stern regard thus Gabriel spake... In progress through the rode of Heav'n Star-pav'd'). Show how Milton contrasts the two angels using description as well as their language. Which rhetorical devices are used, and with what effect?

5

Adam, Eve and their Perfect Paradise

Book 4. 204–51 ('Beneath him with new wonder ... of delicious taste')
Book 4. 288–324 ('Two of far nobler shape ... fairest of her Daughters Eve')
Book 5. 35–93 ('Close at mine ear one call'd ... To find this but a dream!')

In this chapter we turn our attention to the protagonists of Milton's epic drama. The paradise that is lost is theirs; and theirs is the responsibility for losing it. We will consider their ideal garden, their relationship with each other, and their relationship with God. Their loss of paradise we will defer until Chapter 6.

The question of perspective that occupied us in our discussion of Satan is equally important in Milton's presentation of Adam and Eve. In the structure determined by Milton, we do not meet them until Book 4; and we meet them in the context of their environment, which is described first; and their garden environment we explore for the first time through the eyes of none other than Satan. The structure of the poem thus presents an Adam and Eve set in the context of the divine will and the satanic plot. It is as if they are puppets on a stage, and only we, the audience, can see all that is happening in the wings and in the gods.

The Garden of Eden

For our first extract we will look at the description of paradise as Satan sees it from the crown of the Tree of Life:

Beneath him with new wonder now he views
To all delight of human sense expos'd
In narrow room Natures whole wealth, yea more,
A Heaven on Earth, for blissful Paradise
Of God the Garden was, by him in the East
Of Eden planted; Eden stretchd her Line   210
From Auran Eastward to the Royal Towrs
Of great Seleucia, built by Grecian Kings,
Or where the Sons of Eden long before
Dwelt in Telassar: in this pleasant soile
His farr more pleasant Garden God ordaind;
Out of the fertil ground he caus'd to grow
All Trees of noblest kind for sight, smell, taste;
And all amid them stood the Tree of Life,
High eminent, blooming Ambrosial Fruit
Of vegetable Gold; and next to Life   220
Our Death the Tree of Knowledge grew fast by,
Knowledge of Good bought dear by knowing ill.
Southward through Eden went a River large,
Nor chang'd his course, but through the shaggie hill
Pass'd underneath ingulft, for God had thrown
That Mountain as his Garden mould high rais'd
Upon the rapid current, which through veins
Of porous Earth with kindly thirst up drawn,
Rose a fresh Fountain, and with many a rill
Waterd the Garden; thence united fell   230
Down the steep glade, and met the neather Flood,
Which from his darksom passage now appeers,
And now divided into four main Streams,
Runs divers, wandring many a famous Realme
And Country whereof here needs no account,
But rather to tell how, if Art could tell,
How from that Saphire Fount the crisped Brooks,
Rowling on Orient Pearl and sands of Gold,
With mazie error under pendant shades
Ran Nectar, visiting each plant, and fed   240
Flours worthy of Paradise which not nice Art
In Beds and curious Knots, but Nature boon
Powrd forth profuse on Hill and Dale and Plaine,
Both where the morning Sun first warmly smote
The open field, and where the unpierc't shade

Imbround the noontide Bowrs: Thus was this place,
A happy rural seat of various view;
Groves whose rich Trees wept odorous Gumms and Balme,
Others whose fruit burnisht with Golden Rinde
Hung amiable, Hesperian Fables true,   250
If true, here onely, and of delicious taste:

(4.205—51)

This is a more purely descriptive piece of writing than the passages
we have examined previously, and may to that extent appear simpler.
We will nevertheless adopt our standard procedure and analyse the
passage logically to ensure that we understand its meaning. We can
probably agree on six sections:

1. Satan in the form of a cormorant looks down from his perch to see
   the riches of Eden stretched out before him (205–10).
2. The extent of Eden and the location of Paradise are described. Most
   students will need to check on the references to Auran, Seleucia
   and Telassar (210–15).
3. The trees of Eden are described, with particular reference to the
   Tree of Knowledge and the Tree of Life (216–23).
4. We follow the course of the river that flows through Eden, as if Satan's
   eye is tracing its course: it disappears underground, where it mois-
   tens the garden by means of a fountain, emerging to flow through a
   varied landscape before dividing into four streams (223–35).
5. A description of how the streams nourish the rich vegetation of the
   fertile garden (235–46).
6. The passage concludes with a more general view of Eden, comparing it with the legendary islands of the Hesperides (246–51).

We can see from this simple summary that the passage, though part
of a large structure, has a circularity that gives it some semblance of
completeness in itself. It begins and ends with a broad view of Eden,
moving from 'A Heaven on Earth' (208) to 'A happy rural seat' (247).
Within this framework, we hear about the trees of Eden, its river, and
the flowers of Paradise. It is as if, through the eyes of Satan, we gain
sight of, then explore, and then sum up a first impression of God's
new creation.

Perhaps the most marked feature of this vision is its sensuousness. In the garden grow trees 'of noblest kind for sight, smell, taste' (217), and as the passage develops we see this general statement borne out by detailed reference. The garden appeals to the eye with its 'vegetable Gold' (220), the 'Saphire Fount' (237), the streams rolling on 'Orient [shining] Pearl and sands of Gold' (238) and 'fruit burnished with golden rind' (249). Gold is a dominant impression, symbolising wealth, brilliance, and purity – it is the alchemist's dream, and fabled in the legendary golden apples of the Hesperides, which find reality only here in this paradisal garden. The garden appeals to the sense of taste with its trees producing 'Ambrosial Fruit' (219), its rivers that 'Ran Nectar' (240), and its golden apples 'of delicious taste' (251). The sense of smell is implied in references to fruit and blooming vegetation, and is given actuality in the 'odorous Gumms and Balme' (248) that flow from the trees. Though unmentioned, the sense of touch is particularly powerful in this passage, particularly in the muscularity of the active verbal forms and the sense of movement. There are trees growing and 'blooming' (219), a river that 'went ... Passed ... divided ... wandring ... rowling ... Ran   Nectar ... visiting ... fed / Flours' (223–41 passim). From the earth 'Rose a fresh Fountain' (229) that 'Waterd the Garden' (231) and then 'fell / Down the steep glade' (230–1). Flowers are 'Powrd fourth profuse' (243). Trees 'wept' (248) and fruit 'hung' (250). The sun 'smote' (244) the fields. Even the geography of Eden is muscular when we learn how far the garden 'stretched' (210) its boundary.

It should not escape us that one of the senses is missing from the rich sensual impression of the extract: hearing. The river makes no sound other than by implication, neither by conversational rippling when the current is rapid, nor roaring where it meets the nether flood, nor hissing when it produces a fountain; no wind sighs through the trees; and no birds sing. At this point Eden is a silent world, dreamlike in its hushed vividness.

However, when we consider Milton's versification, sound is perhaps the strongest impression we have. The strongly musical appeal of the extract depends partly on the armoury of poetic devices Milton employs. He makes use of the exotic proper nouns we have met examples of previously: Auran, Seleucia and Telassar (211–14) are more important for their rich sound than their specific meaning. Later, the Hesperides are used partly for their meaning, and partly for their alliterative breath in 'Hung amiable: Hesperian ... here' (250–1). Alliteration appears too in the 'fresh fountain' (229) that waters Eden, in the natural plenty that 'Poured forth profuse on hill and dale and plain' (243), in the shade of 'Embrowned ... bowers' (246), and in the 'various view' (247) that Eden offers. More complex sound patterns underline the meaning of the text in the river that 'Passed underneath engulfed' (225) and in the muddy sounds as it 'united fell / Down the steep glade, and met the nether flood / That from his darksome passage now appears' (230–2). Simpler patterns appear in the comforting 'm' sounds of 'High eminent, blooming ambrosial' (219) or 'the morning sun first warmly smote' (244). Alliterative effects can make a significant contribution to meaning, too. One alliterative pairing reappears three times in the passage: God and Garden (209, 215, 225–6), creator and creation united, the one a direct expression of the other.

Our dominant impression is of an environment rich in every delight – delicious in every way, not merely in taste. Indeed, the words 'delight' (206) and 'delicious' (251) bracket the whole extract. Everything here seems superabundant: 'fertile ground' (216) produces 'noblest' (217) and 'rich' (248) trees; the river 'large' (223) is sucked up into a 'fresh' (229) fountain by the 'kindly thirst' (228) of the soil; the sun shines 'warmly' (244). The colours of the garden match the colours of precious jewels (sapphire and pearl) and gold. Above all this garden is 'pleasant' – a word that is repeated twice in lines 214–15, and suggests that the garden is created to be pleasing to the human inhabitants about to be encountered.

Although as yet we meet no animal life here, the garden itself lives. Consider again the range of active verbs in the extract: 'stood ... grew ... thrown ... raised ... up   drawn ... rose ... fell ... ran ... poured forth ... smote'. In lines 226–7 the garden takes on the character of animal life that experiences thirst and possesses veins. The Garden of Eden presents a picture, then, of rich, abundant, bursting vegetable growth: all seems prepared for the introduction of a new kind of life.

Turning to the thematic aspects of the extract, our overriding impression must be of the idealised nature of the garden. All seems perfect. Yet even here Milton keeps before us the catastrophe to come. Primarily, he does so by means of perspective: we look at the garden through the eyes of Satan. The garden itself, of course, contains the means of the Fall. In the centre, beside the Tree of Life, stands the forbidden tree, the Tree of Knowledge, a point stressed by the dramatic syntax of:

> And next to Life
> Our Death, the Tree of Knowledge, grew fast by.
>
> (220–1)

Here the juxtaposition of 'Life' and 'Death' matches the juxtaposition of the trees. Milton's description of the trees emphasises the difference between them. The Tree of Life matches the rest of the garden in the richness of its 'Ambrosial Fruit' of 'vegetable Gold' (219–20); it stands 'high eminent' (219). In contrast, the Tree of Knowledge goes undescribed: it is simply noted as the means of death, of 'Knowledge of Good bought dear by knowing ill' (222).[1] This imbalance in the description of the trees invites us to see one tree as clearly attractive, the other not at all so. Here the poem already conditions our response to the temptation and Fall that occur later.

If we now look more closely at the diction* of the description of the garden, we notice that amidst the idealised details there are some features that suggest the menace of evil. Among the sunny fields we find a 'darksom passage' (232) and 'pendent shades' (239). Ambiguity colours the course of the 'wandring' river (234), for the word may suggest moral looseness, an idea underlined by the 'mazie error' (239) of its path through the garden: 'error' has its Latin sense of wandering, as well as its contemporary sense of going wrong. In the manner we have seen to be characteristic of the poem, Milton introduces anachronistic elements into the description too. The reference to 'nice art' (241) – the phrase means over-fussy sophistication – recalls landscape designers who developed plant beds in cleverly calculated shapes – 'curious knots' (242) – like the Elizabethan knot-gardens that are still preserved today. Their endeavours suggest the insidious attraction of knowledge leading to artificiality: contrast the 'profuse' (243) naturalness of 'Nature boon' (242), whose plenty requires no false arrangement to render it glorious. Of course, all this ambiguous phrasing purports specifically to isolate the ideal from fallen experience; nevertheless, our fallen consciousness registers these echoes of fallen nature as part of the experience of the garden.

The shifting ambiguities of Milton's language here remind us that his management of perspective is of supreme importance. We listen to a vision of an ideal garden, the paradise of Adam and Eve, but everything we hear about it is conditioned by the perspective of Satan, through whose eyes we perceive it. The garden itself, too, contains within its generous fecundity the seed of destruction. As the description proceeds, Milton introduces further parallels (or anti-parallels) from later times, specifically from classical myth and from landscape gardening, to illustrate the perfection of paradise and the flawed nature of man. Finally, Milton returns to the word 'delight' that introduces the description, but only to reaffirm the bitter perspective of Satan, who 'saw undelighted all delight' (286). Thanks to Milton's manner of presenting the garden, we too view it with conflicting feelings.

Thus the setting in which Milton places the human characters is laden with overtones. When he finally introduces Adam and Eve – and we are nearly a third of the way through the poem when that occurs – the same perspective governs their portrait as governs the picture of the Garden of Eden. And that perspective is, of course – at least initially – distorted by being Satan's as well as Milton's.

Adam and Eve

Let us look now to look at how Milton presents the beings for whom the garden is created. This is a much-discussed part of the poem, partly because there are things here that have stirred the fury of feminist critics. We will, however, resist the temptation to confront that sensitive issue for now and defer discussion of it until Part 2 of this study (see especially Chapter 9). Our business here is to explore Milton's portrait as objectively as we can.

This is how Milton introduces the blessed pair:

> Two of far nobler shape erect and tall,
> Godlike erect, with native Honour clad
> In naked Majestie seemd Lords of all,   290
> And worthie seemd, for in thir looks Divine
> The image of thir glorious Maker shon,
> Truth, Wisdome, Sanctitude severe and pure,

Severe, but in true filial freedom plac't;
Whence true autoritie in men; though both
Not equal, as thir sex not equal seemd;
For contemplation hee and valour formd,
For softness shee and sweet attractive Grace,
Hee for God only, shee for God in him:
His fair large Front and Eye sublime declar'd   300
Absolute rule; and Hyacinthin Locks
Round from his parted forelock manly hung
Clustring, but not beneath his shoulders broad:
Shee as a vail down to the slender waste
Her unadorned golden tresses wore
Dissheveld, but in wanton ringlets wav'd
As the Vine curles her tendrils, which impli'd
Subjection, but requir'd with gentle sway,
And by her yeilded, by him best receivd,
Yeilded with coy submission, modest pride,   310
And sweet reluctant amorous delay.
Nor those mysterious parts were then conceald,
Then was not guiltie shame, dishonest shame
Of natures works, honor dishonorable,
Sin-bred, how have ye troubl'd all mankind
With shews instead, meer shews of seeming pure,
And banisht from mans life his happiest life,
Simplicitie and spotless innocence.
So passd they naked on, nor shund the sight
Of God or Angel, for they thought no ill: 320
So hand in hand they passd, the lovliest pair
That ever since in loves imbraces met,
Adam the goodliest man of men since borne
His Sons, the fairest of her Daughters Eve.

                                    (4.288–324)

We can analyse the logic of this passage in four stages, taking the opening two sentences together as the first stage:

1. Adam and Eve are distinguished from the other creatures of the garden by their nobler and erect posture. Though naked, they look and behave like the lords of their environment because in their appearance they are the image of God (288–95).

2. The long third sentence details the masculine and feminine qualities of body and mind that distinguish Adam and Eve from each
other (295–311).
3. The nakedness of Adam and Eve inspires a reflection, tinged with
regret and outrage, on the dishonesty of later times (312–18).
4. The passage concludes by repeating the superiority of Adam and
Eve (319–24).

Even this bare summary shows that a question of changing perspective arises here. As we have seen, Satan's eye leads us first to notice
the two protagonists of the poem, and the picture that Milton paints
of them concludes, sixty lines later, with Satan's comment on it ('O
Hell! What doe mine eyes with grief behold?', 358). In this extract,
however, the narrative voice has taken over. Only the narrator's voice
bewails the loss of innocence in the third section of the passage: only
he can view Adam and Eve with such approval; Satan's perspective has
been set aside.

Praise of the human characters frames the passage. At the beginning, the word 'erect' is repeated, seemingly emphasising both their
physical ('tall') and their moral ('Godlike') qualities. They appear
physically and morally impressive, clothed only in 'naked Majestie'
and 'native Honour', they appear 'divine'. Their moral qualities are
the puritan ones: 'Truth, Wisdome, Sanctitude' (293); the epithet
'severe' appears twice (293–4) in a complimentary sense. The conclusion of the passage is more general. The mutual amity of Adam and
Eve appears in their clasped hands, and in the reference to them as 'the
loveliest pair' (321). The passage closes with a formally structured,
self-reflecting syntax:

> Adam, the goodliest man of men since born
> His Sons, the fairest of her Daughters Eve.

> (323–4)

The ceremonial phrasing of these two lines suggests deference before
natural dignity, after which Milton can go on to a less formal description of Adam and Eve among the animals in the garden.

Adam and Eve are not identical. Milton's word is 'equal' (296),
but this should not lead us to think of the word in terms of current

issues of gender discrimination.[2] Adam and Eve are different because of their different sexual functions, and because of their different origin: whereas Adam was fashioned directly by God, Eve grows as a secondary creation from Adam. Thus 'filial freedom' (294), the duty willingly offered by a son to his father as a creature to his creator, is different for Adam and Eve: he owes reverence to God; she owes reverence to Adam and to God. Milton encapsulates this idea elliptically in 'Hee for God only, shee for God in him' (299).

Milton picks out several physical distinctions that match the psychological differences between them. Adam has a 'fair large front' (forehead) and eyes uplifted ('sublime') to the heavens. He has hair of modest length, parted at the front,[3] whereas Eve's hair hangs to her waist in ringlets. His 'shoulders broad' (303) contrast with her 'slender waste' (304). Psychologically, Adam is suited to logic and bravery ('contemplation ... and valour', 297), while Eve is better fitted to emotion and beauty ('softness' and 'Grace', 298). Adam's appearance suggests 'Absolute rule' (301) which Eve accepts with 'coy submission' (310).

Although elements in this extract touch our modern sensitivity about issues of gender discrimination, we need to try to treat the passage on Milton's terms. The point Milton stresses here is not the inequality of Adam and Eve, but their matching each other. Clearly, Milton suggests that Adam's intellectual abilities are superior to Eve's, and later in Book 4 we will hear her deferentially asking him to explain the nature of the universe to her; when Raphael comes to visit them in Book 5, Adam sends Eve off to prepare dinner, and in Book 7 she leaves Adam and Raphael alone to discuss matters of astronomy. In Book 9, however, crucially and disastrously, Eve is able to outwit Adam in discussion about how to divide their labours. In the current passage, Milton focuses our attention on the reciprocal nature of the relationship of Adam and Eve. Each answers the other's need: together they form a perfect alliance, an ideal image of human life. The stately syntax of the passages describing Adam and Eve expresses the balance of their relationship:

> 'For contemplation hee ... / For softness shee ...' (297–8)
> 'Hee for God only, shee for God in him' (299)
> 'Subjection ... sway' (308)
> ' ... by her yeilded, by him best receivd' (309)

This syntactical poise reaches its climax in the final two lines of the passage ('Adam ... goodliest ... fairest ... Eve'). This balance reflects their mutual dependence: we see this 'loveliest pair' walking 'hand in hand' through the Garden.

There is a further political aspect to this relationship that extends beyond the sexual. Here, in Eden, Milton gives a picture of an ideal world. Here a man deeply embroiled in the republican and royalist conflicts of his time presents his vision of the basis of a civilised world. What we discover is not a world of complete equality, without authority or subordination, but one in which authority is 'gentle', and submission voluntary ('yeilded') and that submission valued and respected ('best receivd'). This relationship reflects another that we have already met in the poem: the relationship between God and the Son. On both human and divine levels, authority exists without exploitation, and submission exists without humiliation. The clasped hands of Adam and Eve here symbolise a relationship of mutual love, respect and generosity.

The portrait is not without irony, for the phrase 'hand in hand' appears also in the penultimate line of the whole poem, in a very different mood. Throughout this superficially idyllic passage, Milton finds ways to remind us of the negative possibilities in his portrait. The relationship between Adam and Eve expresses perfect innocence. They are naked but unembarrassed at being visible to God or angel, for they are unable to imagine sin or evil ('they thought no ill', 320). Milton stresses the naturalness of their relationship. Adam's hair is 'Hyacinthin' (curled); Eve's hair is 'unadorned' (305), 'Disheveld' (306), comparable with a vine. At the same time, however, we notice the ambiguities of Milton's phrasing. There is his description of Eve's hair in 'wanton ringlets' (306), where 'wanton' means 'loose' but both 'wanton' and 'ringlets' may suggest post-lapsarian sexual laxity. A similar ambiguity appears in the 'coy submission' (310) with which Eve accepts Adam's authority, where 'coy' may mean either 'demure' or 'provocative'. In this extract, then, as in the reference to 'nice art' that occurred in the first extract we discussed in this chapter, the ideal picture Milton paints contains hints of its destruction. So, for example, though 'Disheveld' means that Eve's hair is allowed to fall naturally, without artifice, the word may also suggest disorder.

Much more obvious than these hints, however, is Milton's outburst in lines 312–17. Here he fulminates against the rampant evils of his own time, in particular its hypocrisy. Whereas the parts of the extract describing Adam and Eve are marked by balance and dignity, here all is disrupted with brutal repetitions ('guiltie shame, dishonest shame', 'honor dishonorable', 'shews...meer shews') and broken rhythms ('honor dishonorable / Sin-bred. How have ye troubl'd all mankind') as Milton exclaims against the corruption of the modern world. In this extract, as we have seen in earlier discussions, Milton writes about several eras at once – though the classical world is alluded to here only by the use of the word 'hyacinthine', which is used by Homer to describe the hair of Odysseus.[4]

Although the sense of Satan's observing eye is lost in this extract, therefore, the sense of sin and doom remains present, even at this most idyllic of moments. Soon afterwards, Satan's perspective returns, and after a dialogue between Adam and Eve, Milton gives us Satan's ominous realisation that God's prohibition can provide 'fair foundation...whereon to build / Their ruin' (521–2). The ambiguous tone of the extract darkens in the rest of Book 4. Later, when Adam and Eve retire to their bower, Milton sings a hymn to the ideal of wedded love – but cannot resist accompanying it with a diatribe against harlots and masques (see 4.750–75, a passage that will repay close study and therefore appears in the suggestions for further work at the end of this chapter). Finally, Satan takes the form of a toad to squat at Eve's ear trying corrupt her dreams, until he is disturbed by Ithuriel and Zephon.

Eve's Dream

It is the aftermath of this incident that we consider in the final extract, which comes from the beginning of Book 5. Here Eve relates to Adam the dream that Satan-in-the-toad has insinuated into her sleep:

> ...methought
> Close at mine ear one call'd me forth to walk
> With gentle voice, I thought it thine; it said,
> Why sleepst thou Eve? now is the pleasant time,

The cool, the silent, save where silence yields
To the night-warbling Bird, that now awake   40
Tunes sweetest his love-labor'd song; now reignes
Full Orb'd the Moon, and with more pleasing light
Shadowie sets off the face of things; in vain,
If none regard; Heav'n wakes with all his eyes,
Whom to behold but thee, Natures desire,
In whose sight all things joy, with ravishment
Attracted by thy beauty still to gaze.
I rose as at thy call, but found thee not;
To find thee I directed then my walk;
And on, methought, alone I pass'd through ways   50
That brought me on a sudden to the Tree
Of interdicted Knowledge: fair it seem'd,
Much fairer to my Fancie then by day:
And as I wondring lookt, beside it stood
One shap'd and wing'd like one of those from Heav'n
By us oft seen; his dewie locks distill'd
Ambrosia; on that Tree he also gaz'd;
And O fair Plant, said he, with fruit surcharg'd,
Deigns none to ease thy load and taste thy sweet,
Nor God, nor Man; is Knowledge so despis'd?   60
Or envie, or what reserve forbids to taste?
Forbid who will, none shall from me withhold
Longer thy offerd good, why else set here?
This said he paus'd not, but with ventrous Arme
He pluckt, he tasted; mee damp horror chil'd
At such bold words voucht with a deed so bold:
But he thus overjoy'd, O Fruit Divine,
Sweet of thy self, but much more sweet thus cropt,
Forbidd'n here, it seems, as onely fit
For Gods, yet able to make Gods of Men: 70
And why not Gods of Men, since good, the more
Communicated, more abundant growes,
The Author not impair'd, but honourd more?
Here, happie Creature, fair Angelic Eve,
Partake thou also; happie though thou art,
Happier thou mayst be, worthier canst not be:
Taste this, and be henceforth among the Gods
Thy self a Goddess, not to Earth confind,
But somtimes in the Air, as wee, somtimes

Ascend to Heav'n, by merit thine, and see 80
What life the Gods live there, and such live thou.
So saying, he drew nigh, and to me held,
Even to my mouth of that same fruit held part
Which he had pluckt; the pleasant savourie smell
So quick'nd appetite, that I, methought,
Could not but taste. Forthwith up to the Clouds
With him I flew, and underneath beheld
The Earth outstretcht immense, a prospect wide
And various: wondring at my flight and change
To this high exaltation; suddenly 90
My Guide was gon, and I, me thought, sunk down,
And fell asleep; but O how glad I wak'd
To find this but a dream!

(5.35–93)

We can analyse the structure of this extract most simply by marking the passages of narrative and speech thus:

1. In a dream Eve imagines that she hears a voice which she thinks to be Adam's calling her (35–7).
2. The voice draws her attention to the pleasures of the time – the song of the nightingale, the moon and stars – and refers to Eve's own beauty (38–47).
3. In the dream, Eve rises, but failing to find Adam with her, explores the garden until she finds herself at the Tree of Knowledge, where there waits a seeming angel (55–7).
4. The angelic figure addresses the tree in a formal apostrophe* (speaking to the tree as if it were a person), questioning the prohibition against eating its fruit (58–63).
5. Eve is horrified when the angel takes and tastes the fruit (64–6).
6. The angel expresses delight in the fruit, and invites Eve to take some and become god-like (67–81).
7. The angel offers Eve the fruit. Its aroma stimulates her appetite and tempts her to taste. At once, she flies up and sees the panorama of the earth. Suddenly, however, the vision ends and Eve is once again earth-bound, and awakened to find, to her relief, that everything she has experienced has been a mere dream (87–93).

The extract ends, as does the dream, at the point in Book 4 where Satan, discovered in the form of a toad at Eve's ear, returns to his natural shape at the touch of the tip of Ithuriel's spear.

The extract highlights the self-allusive nature of the poem – that is, Milton's way of making different parts of the poem reflect each other and so comment on each other – and this is the aspect that we shall concentrate on here.

The most obvious of these allusions relates to the passage as a whole, which, of course, prefigures the actual temptation that will form the subject of the next chapter of this book. The prefiguring extends beyond situation to linguistic detail when Milton describes the fateful deed with dramatic economy: Satan's model phrase, 'He pluckt, he tasted' (65) foreshadows Eve's imitation in Book 9, 'she pluck'd, she eat' (9.781). Here, however, Eve does not, even in dream, taste the fruit of the forbidden tree. She comes to the point of tasting, but before she can do so is transported upwards with Satan to behold the earth spread out before her. There follows an abrupt change of direction. Line 86 contains a caesura that cuts not only metre and line and sense, but seems also to cut the narrative, as if a part of the poem has been lost. At one moment Eve imagines that she 'Could not but taste' (86) the fruit offered to her; the next she flies 'up to the Clouds'. There is, in fact, no break in the action: the word 'Forthwith' makes this clear. There is, instead, a turning away and a concealment; Eve must not at this point experience, even in the form of a dream, the dire consequence of eating the forbidden fruit. On the contrary, the whole point of Satan's intrusion is to generate a sense of promise, to minimise the anxiety of transgressing God's prohibition, and to make the eating of the fruit attractive in prospect. The risks of Satan's ploy are evident in Eve's waking response to the dream. Nightmares, we must presume, do not occur in Paradise. Even so, Eve finds the dream disturbing and is 'glad [she] wak'd / To find this but a dream' (92–3). In contrast, the effect of the actual eating of the fruit in Book 9 will awaken Eve and Adam to the nightmare of a reality in which paradise itself will seem a dream, and an ideal state from which they are to be forever excluded.

Let us now explore the dream in more detail, to see how its references to other parts of the poem reveal the manner in which Satan seeks to weaken Eve's resistance to temptation.

The most striking of these allusions relates to the manner in which Satan presents himself. We understand from what is said earlier in the poem that Lucifer, the bright angel, is not what he was in his unfallen state. Zephon advises him scornfully to 'Think not... thy shape the same / Or undiminisht brightness' (4.835–6), and his physical form as Eve dreams is 'Squat like a Toad' (4.800). Yet the figure that Eve perceives in her dream is that of an angel, 'shap'd and wing'd like one of those from Heav'n' (55) with 'dewie locks' (56) scented with ambrosia. When she first hears the whispers of Satan-in-the-toad, it seems no harsh croaking but a 'gentle voice' (37). Eve's dream thus begins with a dangerous illusion, that the angel inspiring her dream is beautiful, when in fact he is fallen. This is only the beginning: as we shall see, the whole dream is compounded of illusions.

The development of these illusions is nurtured in the rest of the extract by Satan's rhetoric and Eve's naivety together. His subtlety plays effectively against her inexperience and innocence. We have observed in the opening books of the poem, where he stirs his legions to renewed fight, how effective is Satan's oratory, how potent his rhetoric. Here he employs his powers to different effect.

In the second section of the extract, Satan's gentle voice calls Eve to wakefulness, appealing to her senses in mellifluous verse: only the nightingale ('the night-warbling bird', 40) disturbs the silence of a night illumined by the light of the full moon. The setting is romantic, and Satan's language suggests the flattery of the courtly lover. He describes the nightingale's melody as a 'love-labor'd song' (41), and speaks of the stars metaphorically as heaven's eyes, waking for no other purpose than to see the beauty of Eve ('Natures desire', 45), in whom 'all things joy [take pleasure], with ravishment' (46). 'Ravishment' is a powerful word: all of creation, Satan says, is enchanted by Eve's beauty; but there is also a sexual tone in the word, presenting Satan as a lover tempting Eve to stray from her fidelity to Adam. The romantic element in Satan's treatment of Eve continues into the actual temptation scene in Book 9, where he encourages her to think of the eating of the forbidden fruit as an adventure rather than simple disobedience.

We should note here a further allusion to Eve's narrative of her first consciousness in Book 4. There she describes how she saw her own image in the waters of a lake, and was so captivated by its beauty that she might have remained there forever 'fixt... pin[ing] with vain desire' (4.465–6), lost in worship of her own reflection. She was saved from this fate only by a warning voice that distracted her and brought her to Adam, who became the focus of her devotion when she was persuaded that her beauty was secondary to Adam's 'manly grace / And wisdom, which alone is truly fair' (4.490–1). In Eve's dream, then, Satan tries to reawaken the impulse to vanity that she initially felt, and that has since been submerged in her love for Adam.

Another allusion in the extract indicates a parallel between Satan and Adam, whom we may see in the role of husband, lover or suitor of Eve. Adam, however, is not presented as a lover in the style that Satan adopts, as we can see a little earlier in Book 5, when Adam calls Eve to wakefulness in much more straightforward terms than Satan uses:

>   ...Awake
> My fairest, my espous'd, my latest found,
> Heav'ns last best gift, my ever new delight,
> Awake!
>
>   (5.17–20)

These words contrast with the dream of Satan in significant ways. Here Adam stresses not Eve's beauty, but his own delight in her; there is no appeal to her vanity. His reference to heaven means God, in contrast with Satan's use of the word, which refers only to the night sky. In the following lines, he calls her not to a lover's serenade, but to work in the garden and to admire its beauty rather than her own. There is no talk of ravishment here, but only of his relationship with 'my espous'd' – that is, a union blessed by God. We may recall in this context Milton's earlier paean to wedded love, which he contrasts with 'Casual fruition ... Court Amours' (4.767); for while Adam addresses Eve, in what might be considered courtly terms, as 'Fair Consort' (4.610), Milton is generally careful to insist on the formal nature of their relationship, referring to it as 'connubial' (4.743) or 'conjugal' (4.493 and elsewhere).

A further element here recalls Book 4. Satan's depicting of the heavens as focused on Eve's beauty contrasts directly with Adam's explanation of the stars to Eve. In answer to her question about why the stars shine when there is no one to see, he explains that they are for the benefit of the whole of creation; whether visible or invisible to human eyes (see 4.657–87) matters not. As Satan presents the heavenly objects, in contrast, the moon shines 'in vain, / If none regard' (43–4); and the stars, he suggests, come out just to catch sight of the incomparable Eve ('Heav'n wakes with all his eyes, / Whom to behold but thee' 43–4); she alone is 'Natures desire' (44).

All these allusions indicate that Satan's words are as deceitful as they are flattering. Their insidiousness is prepared from the beginning, where, in contrast with Adam's straightforward 'Awake!' (5.17), Satan begins with the enticing rhetorical question, 'Why sleepst thou Eve?' (38). Then, while Adam calls her to their work in the garden, Satan calls her to play in the evening, 'the pleasant time' (38). The Satan of Eve's dream, that is, introduces the notion of the illicit lover, full of alluring promise, actually tempting her to betrayal. Essentially, the parallel in the wording of Satan's and Adam's speeches to Eve stresses the simplicity of Adam's relationship with Eve and contrasts it with the subversive dishonesty of Satan's flattery of her.

Moving on now to the third section of the extract, where Eve sees an angelic figure beside the Tree of Knowledge, we find two further elements in Satan's tangle of deceits. Of his appearance to Eve as one of the heavenly angels we have already spoken and need say nothing further. Her perception of the Tree of Knowledge, however, deserves attention. While Eve recognises it for what it is, the 'interdicted' (forbidden, 52) tree, it seems, strangely, 'Much fairer to my fancie then by day' (53). By 'fancie' Milton means her imagination, but the word also has implications of delusional thoughts, of wild and corrupt fantasies; after Eve wakes up, Adam explains the operation of fancy to her at some length (see 5.100–19). That her visions are no more than that is apparent from the description (or rather lack of it) of the same tree in Book 4. There, as we have seen above, after a glowing description of the Tree of Life with its 'Ambrosial Fruit / Of vegetable Gold' (4.219–20), Milton dismisses its companion merely as 'Our Death, the Tree of Knowledge' (4.221). Again, the linking of two references illuminates the fraudulence of the picture Satan introduces into Eve's mind.

In the fourth section of the extract, Satan develops the illusion of the tree as desirable with suggestions both intellectual and sensual. He refers to the abundance of fruit on the 'surcharg'd' (58) tree, and its 'sweet' (59) flavour. He suggests that to have forbidden the tasting of this delicious fruit can only have been the result of 'envie or ... reserve' (61) on the part of God. He invites Eve's agreement with a series of rhetorical questions: 'deigns none to ease thy load?' (59) he asks, as if the tree were a conscious being labouring under a weight of fruit that it would be only kindness to lighten; 'Is knowledge so despis'd?' (60) he wonders, implying the foolishness or malignity of whoever forbade it. Finally, he offers Eve his example as he plucks and tastes the fruit.

The fifth section of the extract introduces a new element into Satan's attack when he speaks of the effect of the fruit. First, his appeal grows more direct as his rhetorical questions give way to urging Eve to 'Partake ... also!' (75). At the same time, his flattery oozes more unctuously in 'happie Creature, fair Angelic Eve' (74). In this and the previous section, Satan avoids reference to God, instead minimising the Creator's authority by referring ironically to the 'Fruit Divine' (67), and using the word 'god', which should in Christian thought relate to a unique being, in a generic sense (as in the classical world) in the phrase 'Nor God, nor Man' (60). This is an important idea for Satan's argument, for he wishes to suggest that the fruit can 'make Gods of Men' (70). If she tastes the fruit, she can be 'among the Gods / Thy self a Goddess' (77–8). The section concludes in exclamatory style, looking forward to a future living among the gods: 'such live thou' (81).

Ironically, it is not this powerful plea sways Eve, but the earlier appeal to her taste-buds. In the final section of the extract, she refers only to the 'pleasant savorie smell [that] quicken'd appetite' (84–5) as the reason that she 'could not but taste' (86). Before she can do so, she is swept up to view earth from afar; from one point of view, she sees the world as a god might view it; from another, she is faced with the panoramic prospect of the earth as her own future environment after the Fall. However, she is unaware of these implications: it is the more basic and simple attraction of the senses that draws her into Satan's deception.

If we now look back over the extract, it will be apparent that the duality of Satan's appeal to Eve threads the whole. This is a richly sensuous passage. Satan first stirs Eve's ear with the sounds of the night, silent save for the nightingale that 'Tunes sweetest his love-labour'd song' (41). The music flows in Satan's honeyed flattery, too, with its unusual compound words ('night-warbling' and the alliterative 'love-labour'd'). He proceeds to dazzle her eyes with the beauty of the moon and stars, and, of course, Eve's own beauty, and his own angelic form. He soothes her skin with the cool of the evening, invites her to feel the 'load' (59) of the fruit on the tree; she imagines, with Satan's act, the plucking and tasting of the forbidden fruit, even to the point of sensing its shape as 'Even to my mouth [Satan] held part' (83). The word 'taste' echoes through the passage (59, 61, 65, 77, 86), often accompanied by 'sweet' (59, 68 twice), and mingles with the 'pleasant savorie smell' (84) of the fruit. The description of Satan himself refers to his 'dewie locks [that] distill'd / Ambrosia' (56–7): ambrosia is the food of the classical gods of Olympus that conferred immortality on those mortals who ate it; here, however, Milton seems rather to suggest something aromatic or beautiful rather than edible. Against this barrage of sensual enticements, we must set Eve's instinctive revulsion, emphasised with a vivid inversion of word order: 'Mee damp horror chill'd' (65). The occasion of her revulsion is Satan's blatant disregard of the divine prohibition against eating the fruit, but Eve responds physically – it makes her feel chilled – not intellectually: hence her relief at waking to find her experience 'but a dream' (5.93).

Underlying all this sensuousness there lies a deeper, sensual current. In this setting full of romance, with the love-song of the nightingale, the light of the moon, and the enticements to physical pleasure in the shadowy glades, Satan offers himself as a rival to Adam – as we saw earlier, there is a direct parallel between Adam's words to Eve and Satan's. He invites Eve to a betrayal of both God and Adam. Though Eve expresses her awareness only of betraying God, the sense of double betrayal explains the intensity of her reaction – the shivering cold sweat of fear and horror to which Eve is reduced in her dream.

On the other hand, Eve appears unmoved by the intellectual element in Satan's appeal. Milton says only that Eve is 'wondring' (89) at her sudden 'high exaltation' (90), where it cannot be clear that exaltation means anything other than being raised up above the earth that she sees 'outstretcht immense' (88). When Satan invites her to become 'Thyself a goddess' (78), he develops his earlier flattery of her physical form and invites her to a more refined divinity. However, there is no suggestion in the passage, or in its immediate aftermath, that Eve is attracted by this idea.

Much of the passage is dedicated to stressing the emptiness of Satan's offers. All the allusions in this dream speech of Satan's point to this conclusion. We have already seen Adam awakening Eve to labour in an honest way; we have seen Eve in Book 4 rejecting love of self in favour of love of Adam; we know that Satan in reality is no longer the paragon of angelic beauty that he once had been in heaven and that he now seems in Eve's dream. Further, as we have noted, Satan's blurring of distinctions by indiscriminate reference to gods, goddesses, 'Angelic Eve' and 'Fruit Divine' expresses the fraudulence of his advice. These ideas have physical expression at the conclusion of the passage: when 'Suddenly / My Guide was gon, and I ... sunk down' (90–1) prefigures Satan's rapid sneaking from the scene after the actual temptation in Book 9; in both cases, there is a sudden deflation as reality intrudes.

What Satan offers, therefore, is actually nothing but an encouragement to betrayal. When he invites Eve to become a goddess, to experience the heavenly life as one of the gods, he is simply lying. A final cross-reference here makes the point clear, for later in Book 5, Raphael makes a parallel offer to Adam, in very different terms:

> ... time may come when men
> With Angels may participate, and find
> No inconvenient Diet, nor too light Fare:
> And from these corporal nutriments perhaps
> Your bodies may at last turn all to Spirit
> Improv'd by tract of time, and wingd ascend
> Ethereal, as wee, or may at choice
> Here or in Heav'nly Paradises dwell; 500
> If ye be found obedient, and retain
> Unalterably firm his love entire
> Whose progenie you are.
>
> (5.493–503)

Thus, in Milton's religious world – and here again it is not entirely an orthodox one[5] – Adam and Eve have the capacity to become part of the heavenly world through a process of gradual refinement. They may do so, however, only by absolute fidelity to the will of God. What Satan offers is, as it were, a 'quick fix' that will turn out to have exactly the opposite result from the one desired.

To sum up our discussion of this extract: Milton gives Eve a dream – for which there is, by the way, no precedent in the biblical narrative – as a kind of dress rehearsal of the temptation that will occur in Book 9.

In the dream, he gives Satan the most voluptuous language to attract Eve to the decisive act of eating the forbidden fruit. However, he uses methods both within and outside the extract we have discussed to render Satan's perfidy with the utmost clarity. Satan's implicit offer to supplant Adam, his negligent judgements of gods and goddesses, and his fulsome praises of Eve all reveal his dishonesty; in addition, the passage suggests several parallels with other parts of the poem that highlight the dishonesty and emptiness of the plan Satan suggests.

In their innocence, Adam and Eve dismiss her dream, after discussion, as an anomaly arising from the operation of fancy. Only to the reader is the insidious power of the dream apparent.

Conclusions

- Milton varies the perspective of the poem. He speaks at different times in his own voice, or with Satan's, and views events directly or through the medium of Satan's eyes.
- Milton describes the Garden of Eden as a place of abundant life, with emphasis on growth and movement.
- The Garden of Eden is idealised, yet made to seem lifelike.
- Adam and Eve are idealised, yet made to seem human.
- Epic similes are replaced by dissimiles which are more suitable for describing the perfection of Eden.
- Milton brings many poetical resources to bear upon the vivid rendition of the action and ideas of the narrative:
  - Milton's use of language is very inventive. Particularly, he invents compound words ('night-warbling' and 'love-labour'd') to communicate ideas briefly and vividly.
  - We have found several instances of alliteration and syntactical inversion used to bring out the meaning or dramatic effect of the verse.
  - The language frequently contains ambiguities that suggest hidden meanings, particularly in description of the Garden of Eden, when words suggestive of sin or error appear ('mazie', 'wandring').
- Sensuous imagery works alongside controlled meaning.
- The poem is frequently self-allusive: different parts of the poem contain parallel ideas that comment on and illuminate each other.

- Satan is presented as a rival of Adam for the loyalty of Eve.
- Parallel and contrast communicate ideas vividly, as in the opposition between the Tree of Life and the Tree of Knowledge.
- Milton makes frequent appeal to the senses to enhance the impression we have of Eden, or to give Satan's appeal to Eve dramatic immediacy.
- Irony is used constantly, so that Eden's perfection is seen through the corrupt eyes of Satan.

Methods of Analysis

- In each of the extracts in this chapter, we have followed our standard approach of beginning with a structural summary, following up with a fuller discussion of selected parts of the extract, and concluding with a more general discussion of the most significant points that emerge from the analysis.
- We explored the technicalities of Milton's poetry, trying to see how his use of devices communicates his meaning effectively. In particular we looked at:
  o Alliteration
  o Repetition
  o Unusual language
  o Disruptions of normal word order
  o Imagery
  o Wide use of affective language
  o Sensuous appeal
- We discussed the relationship between Adam and Eve, and their difference and equality.
- We compared other parts of the poem that seem to comment on the extract under discussion, and concentrated on this feature of the poem particularly in discussing the third extract.

Further Work

Choose one or two of the following passages for detailed discussion. Note that you do not necessarily need to discuss the whole passage: if you prefer, select a reasonable length at your own judgement.

1. Book 4, lines 325–92 ('Under a tuft of shade ... To do what else though damnd I should abhorre').

This is the continuation of the passage we considered as our second extract in this chapter. The first part of the passage (325–55) develops the picture of Eden. Then Milton recounts Satan's reaction to the vision that he sees (356–92). If you wish, you could select either half of the passage for discussion. However, it is interesting to consider both the vision of Eden and Satan's reaction together, to see how his envy distorts what he sees. In the first part of the extract, look particularly at how Milton appeals to the senses to bring an abstract scene to life, at how he suggests the perfect relationship between Adam and Eve, and yet introduces an ominous element into the description. In the second half of the passage, consider the ironies of the ways Satan views the scene, analyse how Satan justifies his plot, and explore the elements of regret that appear in him.

2. Book 4, lines 440–91 ('O thou for whom ... wisdom which alone is truly fair').

This passage deals with Eve's first coming to consciousness. The major thematic ideas to consider in this passage are the role of Eve in the poem, the relationship between the human characters and their God, and the relationship between Adam and Eve. From the point of view of technique, look particularly at the ways in which Milton vividly dramatises Eve's waking and its aftermath.

3. Book 8, lines 437–99 ('Thus farr to try thee, Adam ... one Flesh, one Heart, one Soule').

This passage recounts God's response to Adam's request for a companion, and recounts the creation of Eve. There are three thematic elements that deserve discussion: God's behaviour towards Adam; Adam's perception of God; and Adam's expectations of Eve. From the stylistic point of view, look for alliterative effects, imagery, and syntactical patterns that are important in developing the varying moods of the extract.

6

The Fall and its Aftermath

Book 9. 494–551 ('So spake the Enemie...at the voice much marveling')

Book 9. 780–833 ('So saying, her rash hand...without him live no life')

Book 12. 610–49 ('For God is also in sleep...took thir solitarie way')

With this chapter we come to the crux of the whole poem. As we saw in Chapter 1, Milton prepares the tragic climax of the poem with a lengthy proem to Book 9. Here, he says, he will speak of 'foul distrust, and breach / Disloyal on the part of Man' and 'On the part of Heaven...Anger and just rebuke, and judgement giv'n' (9.6–10). Milton's moral perspective appears at that point simple: Man commits sin; God punishes him. However, this simple perspective blurs when, immediately after the proem, Milton turns to Satan, just as he did in Book 1. Immediately after the invocation at the beginning of Book 9, the narrative picks up from the end of Book 4, where Gabriel expelled Satan from the Garden of Eden. Here Satan has a further tortured soliloquy in which to reaffirm his desperate purpose: once again, we view events from Satan's – as it were, the wrong – perspective. Later in Book 9, we view events from the point of Eve, then from that of Adam, and the moral clarity of the invocation further loses definition. By the end of the poem, after Michael's review of biblical history and his promise of future hope, the meaning of the Fall itself is far from clear.

The Temptation

The first passage we will discuss occurs well into Book 9, when Satan, having entered the serpent and discovered Eve, sets about entrapping her:

> So spake the Enemie of Mankind, enclos'd
> In Serpent, Inmate bad, and toward Eve
> Address'd his way, not with indented wave,
> Prone on the ground, as since, but on his reare,
> Circular base of rising foulds, that tour'd
> Fould above fould a surging Maze, his Head
> Crested aloft, and Carbuncle his Eyes;   500
> With burnisht Neck of verdant Gold, erect
> Amidst his circling Spires, that on the grass
> Floted redundant: pleasing was his shape,
> And lovely, never since of Serpent kind
> Lovelier, not those that in Illyria chang'd
> Hermione and Cadmus, or the God
> In Epidaurus; nor to which transformd
> Ammonian Jove, or Capitoline was seen,
> Hee with Olympias, this with her who bore
> Scipio the highth of Rome. With tract oblique   510
> At first, as one who sought access, but feard
> To interrupt, side-long he works his way.
> As when a Ship by skilful Stearsman wrought
> Nigh Rivers mouth or Foreland, where the Wind
> Veres oft, as oft so steers, and shifts her Saile;
> So varied hee, and of his tortuous Traine
> Curld many a wanton wreath in sight of Eve,
> To lure her Eye; shee busied heard the sound
> Of rusling Leaves, but minded not, as us'd
> To such disport before her through the Field,   520
> From every Beast, more duteous at her call,
> Then at Circean call the Herd disguis'd.
> Hee boulder now, uncall'd before her stood;
> But as in gaze admiring: Oft he bowd
> His turret Crest, and sleek enamel'd Neck,
> Fawning, and lick'd the ground whereon she trod.

His gentle dumb expression turnd at length
The Eye of Eve to mark his play; he glad
Of her attention gaind, with Serpent Tongue
Organic, or impulse of vocal Air,   530
His fraudulent temptation thus began.
Wonder not, sovran Mistress, if perhaps
Thou canst, who art sole Wonder, much less arm
Thy looks, the Heav'n of mildness, with disdain,
Displeas'd that I approach thee thus, and gaze
Insatiate, I thus single; nor have feard
Thy awful brow, more awful thus retir'd.
Fairest resemblance of thy Maker faire,
Thee all living things gaze on, all things thine
By gift, and thy Celestial Beautie adore   540
With ravishment beheld, there best beheld
Where universally admir'd; but here
In this enclosure wild, these Beasts among,
Beholders rude, and shallow to discerne
Half what in thee is fair, one man except,
Who sees thee? (and what is one?) who shouldst be seen
A Goddess among Gods, ador'd and serv'd
By Angels numberless, thy daily Train.
So gloz'd the Tempter, and his Proem tun'd;
Into the Heart of Eve his words made way,   550
Though at the voice much marveling

                                                    (9.494–551)

The passage falls into the following sections:

1. A description of the serpent (494–504).
2. References to classical myths in which serpents figure (503–10).
3. An epic simile comparing the serpent with a tacking ship (503–18).
4. Eve, preoccupied with her work, ignores the rustling sounds of the serpent (518–22).
5. The serpent redoubles its efforts and eventually begins to speak (523–31).
6. The serpent's address to Eve (532–48).
7. Eve's reaction (549–51).

Rather than following our standard procedure, we will deal with the second section of the extract first. Here Milton presents a brief, condensed series of classical references. I do not propose to examine these in detail: read the notes in a good edition! Essentially, all the references relate to stories in which sexual intercourse with a serpent changes human characters into serpents or introduces a serpent-like quality into them. In one of them, Cadmus changes into a serpent and then, when he embraces his wife, Hermione, causes her to change into a serpent also. Clearly, these references prefigure the dangers for both Eve and Adam of the serpent's temptation.

With this in mind, let us return to the beginning of the extract to examine Milton's presentation of the serpent. We should notice, to begin with, the clear opening statement that the serpent is a vehicle for Satan, 'the Enemie of Mankind' (494), its lugubrious 'Inmate' (495). Then we should note that there are distinct elements in the description: the epic simile which forms a coherent section; description of the serpent's appearance; hints of the serpent's personality; and description of the serpent's manner of approach to Eve. All of these components point to the way in which Eve may be beguiled.

The serpent's superficial beauty is the most obvious of its attractions. It dazzles with radiant colours: it has a 'burnisht Neck of verdant Gold' (501), later described as 'enamel'd' (525, meaning 'variously coloured') and its 'Carbuncle' (500, meaning 'deep red') eyes glow like coals. Condemned to hug the ground after the Fall ('Prone on the ground, as since', 497), this pre-lapsarian serpent sits erect on the spirals of its body. Milton gives the serpent epic stature, so that it 'tour'd / Fould above fould' (498–9) with its head 'Crested aloft' (500); it is 'lovely, never since of Serpent kind / Lovelier' (504–5). The combination of sinuous and towering movement, burnished gold and glowing red light make a compelling portrait.

At the same time, Milton constantly reminds us of the evil embodied in the serpent. The serpent's crested head suggests Satan's sin of pride, particularly since the word 'crest' is often associated in the poem with Satan;[1] so too does the architectural metaphor that Milton applies twice to the serpent's appearance in references to its 'circling Spires' (502) and 'turret Crest' (525).[2] The serpent's twisting coils carry the more insidious implication of moral error, diversion and deceit. Thus its coils become 'a surging Maze' (499), and when he advances upon Eve he moves his 'tortuous Traine' (516) with a 'tract oblique' (510) that suggests indirectness of purpose as well as movement; Milton's vocabulary reiterates the image with 'indented' (496), 'circling' (502), 'side-long' (512) and 'Curld' (517). This theme of indirectness inspires the epic (epic, even though unusually brief) simile (513–15) of the steersman who trims his sail to a veering wind. Like the steersman, Satan will adapt his persuasions to the responses he meets from Eve; directness, straightforwardness, truth – these have no part in his plan.

The simile of the steersman and his vessel brings into focus another, less obvious strand of imagery: the imagery of water, which appears towards the beginning of the extract. It begins with the 'indented wave' (496) of the movement that characterises the serpent after the Fall, continues with 'surging Maze' (499) of the serpent's coils that 'Floated redundant' (503) on the grass. Thus Milton suggests the formlessness of the serpent: it is an impression of moving coils, without constant shape.

I have referred to the serpent thus far as neuter: it is an 'it'. Milton, however, pointedly uses the masculine pronoun: his serpent is 'he'. The serpent's purpose is to attract Eve and overcome her reluctance to eat the fruit of the forbidden tree. The imagery we have discussed above helps him to achieve his aim. However, as foreshadowed in Eve's dream in Book 5, he also has something of the character of a seducer: there is something sexy as well as clownish about this serpent: 'pleasing was his shape, / And lovely' (503–4). His approach to Eve is circumspect, as the formal phrasing suggests when he 'toward Eve / Address'd his way' (495–6), and as the formal epic simile implies when the careful steersman 'side-long … works his way' (512). A little later, growing 'bolder now' (523) he at length stands before her 'in gaze admiring' (524). He tries to attract her attention in a manner that would be comically contemptible were it less appalling in consequence: he bows and licks the ground, 'Fawning' (526), adopting a look of innocence with his 'gentle dumb expression' (525). There is no overt sexuality here, but our reaction to the serpent's behaviour is conditioned by the classical references in lines 505–10, which all involve sexual congress between humans and serpents. In this context, the serpent's behaviour as he 'Curld many a

wanton wreath in sight of Eve / To lure her Eye' (517–18) suggests
the posturing of a potential lover showing off his attractions to win
the approval of his partner or victim. The word 'wanton' has, as
elsewhere in the poem, a double meaning, suggesting both over-
abundance and lust.[3]

All this prepares the reader for the moment when the serpent speaks.
Here the clownishness spills over into something of the nature of a
horror film, with the serpent-zombie acting almost like a human, but
only to remind us by his unnatural behaviour how utterly non-human
he actually is. Here Milton's use of courtly language exaggerates the
serpent's imposture as the courtly lover to and beyond the point of
caricature*. Eve is his 'Sovran Mistress' (532), 'sole Wonder' (533),
'the Heav'n of mildness' (534), 'Celestial Beautie' (540), 'universally
admir'd' (542). The serpent's speech is peppered with the clichés of
courtly love – her 'disdain' (534) and 'awful brow' (537), his behaviour as he 'gaze[s] / Insatiate' (535–6) and fearful of her rejection,
the 'ravishment' (541) of all who look upon her. We have met such
language before, of course, in Eve's dream in Book 5. But there, Satan
took the form of an angel. Here he is a much lesser, more insidious
creature. In contrast, the flattering language of Eve's dream we see
here in a much more florid, exaggerated form than previously. Thus,
for this critical moment, Milton has increased, with the extravagance
of the language of courtly love, the grotesqueness of the situation.
Throughout the flattery, we can hardly forget the vivid description
of the source of these fulsome utterances – the serpent – and we can
hardly ignore the horrifying inappropriateness of the words to their
speaker. Here Milton has succeeded in conjuring up a truly revolting
picture.[4]

If we now think back to the detail of our discussion of Eve's dream
in Chapter 5, where Satan in the guise of a good angel spoke to Eve,
we can see how carefully Milton has magnified the actual temptation, making it both more vivid and more disgusting than the dream.
The rhetorical element in the serpent's speech intensifies too. There is
the same unctuous flattery, and rhetorical questions again invite Eve's
acquiescence in his argument. Even the phrasing of one key idea recurs
in the serpent's encouragement to Eve to see herself as 'A Goddess
among Gods' (547), echoing 'among the Gods / Thyself a Goddess'
(5.77–8). But the Book 9 episode differs radically from Book 5.

Here, the serpent acknowledges God. He addresses Eve as 'Fairest resemblance of thy Maker faire' (538) and his language acknowledges heaven obliquely when he pays homage to her 'Celestial Beautie' (540) and her 'Heav'n of mildness' (534). These references reassure and challenge in equal measure. On the one hand, the serpent enlists himself with God, and renders himself more acceptable and safe; on the other, he invites Eve, as he questions her situation, to accept his view as an alternative to God's. Milton uses the archaic word 'glozed' (549) to describe what the serpent does in this speech, suggesting a mixture of flattery, persuasion and deceit.

In this crucial passage, then, we see Milton using together many of the techniques we have explored in previous chapters. We find here varieties of repetition, used to communicate the idea of abundance in 'foulds that tour'd / Fould above fould' (498–9), or to intensify an idea in 'Thy awful brow, more awful' (537); words used in different senses to disarm ('Wonder not … sole Wonder', 532–3); inversion of word order for dramatic effect ('Pleasing was his shape', 503); alliteration used to intensify an image in the serpent's 'tortuous traine' (516); and a combination of alliteration and repetition to emphasise an essential idea in 'Beautie adore / With ravishment beheld, there best beheld' (540–1). As we have seen, the extract also contains classical references, an epic simile, vivid description, rhetorical effects, allusions to other parts of the poem. This remarkable battery of poetic and syntactical devices is employed not for its own sake, but to create a powerful impression both alluring and sickening. The effect on Eve is communicated in the elliptical concluding line of the extract, 'Though at the voice much marveling' (551).

So emphatic is the description of the posturing of the serpent in this extract that many readers have seen deeper meanings in the picture Milton paints. Thus we may think of the spires of the serpent's folding coils as intended actually to suggest a magnificent cathedral – precisely the kind of house of worship that was alien to Milton's Puritan ideas. If we look at the rest of the description in this light, we may feel that the grandeur of the serpent's colours and spires could suggest the fine vestments of a Catholic priest celebrating the Mass. Then the bowing and scraping with which the serpent's display concludes may suggest the bowing and genuflecting of a Catholic religious service. In short, the description of the serpent is a parody of the Catholic practices, splendour and ceremony that Milton despised.[5] This symbolic element in the extract has a further dimension if we consider it in relation to the thematic opposition between good and evil. In this context, we may see Satan as an opponent of God, of course, but also more pointedly as an opponent and rival of the Son. In the extract, Milton gives physical form to this opposition in the form of parody: Satan's incarnation in the shape of the serpent reflects in a spectacularly repellent manner the incarnation of the Son as Jesus Christ.

Even setting aside the deeper layers of meaning in the extract, this is clearly a crucial part of the poem, and will repay close study. In the Further Work section at the end of this chapter, you can explore how the temptation develops by studying the dialogue that follows.

Original Sin

We move on now to consider the moment when Eve, urged on by the serpent, eats the fruit of the forbidden tree. Here the 'breach / Disloyal' that Milton has spoken of in the proem to Book 9 takes on form and substance, and in the process comes to seem much less simple than the proem suggested.

> So saying, her rash hand in evil hour   780
> Forth reaching to the Fruit, she pluck'd, she eat:
> Earth felt the wound, and Nature from her seat
> Sighing through all her Works gave signs of woe,
> That all was lost. Back to the Thicket slunk
> The guiltie Serpent, and well might, for Eve
> Intent now wholly on her taste, naught else
> Regarded, such delight till then, as seemd,
> In Fruit she never tasted, whether true
> Or fansied so, through expectation high
> Of knowledg, nor was God-head from her thought.   790
> Greedily she ingorg'd without restraint,
> And knew not eating Death: Satiate at length,
> And hight'nd as with Wine, jocond and boon,
> Thus to her self she pleasingly began.
> O Sovran, vertuous, precious of all Trees
> In Paradise, of operation blest

To Sapience, hitherto obscur'd, infam'd,
And thy fair Fruit let hang, as to no end
Created; but henceforth my early care,
Not without Song, each Morning, and due praise   800
Shall tend thee, and the fertil burden ease
Of thy full branches offer'd free to all;
Till dieted by thee I grow mature
In knowledge, as the Gods who all things know;
Though others envie what they cannot give;
For had the gift bin theirs, it had not here
Thus grown. Experience, next to thee I owe,
Best guide; not following thee, I had remaind
In ignorance, thou op'nst Wisdoms way,
And giv'st access, though secret she retire.   810
And I perhaps am secret; Heav'n is high,
High and remote to see from thence distinct
Each thing on Earth; and other care perhaps
May have diverted from continual watch
Our great Forbidder, safe with all his Spies
About him. But to Adam in what sort
Shall I appeer? shall I to him make known
As yet my change, and give him to partake
Full happiness with mee, or rather not,
But keep the odds of Knowledge in my power   820
Without Copartner? so to add what wants
In Femal Sex, the more to draw his Love,
And render me more equal, and perhaps
A thing not undesireable, somtime
Superior; for inferior who is free?
This may be well: but what if God have seen,
And Death ensue? then I shall be no more,
And Adam wedded to another Eve,
Shall live with her enjoying, I extinct;
A death to think. Confirm'd then I resolve,   830
Adam shall share with me in bliss or woe:
So dear I love him, that with him all deaths
I could endure; without him live no life.

(9.780–833)

The extract clearly splits into two sections. The first, which describes
the eating of the fruit and its immediate aftermath, is best treated

as a unit, but it is worth isolating individual parts of the second paragraph.

1. Eve eats the fruit and we are told of the immediate aftermath: the serpent disappears, and nature groans (780–94).
2. Eve praises the virtues of the tree and its fruit (795–808).
3. Eve praises 'Experience' as her guide (808–10).
4. Eve wonders whether her deed is known to God (811–16).
5. Eve considers her relationship with Adam (816–33).

Like the first section, the second deals with the immediate effects of Eve's transgression, and we can already see from a simple summary, how far they range.

The phrase Milton uses to narrate Eve's act in taking the forbidden fruit – 'she pluck'd, she eat' (781) – is, as we have seen, a repeated formula: Eve is copying what Satan did in her dream (5.65) and what the serpent tells her he did to gain the powers of understanding and speech (9.595). Her act is almost involuntary, performed not so much by Eve as by 'her rash hand' (780) seemingly with a will of its own. But in truth her mind and heart are in it.

We sense Eve's mood in the diction of this crucial moment – particularly in Milton's choice of language in the phrasing of plucking and eating that we have met more than once. 'Plucking' is an active word: so much more than a Sunday afternoon at the fruit-picking centre. 'Pick' would be closer to neutral. In 'pluck' there is muscle and there is a touch of violence: the word even suggests greed. We pluck a chicken, or remove its innards (the 'pluck'); or thieves may pluck their victim. In *Paradise Lost*, the word is usually used of the forbidden fruit, though it has other violent contexts. In Book 6, it refers to the uprooting of mountains, and in Book 11 to premature death:

> So maist thou live, till like ripe Fruit thou drop
> Into thy Mothers lap, or be with ease
> Gatherd, not harshly pluckt, for death mature.

> (11.535–7)

The linking of 'pluckt' with 'harshly' here sufficiently illustrates Milton's feeling for the word. We are justified, therefore, in responding to the tones of violence the word contains. The harsh muscularity of the word dramatises Eve's will and energy in disobedience.

If we glance forward to the second section of the extract we see that Eve expects the same kind of reward as the serpent claims to have experienced; here in the first paragraph, however, the narrative focuses on the ugly effects of her act, showing how radically her disobedience has altered the balance of the created world. Her act is felt as a 'wound' by the Earth (782), and brings forth a great sighing from nature, which gives 'signs of woe' (783). What these signs are is not stated for in what follows Milton describes the signs of woe in Eve herself; but the reason for the upheaval in nature is clearly summed up in the recognition 'That all was lost' (784). Here Milton adopts a view of creation comparable with the mediaeval theory of the Chain of Being, in which a disturbance in one link of the chain of the created world inevitably results in disturbance everywhere else; Milton's creation is a single monistic texture,[6] and Eve's transgression at once destroys the harmony of the whole.

Eve has taken the fruit; and the fruit immediately takes her for its slave. The serpent that appeared recently so impressive, gorgeous, eloquent and confident dematerialises in a brief contemptuous sentence ('Back to the Thicket slunk / The guiltie Serpent', 784–5). The serpent's departure goes unnoticed by Eve, who is now absorbed in the fruits of her transgression. At once, its effects are apparent. In contrast with the moderate habits of Adam and Eve earlier,[7] she eats 'Greedily... ingorg'd without restraint' (791) until she is 'Satiate... height'ned as with Wine' (792–3): thus the sin of gluttony is born. The evil character of her ecstasy is underlined by Milton's use of the word 'satiate', which recalls the serpent's reference to his own 'Insatiate' (536) admiration of Eve. Her clarity of judgement is gone too: she can think of nothing but eating; she is 'wholly' (786) absorbed in it, to the point that she 'nought else / Regarded' (786–7). The essential irony here is that while Eve feels transported above herself, Milton reveals her as reduced, even debased. Milton shows her, drunk with delight, succumbing to the vagaries of a fallen imagination. The telling phrase 'as seemd' (787), interpolated in the statement that Eve has not previously tasted such fruit implies the possibility of delusion, and develops into 'whether true or fansied so' (788–9): Eve can no longer distinguish reality from illusion. She imagines herself embarking on the route to perfect knowledge, even to 'God-head' (790) while she is in fact destroying herself. Milton points the irony with powerful ellipsis in '[she] knew not [that she was] eating [her own] Death' (792). The alliteration in lines 790–1 ('God-head ... G reedily ... ingorg'd') underlines the same idea more brutally, showing Eve dreaming of godliness while wolfing the fruit like an animal. This is no single delicate, demure and innocent bite of an apple that Eve takes. She gluts herself to repletion.

Appetite, then, lies at the heart of Eve's transgression. It was appetite for knowledge and its advantages, as well as the simple pleasure of taste that led to her fall, and it is appetite that consumes her immediately after it. One sin, however, leads to others, and one weakness opens the door to companions. In the second section of the extract, Milton shows Eve drifting ever more deeply into the confusion that sin brings in its train. Those who are guilty of one deadly sin are also guilty of all the others. We already see here pride and gluttony. Idolatry comes next.

Eve's first act, after eating her fill, is to express her gratitude to the tree. The lines are a little difficult, and we need to be sure we understand them. In the first, we need to recognise an ellipsis: Milton uses a sequence of three positive adjectives, omitting the 'most' which would render them more obviously superlatives: '[most] Sovran, [most] vertuous, [most] precious of all Trees' (795). Exactly where the 'most' may best be is open to question, but makes little difference. What is clear is that Eve's words represent genuine gratitude, even veneration. The language is heavily ironic. It is actually the Tree of Life that is most sovereign and most precious. In addition, the word 'vertue' is ambivalent: the tree has the power to change, but it certainly has no moral goodness. Eve's addressing the tree as 'of operation blest / To Sapience' (796–7) is less helpfully ambiguous, meaning either 'blessed in its uses for those wise enough to eat the fruit' or 'blessed in giving wisdom'. In either case, the word 'blest' is again ironic. Milton's irony goes beyond these details, however: the whole of the second section of the extract constitutes a parody of Christian beliefs and, more specifically, Christian hymns.[8] The section as a whole shows Eve offering to the tree the praise that should be reserved for God, and promising it the careful labour that should be reserved for the other trees in the garden. Thus she is the first idolater. In her mind the tree supplants

God, whom here she refers to with deliberate and pagan vagueness as 'the Gods' or 'others [who] envie [the wisdom] they cannot give' (804–5). She follows Satan's own error in his rebellion against God, when she expects to rival God himself – to 'grow mature / In knowledge as the Gods' (803–4). We may see this, perhaps, as one effect of her substituting the Tree of Knowledge for God as the object of her worship.

The next section of the passage deepens Eve's alienation from God. Having praised her favourite tree, she goes on to express her debt to 'Experience' (807) as her 'Best guide' (808). This idea marks a fundamental change in her perceptions. Hitherto, she has looked up to Adam as her mentor and guide; he, for her, represents the authority of God ('Hee for God only, shee for God in him', 4.299): now the highest authority she recognises is herself – her own ideas, her own feelings, her own experience. The authority of God's law has thus been supplanted by the authority of her own mind. Without hesitation, Eve rejects the principle of obedience on which the order of the created world is founded. The significance of this idea for Milton's own time is great: for the Puritans, the word of God as revealed in the Bible is the pre-eminent authority by which to judge moral behaviour; Eve's apotheosis of self gives her the status of the first of those who deliberately obfuscate, pervert, or deny the word of God. For her, the principle of obedience has become anathema, so that she identifies God merely as 'Our great Forbidder' (815). His realm, she decides, is too 'high, / High and remote' (811–12) to have any interest in her: there is derision, here, and scorn in the repeated 'high', even though Eve's anxiety that her transgression should go unnoticed, should remain 'secret' (811), shows that she still retains understanding of what she has done; but high and remote too, from her new perception of the world, are the demands of God's law.

In lines 795–816, hence, Milton presents Eve's transgression as a complete betrayal. To that extent, he gives form to his initial description of 'foul distrust and breach'. This is no mere half-accidental error: Eve delights in the fruit, eating greedily, rejoices in prospect of the wisdom she thinks she is about to attain, and anticipates with excitement taking her place as a goddess among gods. She rejects God's law and Adam's will. In their place she worships the gods of her own appetite and her own will. The old order of creation is gone at a stroke:

looking back to the beginning of the extract, we can see that this is why 'Earth felt the wound, and Nature...gave signs of woe' (782–3). In these lines, Milton explores the full meaning of the simple phrase with which these ideas are introduced: 'all was lost' (784).

In the remainder of the extract, Milton explores the effect of Eve's transgression on her relationship with Adam. In essence, this means showing how the simplicity of their relationship up to this point has been corrupted. The questions Eve asks in lines 816–27 – how shall she appear to Adam? Should she invite him to join her in eating the forbidden fruit? Or should she keep her new-found knowledge to herself? But what if death results? – show a new kind of confusion clouding the clear mind that she ironically imagines now to be on the verge of attaining a higher, yet clearer state. The old simplicity is gone. In its place, doubts and anxieties reign.

The first question Eve asks indicates the depth of her change. In asking herself 'in what sort / Shall I appeer?' (816–17) to Adam, she reveals her descent from grace in two ways. Firstly, her relationship with Adam is no longer straightforward. Secondly, in envisioning herself behaving in a manner intended to deceive, she reveals that she is divided within herself. It is as if, instead of behaving spontaneously, she has now become an actor playing someone else's role in a drama staged inside her head. In brief, plain honesty has deserted her. She has begun already to live a lie.

Things go from bad to worse. From questioning whether she can be honest with Adam, she begins to think of deliberately denying him the advantages she thinks she has gained from her transgression. She thinks to 'keep the odds of Knowledge in my power / Without Copartner' (820–1), so that she can become the 'more equal' (823) partner in her relationship with Adam; she thinks it 'not undesireable [that she may become] sometime / Superior' (824–5). No longer is she 'for God in him' (4.299); no longer can it be said that she 'thought no ill' (4.320), for she has discovered both envy and jealousy. Their hitherto harmonious relationship has become a potential battleground.

Finally, thinking of the possible fatal consequences of eating the forbidden fruit, Eve becomes prey to sexual jealousy as she imagines Adam (however improbably given their situation!) 'wedded to another Eve...I extinct' (828–9). It is this idea – 'A death to think' (830) – that finally convinces Eve that she had better share the fruit with Adam:

then at least, if indeed 'death ensue' (827), neither of them will survive! Eve has indeed 'thought death'.

The completeness of Eve's corruption is thus depicted with devastating precision. However, there is a redeeming feature, we may feel, at the conclusion of the extract, where Eve declares her absolute love for Adam, with whom 'all deaths / [she] could endure, without him live no life' (832–3). Indeed, in her determination that Adam shall share with her 'in bliss or woe' (831), we can hear an echo of the marriage service in the Book of Common Prayer, which is still used today.[9] However, this new kind of love, realised only at the conclusion of the series of delusions and illusory hopes and fears that have crossed Eve's mind in the aftermath of her eating the forbidden fruit, will not redeem either of them in the Christian sense without the additional sacrificial divine love with which *Paradise Regained* deals.

Milton's language in this final section of the extract reveals Eve's debasement with remarkable economy and dramatic conviction. Her questions show her convincing herself, and skirting round the truths that at some level she still understands. There is a lawyerly indirectness in her circumlocutions and euphemisms* as she debates the case with herself: 'shall I make known to him ... give him to partake' (817–18): contrast the brevity of 'for inferior who is free?' (825). She carefully understates her sin as 'my change' (818); she uses a euphemistic negative in thinking that superiority to Adam would be 'A thing not undesireable'; the illogical 'more equal' (823) may be viewed as an ellipsis of 'more nearly equal' but carries for us an uncomfortable and not entirely inappropriate reminder of Orwell's doublethink.[10] When Eve expresses her horror at the prospect of Adam wedded to another Eve, we can hear an open mouth gasping in the gaping vowels of 'And Adam ... another Eve ... enjoying, I extinct' (828–9) – say the last three words yourself, to see the effect. Her confusion and doubt and indecision are aptly represented in a 'Shall I/ shan't I' sequence in 'Shall I ... shall I ... or rather not ... but ... (817–20). Further, we can sense panic and desperation in the wild way she juggles the words and meanings of 'death' and 'life' in lines 827–33. Here, at the end of the extract, we return to the central meaning of this climactic point: the exchange of life for death. As a formal epic poem, *Paradise Lost* establishes an appropriate ceremonial mood and adopts generally a solemn pace; yet within that formal framework, Milton is able here – as often elsewhere in the poem – to generate emotional power and dramatic conviction in rendering a lifelike state of mind in verse.

The Loss of Eden, and the Promise of the Future

In the aftermath of this episode in Books 9 and 10, Milton dramatises the effects that we have seen adumbrated. He recounts the judgement of God upon Adam and Eve, whose retribution is tempered by mercy, and upon the fallen angels, who are reduced to serpents as a punishment. We witness the new difficulties in the relationship between Adam and Eve: their recriminations and reconciliations, accusing each other and themselves, and complaining against the 'cruel Serpent' (10.927). Adam bewails his fallen lot in language that echoes that of Satan: compare Adam's 'O miserable of happie!' (10.720) with Satan's 'O me miserable!' (4.74). Eve confesses that she has sinned, and condemns herself for committing a greater sin than Adam's, having betrayed him as well as God ('Both have sin'd, but thou / Against God onely, I against God and thee', 10.930–1).

Milton dramatises the change in the relationship between Adam and Eve by contrasting their behaviour before the Fall and subsequently. In Books 4 and 5, we see them behaving in a mutually respectful manner. When they retire in the evening to their 'blissful Bower' in Book 4, they are 'talking hand in hand' (4.689-90), discussing the stars; their hands symbolise their relationship, which Adam describes as 'mutual love, the Crown of all our bliss' (4.727–8). We see this mutual love in operation at the beginning of Book 5, when Adam wakes Eve gently, calling her 'Heav'ns last best gift, my ever new delight' (5.19); she in turn addresses Adam as 'O Sole in whom my thoughts find all repose, / My Glorie, my Perfection' (5.28–9). Later, however, they have a problem to deal with in the shape of Eve's troubling dream. After she has described it to him, Adam comforts her, as 'Best Image of my self and dearer half' (95), sadly suggesting that the source of her dream must be evil, even though he can hardly imagine its source ('Yet evil whence?', 99). Having averred that 'in thee can harbour none / Created pure' (99–100), he suggests that her evil dream may have found access to her mind through one of the

'lesser Faculties', which he calls 'Fansie' (101–2); but he confidently
reassures her with the following extraordinary idea:

> Evil into the mind of God or Man
> May come and go, so unapprov'd, and leave
> No spot or blame behind.
>
> (5.117–19)

Extraordinary as this idea seems, it is entirely in keeping with Milton's
theology. Evil must have a place in the mind of God: else how can it
emerge in his works? And it does emerge, in heaven in the form of
Satan, and in Paradise – again in the form of Satan, but also in Eve's
suggestibility. Equally, however, the presence of evil does not make
God or Eve evil: Eve becomes prey to evil only when she acknowledges and acts upon the suggestions of the devil.

How different is their behaviour after the Fall! We have seen how Eve
becomes at once prey to sin. Adam, like her, eats greedily of the fruit
that Eve offers him, 'Eating his fill' (9.1005) while Eve keeps pace with
him, continuing 'to iterate / Her former trespass fear'd' (9.1005–6).
Lust follows at once, when Adam begins to 'cast lascivious Eyes' on Eve
(9.1014). When they wake, they wake to their new state, 'destitute and
bare / Of all thir vertue' (1062–3). Thence they fall to disputing their
responsibility for their loss, and Book 9 ends with a summary:

> Thus they in mutual accusation spent
> The fruitless hours, but neither self-condemning
> And of thir vain contest appeer'd no end.
>
> (9.1187–9)

This is a complete reversal of their earlier state. Milton stresses their mutuality still, in 'mutual' and 'neither', but now their rending arguments produce only bitterness. As the reward for their transgression, they win not
an eternity of bliss as demi-gods, but endless wrangling. Their dispute
gains nothing: Milton calls it 'vain' and, with an ironic pun, 'fruitless';
the word 'spent' implies waste of time. However, he hints at a means of
escape from the circle of recrimination in the enjambement of the final
two lines. The phrase 'neither self-condemning' runs straight on to 'And
of thir vain contest' without significant pause. A comma at the end of

line 1188 would have linked 'neither self-condemning' with the 'mutual accusation' of the preceding line. As it is, however, the enjambement hints at a causal relationship between 'neither self-condemning' and the endlessness of their dispute: the 'And' of the final line becomes by implication a 'So' or an 'And therefore'. However, we have to wait until Book 10 before confession of guilt opens a possible route to redemption. As in Book 9, Milton presents the further development briefly:

> But rise, let us no more contend, nor blame
> Each other, blam'd enough elsewhere, but strive
> In offices of Love, how we may light'n
> Each others burden in our share of woe

> (10.958–61)

Here Adam invites Eve to join with him in sharing the punishment for their sin. The positive mood emerges from the strong verbs he uses – 'Rise … strive … light'n' – and in his reference to their love. There remains a sense of doom and darkness in the 'burden' and 'woe' that they must look forward to. Both aspects of these lines find expression in the double use of 'blame': they should not accuse each other; instead, they should find ways to alleviate the blame that they receive from 'elsewhere' – meaning God's judgement, since heaven is spoken of as 'the place of judgement' (10.932) a little earlier.

Most of Books 11 and 12 expand on the negative effects of the Fall, taking in the impending expulsion from the Garden of Eden, and the fortunes of Eve's children and their descendants. In this way, Milton spells out the 'rebuke and judgement' that he has spoken of in the proem to Book 9. In actuality, however, once mutual accusation has given way to self-accusation, and Adam and Eve acknowledge their own guilt, the expulsion from the garden is much less clear in its implications than the proem of Book 9 suggests.

For our final extract we take the conclusion of the poem, dealing with the immediate personal effect of the Fall as Adam and Eve make their exit from the Garden of Eden:

> For God is also in sleep, and Dreams advise,   610
> Which he hath sent propitious, some great good
> Presaging, since with sorrow and hearts distress
> Wearied I fell asleep: but now lead on;

In mee is no delay; with thee to goe,
Is to stay here; without thee here to stay,
Is to go hence unwilling; thou to mee
Art all things under Heav'n, all places thou,
Who for my wilful crime art banisht hence.
This further consolation yet secure
I carry hence; though all by mee is lost,   620
Such favour I unworthie am voutsaft,
By mee the Promis'd Seed shall all restore.
So spake our Mother Eve, and Adam heard
Well pleas'd, but answer'd not; for now too nigh
Th' Archangel stood, and from the other Hill
To thir fixt Station, all in bright array
The Cherubim descended; on the ground
Gliding meteorous, as Ev'ning Mist
Ris'n from a River o're the marish glides,
And gathers ground fast at the Labourers heel   630
Homeward returning. High in Front advanc't,
The brandisht Sword of God before them blaz'd
Fierce as a Comet; which with torrid heat,
And vapour as the Libyan Air adust,
Began to parch that temperate Clime; whereat
In either hand the hastning Angel caught
Our lingring Parents, and to th' Eastern Gate
Let them direct, and down the Cliff as fast
To the subjected Plaine; then disappeer'd.
They looking back, all th' Eastern side beheld   640
Of Paradise, so late thir happie seat,
Wav'd over by that flaming Brand, the Gate
With dreadful Faces throng'd and fierie Armes:
Som natural tears they drop'd, but wip'd them soon;
The World was all before them, where to choose
Thir place of rest, and Providence thir guide:
They hand in hand with wandring steps and slow,
Through Eden took thir solitarie way.

(12.610–49)

It is convenient to treat this extract as four sections:

1. Eve greets Adam with the assurance that she knows the substance of
   his dialogue with Michael, having been informed of it in a dream,

affirms her fidelity to Adam, admits her culpability in his expulsion from the garden, and repeats Michael's promise that she as mother of mankind will be the means of the restoration of paradise (610–24).

2. The legion of the cherubim approaches preparing to escort Adam and Eve from the garden (624–36).
3. Michael takes Adam and Eve by their hands and leads them out of paradise, which is now guarded by a gate with armed defenders, overhung by a flaming sword (636–43).
4. Adam and Eve shed tears, but soon turn towards the opening terrain of the world beyond the Garden of Eden (645–9).

This bare summary is sufficient to show that the mood of the end of the poem is ambiguous. Paradise is lost, but, strangely, Adam and Eve leave the garden in a spirit far from despair.

The opening paragraph of the extract, indeed, presents Eve in a mood of unprecedented purpose and energy. We see it not only in what she says, but in the brevity and incisiveness of her manner. What has passed between Adam and Michael, she says, 'I know' (610). Focused on the future, she commands Adam to 'lead on' (614), and explains elliptically, 'In mee is no delay' (615). At this point, their recriminations are behind them: they have acknowledged the sins they have been guilty of and they are resolved to face the future together with optimism. Devotion to each other is crucial to their resolve. Michael has offered to Adam the prospect of a different kind of paradise from the one he has lost – 'A Paradise within thee, happier farr' (12.587) – and Eve seems to echo the idea in her declaration of dedication to Adam. To be with him, she says, is her paradise ('With thee to goe, / Is to stay here', 615–16); for her, he is 'all things under Heav'n, all places' (618). These fervent phrases echo biblical and classical sources[11] (though they may equally remind us of John Donne's 'The Sun Rising', in which he declares of his lover 'She's all states, all princes I; / Nothing else is'[12]). They also recall Eve's formal song of love to Adam in Book 4 (639–58) in the time of their innocence prior to the Fall. However, the mood has changed. Eve's devotion registers in the phrase 'under Heav'n' (618) both the inclusiveness and the limitation of her relationship with Adam. Further, it is as much the product of that relationship as the relationship itself that lies at the root of Eve's optimism: she concludes her speech with the idea that her progeny shall restore paradise. The pattern of events emerges from the parallelism in lines 620—3: 'all by me ... lost ... By me ... all restore.' Thus she sees in herself the means to redeeming her error. The submerged metaphor of pregnancy in 'I carry hence ... the Promis'd Seed' (621, 623) looks forward through the generations to the incarnation of the Son as Jesus Christ, the redeemer of mankind. This is the 'consolation yet secure' (that is, the hope still guaranteed, 620) that allows her to look to the future with confidence.

Despite its direct emotional appeal, Eve's speech contains much underlying artistry, based mainly on sharp oppositions. She contrasts 'some great good' (612) with 'sorrow and hearts distress' (613); her 'wilful crime' (619) with 'further consolation' (620); and, as we have seen, all that has been lost and all that will be restored. Her language is paradoxical: 'With thee to goe, / Is to stay here', and 'without the here to stay / Is to go hence unwilling' (615–17). Thus Eve, juggling two meanings of paradise as a place or as a state of mind, supports the promise of the 'paradise within' that Michael has promised. Finally, there is the contrast between her 'unworthy' (fallen, 622) nature and the hope she brings for the future.

That is the last we hear from Adam and Eve. But Milton's portrayal of the setting in which their departure from the garden occurs conveys a great deal. Before we watch them leave, our attention is drawn, with theirs, to the brilliant display of the cherubim gliding down to escort the couple from paradise. The vision is apocalyptic and paradoxical, brightly lit and gloomily obscured, comprehending both arid desert and soggy swamp. On the one hand we see the cherubim 'in bright array' (627), led by a blazing sword, yet 'meteorous [meaning fleeting like the light of meteor] as evening mist' (629); paradise, so recently 'thir happie seat' (the home of their ideal life, 642), now appears to Adam and Eve only as a menacing 'gate / With dreadful Faces throng'd and fierie Armes' (643–4). Milton's similes in the second and third parts of the extract gesture towards the fallen lives of Adam and Eve and their descendants. The parched Libyan terrain suggests the tribulations of a hostile world. The labourer, at whose heel the marsh ('marish') mist gathers as he returns home, seems a symbol of all the masses of mankind, struggling to emerge from the mists of sin to return to the state of virtue that is their true heavenly home.

(He calls to mind, too, the 'Peasant' referred to in an epic simile near the end of Book 1.)

In contrast with the optimism of Eve's speech, the mood in this second section of the extract is one of regret, as the couple look back at the region they have lost. Their 'lingring' (637) implies unwillingness to leave. However, the 'hastning angel' (636) propels them 'as fast' (639) to the plain below paradise. Milton's Latinate word 'subjected' (640) means 'lying below' the garden, but also carries implications of inferiority and of submission: Adam and Eve, having accepted their punishment, go now to a lowlier world than they have possessed heretofore. So long in coming, the expulsion from paradise is over in a few lines.

The conclusion of the poem builds on the themes and contrasting moods established in the earlier lines of the extract. It focuses on the contrast of regret and hope in the human characters, on their devotion to each other, on their imperfection, on the hostility of the world they are entering, and on the protection of their creator. The conclusion emphasises the human scale. Adam and Eve weep, but dry their eyes, appearing suddenly like children comforted after an injury, and we see them making their way through Eden 'hand in hand' (648) with the promise of mutual comfort. The world is wide and unknown, but they have 'Providence [as] thir guide' (647).

Milton's language is full of ambiguities. The tears of Adam and Eve are 'natural' in two senses: understandably, the couple are sad to be leaving paradise; and these are the tears to which human nature will always be prone because of the Fall. How, though, should we interpret 'The World was all before them' (646)? Should we think of it as meaning that the fallen world is the only world remaining to them, or that a world of great promise awaits them, or that a world of menace and uncertainty threatens them? There is, I think, no straightforward answer to this question: Milton allows our minds to range over the many possibilities. A smaller uncertainty colours the statement that Adam and Eve are free to 'choose / Thir place of rest'. The phrase means not, surely, merely a bed for the night, but a place of serenity that they build for themselves, or perhaps commitment to a rewarding mode of life – with the implication that their choice may be either good or bad, since providence is no more than a 'guide'. Similar doubts underlie the description of the 'wandring steps and slow' (648) with which Adam and Eve make their journey. The confidence of Eve's speech is gone: 'wandring' suggests uncertainty, and, as we have seen in earlier discussion, implies the possibility of moral error as well as losing one's way in the material world. It remains unclear whether Milton intends us to understand 'wandring' in its innocent or its fallen sense. Equally unclear is the range of freedom of their wandering under the aegis of 'Providence thir guide'. And how can they then be truly 'solitarie'? What are we to think of Milton's matching up the ending of Book 12 with the ending of Book 1 by means of reference to the peasant and the labourer?

There is, therefore, much more to the expulsion from the Garden of Eden than simple rebuke and judgement. Adam and Eve are escorted as much in protection as in punishment. There is a promise of future reward as well as rebuke for past transgression. Above all, this ending reasserts nothing more definitely than the uncertainties that have coloured the poem as a whole.

This is a richly suggestive ending – if ending it truly is at all. How does the conclusion answer Milton's determination, expressed at the beginning of the poem, to justify the ways of God to men? In the course of reading the poem, we have seen God's plan and his foreknowledge, we have witnessed his anger at the transgression of his new creatures and the punishment meted out to the rebel angels for their part in the Fall, and we have noted that his judgement against Adam and Eve has been tempered by mercy. On the part of Adam and Eve, too, we have registered changes of outlook. From their pristine state of submissive innocence, we have watched Eve learning to think of God as the Forbidder – almost as the warden of their Eden-prison; we have seen the resulting altercation and dispute between her and Adam, until then the object of her devotion; and we have seen their reconciliation. At the end of the poem, they are once again companionably 'hand in hand' (648), as they last were in Book 4;[13] once again, they are reconciled also with God ('Providence thir guide'). However, these are reconciliations tempered by experience, and thus no longer changeless: innocence, once lost, is not recoverable. The ambiguities of the conclusion, therefore, reinforce the uncertainties that Adam and Eve face: the hesitancies of the last two lines conclude with 'way' – an interminably long open syllable that points forward through a long historical perspective.

Nothing, then, is finally resolved. Milton's ambitious plan requires *Paradise Regained* for its completion.

Conclusions

- Milton deploys all the techniques at his disposal to render the temptation vivid.
- The serpent – with the voice of Satan – is presented as a masterly rhetorician.
- Milton presents the serpent as beautiful while simultaneously bringing out the evil nature of its inhabitant.
- Though the serpent's temptation is powerful, there is no doubt that it is Eve's free choice to eat the apple. She does so with the clear idea that she will achieve the status of a goddess, and refers to God's prohibition with resentment.
- The effect of Eve's transgression is immediate: a mood of doubt, fear, and uncertainty enters her heart for the first time – she doubts Adam's fidelity, and is uncertain how to behave towards him. She has learnt to fear the future. God's judgement, and the expulsion from the garden, are in a sense merely a formal ratification of what Eve has done of her own volition.
- The imagery of knots – symbolic of confusion – appears frequently: in the snake, in the convoluted reasoning of Eve, in the meandering route taken by Adam and Eve as they leave the garden.
- Milton enhances the dramatic effect of this part of the poem with a broad range of poetic and rhetorical effects, among which we may note especially:
  - Puns focus essential ideas: fruit/fruitless, Eve/evil.
  - Strong parallels and contrasts occur: Eve and the serpent, Adam with or against Eve, love versus enmity, the grandeur of the serpent and its undignified exit, hope and despair, innocence and evil, for example.
  - Paradox is used to highlight the irony of Eve's expectations and the mutual need of Adam and Eve.
  - Milton makes frequent use of inversion, repetition and ellipsis.
  - There is rich imagery and symbolism.

o Classical references and epic simile broaden the significance of the events.

- Milton's personal ideas emerge strongly in this part of the poem. In particular, his anti-Catholic views colour, perhaps even define, the way he presents Satan.

- The conclusion of *Paradise Lost* is not the conclusion of Milton's plan of justifying the ways of God to men. *Paradise Regained* is required to complete the pattern.

- The Fall may be seen as illustrating the conflict between mediaeval and Renaissance worlds. Adam and Eve, in their unquestioning acceptance of God's plan, reflect a world in which the authority of the church was absolute. Eve, in her rejection of God's prohibition, illustrates the independent spirit of the Renaissance world.

- Adam and Eve take the first step towards regeneration when they acknowledge their own fault and accept the blame for it.

- Hope is explicit in the expulsion of Adam and Eve from the Garden of Eden. Michael promises them the possibility of achieving a new and better 'paradise within'. Eve looks forward to the future with confidence.

Methods of Analysis

- We continued to begin the discussion of each extract with a structural analysis of its content, and proceeded, as before, to explore the meaning of each section before reviewing the whole.

- In this chapter, however, we have focused particularly on the symbolic aspects of Milton's writing. We explored the meanings implicit in the embodiment of Satan in the serpent in the case of the first extract, and on the implications of the setting in our analysis of the conclusion of the poem.

- We explored the dramatic way in which Milton realises the contrast between the pre-lapsarian and post-lapsarian relationships of Adam and Eve.

- We have also looked for ambiguities and paradoxes and other conceptual properties of the verse, and tried to see how these relate to the emotional effect of the events.

- We considered Milton's use of colour and action to convey vividly the biblical events.
- In this chapter in particular we have considered the way in which Milton uses the characters own words to carry his theme.

Further Work

1. Analyse the part of the poem in which Satan seeks out Eve: 'For now, and since first break of dawne ... Of pleasure not for him ordain'd' (Book 9, lines 412–70).

   You could explore the whole of this passage, or restrict yourself to only half of it: it could be conveniently split at line 444. Both parts of the extract deal with Satan's view of Eve, but the first focuses rather on him, and the second on her.

   In either case, think about how Milton uses direct description and the environment of the garden to emphasise the innocence and beauty of Eve and thus render the evil intent of Satan all the darker. The passage is full of sharp contrasts, representing the essential opposition of evil against innocence.

2. Look at the continuation of the dialogue between Satan and Eve that we chose for our first discussion in this chapter. Begin at Eve's response, 'What may this mean?' and continue to the end of Satan's response, 'Sovran of Creatures, universal Dame' (Book 9, lines 553–612). Consider how Eve's attention is caught, and look at the way in which Satan deploys subtle rhetorical skills to disarm Eve, make her trust him, and encourage her to see the forbidden fruit as harmless.
3. Study the passage in which Satan brings Eve to the tree, and she rejects his suggestion that she should eat: 'Lead then, said Eve ... Thereof nor shall ye touch it, least ye die' (Book 9, lines 631–64). Look at the means by which Milton vividly conveys Eve's changes of mood and controls the pace of the dialogue.
4. Study Satan's address to the tree, concluding with the temptation, 'O Sacred, Wise, and Wisdom-giving Plant ... Goddess humane, reach then and freely taste' (Book 9, lines 679–732). Consider the

range of rhetorical tricks Satan uses to dispel Eve's doubts, such as affirming God's care while redefining the terms of God's prohibition and diminishing God's authority.

5. Choose a paragraph from the conclusion of Book 9 to show how Milton presents the aftermath of the Fall. You might like to study the narrative in lines 1099–131 ('So counsel'd he ... Superior sway'), or the bitter dialogue in lines 1134–89 ('Would thou hadst heark'nd to my words ... And of their vain contest appeer'd no end'). In very different ways, these parts of the conclusion illuminate the consequences of the Fall, both for Adam and Eve, and for later times.

6. Book 10 details the after-effects of the Fall, including God's judgement on Adam and Eve and the human race. It is probably best to take for detailed study a passage from the end of the book after all the consequences of the Fall have been made clear. For example, you could explore Adam's despairing soliloquy in lines 720–844 ('O miserable of happie ... from deep to deeper plung'd!'). Read the whole speech first, and then select either lines 720–70 or lines 721–42, or lines 743–70 for close study. This passage, full of questioning and recrimination, is crucial to the question of how to justify the ways of God to men.

7. Later in Book 10, Adam and Eve become reconciled both to their fate, and with each other. Here the dramatic qualities of Milton's verse emerge powerfully. Study the effectiveness of his dramatisation of the scene in lines 909–65 ('He added not, and from her turn'd ... And to our Seed (O hapless Seed!) deriv'd').

8. After Michael's account of biblical history in Book 11 and the earlier part of Book 12, the mood of the poem lightens. Perhaps the most interesting passages for close study occur in the latter part of Book 12. Analyse lines 451–97 ('Then to the Heav'n of Heav'ns he shall ascend ... Thir proudest persecuters'), in which Michael recounts the Son's triumph over death and Adam's doubtful rejoicing. This passage, too, relates directly to Milton's purpose in *Paradise Lost*.

9. A further choice is the conclusion of the dialogue between Michael and Adam, which summarises the meaning of what has occurred. Analyse lines 552–605 ('He ended; and thus Adam last reply'd ... With meditation on the happie end'). Both this and the preceding extract focus on the problematic concept of the *felix culpa*, or happy fault: the idea that good can emerge from evil.

10. Finally, an interesting subject for a general essay on *Paradise Lost* would be to compare the responses of Satan and Adam to their punishment. This could, of course, be treated as an essay ranging over all the relevant parts of the poem. Alternatively, and more suitably from our point of view in this book, it might take this form:

Compare the soliloquy of Satan in Book 4 (lines 32–113) with the soliloquy of Adam in Book 10 (lines 720–844), explaining how and why they react differently to their punishment.

PART 2

THE CONTEXT AND THE CRITICS

7

Milton's Life as it Relates
to *Paradise Lost*

In this chapter we will largely restrict ourselves to considering how Milton's life was affected by the writing of *Paradise Lost*, and how the poem reflects his life. For a thumbnail picture of Milton's life and times, you may wish to consult the brief chronologies available in the Fowler and Lewalski editions of the poem. A useful and compressed narrative appears in *A Companion to Milton*.[1] There are many full biographies, among which Anna Beer's *Milton: Poet, Pamphleteer and Prophet* is a very readable choice.[2]

From an early age, Milton was confident of his destiny as a writer. He wrote in *The Reason of Church Government* (1642)[3] that he came to accept the favourable view that Italian masters took of his early writings:

> I began thus far to assent both to them and to divers of my friends here at home, and not less to an inward prompting which now grew daily upon me, that by labor and intense study, (which I took to be my portion in this life,) joined with the strong propensity of nature, I might perhaps leave something so written to aftertimes, as they should not willingly let die. (*The Reason of Church Government Urged Against Prelaty* (1642))

These thoughts, he goes on to say, 'at once possessed me'. Milton goes on to amplify this general ambition by suggesting that he may be able to achieve as much as the great writers of the past:

> ... what the greatest and choicest wits of Athens, Rome, or modern Italy, and those Hebrews of old did for their country, I, in my proportion,

and with this over and above, of being a Christian, might do for mine; not caring to be once named abroad, though perhaps I could attain to that, but content with these British islands as my world ... (Ibid.)

Two significant points arise here. Firstly, Milton makes a comparison with the writers of ancient times: he implies that he can enhance the reputation of his homeland in much the same way as the classical writers; immediately afterwards, he contrasts the way that Athens had been glorified by its writers, with the way England in his view had been 'made small by the unskilful handling of monks and mechanics'. Secondly, Milton pointedly emphasises his Christianity as something 'over and above' other considerations: Milton had been intended for holy orders, though he never took them; but whatever else we may think of Milton and his works, the moral seriousness and integrity of his intent as a sincere and undeviating Christian can hardly be doubted. Nowhere in Milton's works are his literary ambition and his Christian stance and his moral integrity more essential and more evident than in the poetic works of his maturity, *Paradise Lost, Paradise Regained*, and *Samson Agonistes*.

The Genesis of *Paradise Lost*

Milton's ambition of writing a work to rival the *Odyssey* or *Iliad* or *Aeneid* required a long period of gestation. Milton tells us in the proem to Book 9 of *Paradise Lost* that the subject he eventually settled on was 'long choosing, and beginning late' (9.26). In fact, though the poem did not reach its final form until 1674, there is evidence that Milton was considering his project when he was still a student, at the age of twenty, half a century earlier – even before he went to Italy, where, as he told us above, he was inspired to make writing his vocation.

Milton had in mind a large and serious work – something that would confer on English the same kind of honour that Homer achieved for Greek or Virgil for Latin, something to rival the works of Ariosto or Spenser. The Book of Genesis, however, was not the first 'subject for heroic song' (9.25) that attracted him: about the age of thirty, he was considering writing an Arthurian epic.[4] Nor was epic the form he initially considered for his religious subject: the Trinity Manuscript, written about 1640, contains sketches of a religious drama to do with the Fall. You can find these reproduced in the introduction to the Fowler edition, or the appendix to the Lewalski edition of the poem.[5] The influence of these early sketches is still felt in the vivid drama Milton brought to the epic form he finally selected.

Milton did not begin writing the poem as we now have it until nearly twenty years after his visit to Italy, possibly around 1658. By this time, Milton was around the age of 50, had married three times, fathered five children, travelled in Europe, espoused the republican cause in the civil war, and had published, in addition to his poetry, prose works on a range of divisive issues including civil and religious government, divorce and polygamy, freedom of speech, and education; he had also gone blind.

By this stage his ambition had expanded. Now he envisaged something weightier than Spenser's *Faerie Queene*, and something more serious than the works of such as Ariosto or Tasso. He speaks in the proem to Book 9 of rejecting for his theme 'Warrs, hitherto the onely Argument / Heroic deem'd' (9.28) and 'fabl'd Knights / In Battels feign'd' (9.31) and 'Races and Games' (9.33) with all the paraphernalia of 'Impreses quaint...tinsel Trappings' (9.35–6). These disparaging remarks about the chivalric style of epic seems to dismiss it as, by Milton's standards, lightweight. He intended something larger and grander in scale and purpose. He speaks, again in Book 9, of the 'higher Argument' (9.42: the more noble subject) to which he is called. It was not only the subject matter of the fashionable epics that he eschewed: he also scorned their style. He rejects the rhyming verse in which they were conventionally cast, as 'the Invention of a barbarous Age' (Lewalski, 10) and turns instead to what he thinks of as the greater dignity of 'Heroic Verse without Rime, as that of Homer in Greek, and Virgil in Latin' (Lewalski, 10). He also rejects the themes of the past, describing earlier writers as 'Erring' (1.747) in their accounts.

Once begun, the writing of *Paradise Lost* occupied Milton for the best part of 15 years. Before it was finished, Milton had fled to Chalfont St Giles to escape the bubonic plague of 1665 and remained there during the Great Fire of London in 1666. This was an equally turbulent period politically; whereas in the heyday of Cromwell Milton had rejoiced in the establishment of a republic, later, after the restoration of the monarchy in 1660, he suffered arrest and imprisonment as an active republican and the author of a pamphlet recommending regicide, and was lucky to escape execution. The first edition of *Paradise Lost*, published in 1667 (though perhaps completed some years earlier), consisted of the poem cast in 10 books without any additional material. It was reissued in 1668, with introductory and explanatory material, including Milton's defence of the verse form, and the arguments that summarise the plot of each book. In 1674 the second edition was published, constituting a revision of the poem into 12 books (by the simple expedient of dividing Books 7 and 10) with a few additional lines of verse; the additional material was reorganised so that the Arguments each preceded the appropriate book instead of being printed together at the beginning of the whole, and there were many changes in spelling, punctuation and capitalisation. Having completed his crowning achievement, Milton died before the year was out.

It is reasonable to argue, then, that Milton's life was largely dedicated to the enormous task he set himself early on. He was a prolific writer in the genres of poetry (in English, Italian, Latin and Greek), drama, and polemical prose both in Latin and English, and undertook other major projects. But *Paradise Lost* stands pre-eminent among his achievements. Higher argument it certainly is: nothing less than the story of mankind and his relationship with his creator. Into this universal subject he introduced elements of his own life, commenting particularly on his blindness and on marriage, giving his opinions about elements of religious, secular and political life, and, in Books 11 and 12, summarising a history of the human race. His other publications on a variety of aspects of government and social management show him formulating opinions on the major issues of his time. He saw himself as a historian, and in 1670 published a *History of Britain*, begun some twenty years earlier. In comparison with all these works, however, *Paradise Lost*, encompassing as it does the whole of human and divine history as people of Milton's time perceived it, is still a much grander, more ambitious labour.

Milton's Education

Milton was fitted by nature and nurture for the task he undertook. He was born the son of prosperous parents in London near St Paul's in 1608. Educated by private tutors at first, he entered St Paul's School at the age of 12, proving an adept and almost obsessive pupil; he studied late into the night by candlelight, often until the early hours of the morning. After five years at St Paul's, he entered Christ's College, Cambridge, where his path initially was far from smooth; rusticated temporarily in 1626, he found himself ill-suited temperamentally to his fellow students whom he felt wished him ill; later, however, he began to feel more at ease, gaining his BA in 1629, and receiving an MA *cum laude* in 1632.

The education of Milton's era was essentially classical: this was, after all, still the Renaissance, if late in that period. He studied, of course, the Bible, which was published in its King James version in 1611, three years after Milton's birth – though Milton was also familiar with the earlier Geneva Bible of 1560. He steeped himself in all the great Greek and Roman writers of classical times. Chief among these were the ancient writers of epic poetry, Homer, Virgil and Lucan. *Paradise Lost* draws heavily upon them. The first edition (1667) is structured on the ten-book model of Lucan's *Pharsalia*, an epic poem about the civil war between Julius Caesar and Pompey the Great, while the second (1674) edition is modelled on the 12-book structure of Virgil's *Aeneid*, which deals with the story of Aenaeas as the founder of Rome and is dedicated to honouring the Augustan empire. Milton's work also contains echoes of, or allusions to, works or ideas of Plato, Aristotle, Homer, Hesiod, Herodotus, Horace, Sallust, Ovid, Lucretius, Livy, Pliny and Seneca as well as the European writers of the Renaissance such as Dante, Ariosto, Tasso, Du Bartas and Camoëns, and English writers such as Chaucer, Spenser, Sidney, Donne, Rochester, Dryden, and Shakespeare. *Paradise Lost*, therefore, is the work of a highly erudite man, wellschooled in the culture of his time, and fully conscious of the debt his writing owed to the past.

Milton was also a remarkable linguist. He was familiar with upwards of a dozen languages, and wrote poetry fluently in Italian, Latin and Greek as well as in English. At Cambridge he was accustomed to participating in scholarly disputation using Latin. When he wrote polemical prose for Europe, he wrote in Latin, and used English when he wished to address himself chiefly to his own countrymen. If ever a man understood the meanings of words, and the nuances of language, and the structure of meanings, it was surely John Milton. His sensitivity to shades of meaning and etymology is everywhere apparent in *Paradise Lost*. In our analyses in Part 1 of this book, for example, we found many usages, such as the ambiguous use of the word 'error', that draw on the sources of language; and there are many such subtle uses of diversities of meaning in the poem. We also found habitual use of unusual word-order copied from classical languages, as well as direct quotations from and allusions to classical and Renaissance authors.

European Travel

After leaving Christ's College, Milton spent some years living in London and Buckinghamshire, devoting his time to further independent study, particularly of mathematics, and writing poetry on a variety of subjects; some of his work during this period – including *Comus* and *Lycidas*, for example – is among his finest. In 1638, however, he began on another formative period, when he set out on a continental tour taking in France, Switzerland and Italy. He spent most time in Italy, however, visiting Florence, Siena, Rome, Venice, Milan and Naples. It is assumed that, among other places, Milton visited Vallombrosa, the site of a monastery in a valley about twenty miles from Florence, which provided the basis for the simile in *Paradise Lost* 1.303–5. During the course of this tour, he visited Naples where he met Hugo Grotius, a Dutch scholar and poet; he met Giovanni Battista Mansus, Marquis of Manso, the biographer of Torquato Tasso, and wrote the Latin poem *Mansus* in his honour. He also met Galileo, who was famous (or infamous, in the eyes of some) for his support for the Copernican (heliocentric) view of the universe.

Milton's European tour helped to confirm in him his republican sympathies, while his meetings with Grotius, Manso and Galileo must surely have stimulated his interest in the relationship between authoritarian government and individual freedom that constitutes a significant theme in several of his pamphlets. The relationship between authority and individual freedom finds expression on several levels in *Paradise Lost*, most obviously in the relationship between God and Man, or between God and Satan. It was also a significant issue in Milton's social and political world.

As the only contemporary mentioned by name in *Paradise Lost*, Galileo clearly had special significance for Milton. He is referred to as 'the Tuscan artist' in 1.288, and his ideas pepper the poem.[6] When Milton met him Galileo was, though 77 years old and blind, under house arrest in Florence, as Milton reports ironically in *Areopagitica*:

> [In Italy] I found and visited the famous Galileo, grown old a prisoner to the Inquisition, for thinking in astronomy otherwise than the Franciscan and Dominican licensers thought. (Teskey, 360)

Galileo's conflict with authority stemmed from 1610, when he asserted, following the heretical views of Copernicus, that the universe was heliocentric; for the fathers of the Church of Rome, on the contrary, it was an article of faith that the earth was the centre of the universe, just as man was the focus of God's providence. Thus Galileo was expected to recant, and at first agreed not to publicise his support for the Copernican theory. In 1616, however, he was given permission to publish material that did not directly conflict with the views of the church. Ultimately, in 1632 he published a treatise entitled *Dialogue Concerning the Two Chief World Systems*. In fact, this treatise, far from being innocuous, mocks the traditional Ptolemaic, geocentric view of the universe as foolish. This expression of his heterodox views, then, was the direct reason that Galileo was placed under house arrest by the Inquisition. He was compelled to recant in 1633.[7]

Galileo's experience seems to have sharpened Milton's ideas about the authority of the church, which he expressed in, for example, his tract *Of Prelatical Episcopacy* (1641), which argues against the power of the bishops in the English church. The attempt to muzzle Galileo underlies his savage denunciation of censorship in *Areopagitica* (1644). In *Paradise Lost*, the relationship between God and Satan, and the relationship between God and Adam may both be seen as partial parallels for the relationship between the Church of Rome and Galileo. We may think also of Milton's description of the naked majesty of Adam and Eve who exhibit 'Truth, Wisdome, Sanctitude severe and pure, / Severe, but in true filial freedom plac't; / Whence true autoritie in men' (4.293–4): among men, Milton says, true authority stems only from submission to God. We may recall, too, the fallen Eve's description of God as the 'great Forbidder' (9.815) and Satan's scathing references to God as 'the Thunderer' (2.28) and 'my punisher' (4.103).

Pamphleteer and Political Activist

Milton's lengthy European tour was cut short by news of imminent civil war in England. He returned in 1639 to a country torn by religious and political unrest, and threw himself eagerly into the debates. Poetry continued to occupy him, and in 1645 he prepared his *Poems of Mr. John Milton, Both English and Latin, Compos'd at several times* (dated 1645 but actually published in 1646) but he was more prominently absorbed in the political world.

True to his sympathy with Galileo and his authorship of *Areopagatica*, Milton published his opinions without reserve. He justified wide and uncensored reading in *Areopagitica* in terms that seem to justify also his outspoken conduct:

> I cannot praise a fugitive and cloistered virtue, unexercised and unbreathed, that never sallies out and sees her adversary, but slinks out of the race, where that immortal garland is to be run for, not without dust and heat. (Teskey, 349–50)

Milton practised the advice implied here, and remained anything but cloistered and unexercised. Back in England, we see him sallying out to every field of battle available to him, publicising his views on domestic life, religion and ecclesiastical organisation, and on the structure of civil life. He was magnetically attracted, it seems, to the sound of gunfire.

In the religious field, Milton spoke on both formal and doctrinal aspects of faith and church. He was a puritan. Nowadays the adjective 'puritanical' has associations of narrow-mindedness, prudery, bigotry and aggressive sobriety; indeed, the word had such meanings before the time of Milton – think of Malvolio in Shakespeare's *Twelfth Night*.[8] Milton shared in this tendency towards sobriety, to the extent of disapproval of theatrical entertainment; his late dramatic piece, *Samson Agonistes*, is a verse drama not intended for the theatre. Primarily, however, the Puritans were a loose group of reformers who disapproved of the Church of Rome and its practices, feared that the protestant church had relapsed into Catholic ways, and wanted to establish a simplified form of worship devoid of ritual, mystery and glamour. Above all, they placed reliance on individual – and straightforward – interpretation of scripture without any earthly intermediate authority of the kind vested in Pope or clergy of any denomination. They believed, in short, in individual faith and worship: they rejected organised religion. The anti-episcopal tracts of 1641 adopt a strongly Puritan point of view, denouncing the kind of idolatry associated with Catholicism that we saw parodied in our analysis (in Chapter 6) of the appearance of the serpent in *Paradise Lost*, 9.524ff.. A later tract, *The Likeliest Means to Remove Hirelings out of the Church* (1659), is reflected in the reference in 4.193 to the 'lewd Hirelings' that populate the church. Later in life he summed up his religious views in *De Doctrina Christiana* (Christian Teaching).

In the civil arena, Milton aligned himself firmly with the republican cause. The era of the republic is framed by two publications in which Milton affirmed his loyalty to the cause, and both were linked to the most significant political events of the era – the execution of Charles I and the restoration of the monarchy. In 1649, a fortnight after the execution of Charles I, he published *The Tenure of Kings and Magistrates*, in which he advocated regicide; he had, in fact, written it prior to the execution. This is its lengthy subtitle:

> Proving that it is lawful, and hath been held so through all ages, for any, who have the power, to call to account a tyrant, or wicked king; and, after due conviction, to depose, and put him to death; if the ordinary magistrate have neglected, or denied to do it. And that they, who of late so much blame deposing, are the men that did it themselves.[9]

Ten years later, immediately before the restoration, he published another anti-monarchist tract, *The Readie and Easie Way to Establish a Free Commonwealth* (February, 1660) – a brave, not to say foolhardy act in the circumstances, and one which he came near to paying for with his life. The span of the interregnum is therefore marked by these two pro-republican tracts by Milton.

In the intervening period, Milton continued to argue on behalf of the republic. Following his advocacy of regicide in 1649, Milton published *Eikonoklastes* (Breaker of Icons), a savage riposte to the defence of the king and kingship in *Eikon Basilike* (Image of the King), a work widely considered to have come from the hand of Charles I himself shortly before his execution.

Two years later, in 1651, Milton developed his work for the republican cause by publishing *Defensio pro populo Anglicano* (Defence of the English People), a tract intended to justify the actions of the English republicans to critics in Europe. This called forth a riposte in the form of the tract *Regii sanguinis clamor ad coelum Adversus Parricidas Anglicanos* (The Cry of the King's Blood to Heaven against the English Parricides), written by Pierre du Moulin but published anonymously in 1652. By this stage, Milton was completely blind, and Moulin asserted that this misfortune was God's means of punishing him for his sins. This tract in turn demanded a response, which was published in 1654 as *Defensio secunda*, in which Milton countered that his blindness was a trial from God who had also granted him spiritual illumination.[10]

Milton's final tract advocating republicanism, *The Readie and Easie Way to Establish a Free Commonwealth*, appeared immediately before the restoration. Rather few republicans were imprisoned or executed after the Restoration, Charles's first aim being to consolidate his position as the king of a unified, peaceful country; but one among them was Sir Henry Vane, the subject of Milton's sonnet 'To Sr Henry Vane the younger' in praise of this leading republican. Milton, however, had been incautious to say the least. As a direct result of publicising his opposition to the king, he was forced into hiding; his books were burned; eventually he was discovered and arrested, and, in October, imprisoned. Thanks to the intercession of influential supporters, however, he was released in December of the same year. This is the experience alluded to in the invocation that begins Book 7 of *Paradise Lost*, where Milton rails against his situation, surrounded and beset on all sides, as he saw it, by enemies of his person and opponents of his thinking, 'fall'n on evil dayes…In darkness, and with dangers compast round' (7.25–7).

In the domestic sphere, this period is marked by Milton's hasty and ill-judged marriage to Mary Powell, who was half his age and the daughter of a royalist family. Their marriage took place in 1642, shortly before the outbreak of the civil war. After only a month or so, Mary, motivated perhaps by mixed political and personal reasons, returned to her family home near Oxford, and remained there until 1645, when the couple moved to a house in the Barbican. In the interim, Milton, inspired by his experience of a troubled marriage, published four tracts on the subject of divorce. *The Doctrine and Discipline of Divorce* appeared in 1643, followed in 1644 by *The Judgement of Martin Bucer Concerning Divorce*, and in 1645 by *Tetrachordon* and *Colasterion*. There were four pamphlets rather than one because Milton, advocating essentially divorce on demand, aroused strong opposition in a society in which infidelity or cruelty were the only broadly acknowledged grounds for separation; and the storm of criticisms with which his ideas were greeted required answers. Clearly, by the time Milton composed *Paradise Lost*, his view of marriage had mellowed. He presents a warm picture of the relationship between Adam and Eve, which infuriates Satan as he sees them 'Imparadis't in one anothers arms' (4.506). Milton marks his portrait with a digression on the subject of marriage:

> Haile wedded Love, mysterious Law, true source   750
> Of human ofspring, sole proprietie,
> In Paradise of all things common else.
>
> (4.750-2)

Milton goes on to sing of 'Relations dear and all the Charities / Of Father, Son and Brother' (4.756-7) and to personify love who 'Here...his golden shafts imploies, here lights / His constant Lamp, and waves his purple wings' (4.763-4). As we have seen, Eve plays a role at least equal in importance with Adam's in both the Fall and in their recovery from its effects. Hers is the final speech of the poem, and in it she reaffirms their reciprocal love.

By the time he wrote that passage, Milton's marriage with Mary Powell had born fruit. She gave birth to two daughters, Anne (1646) and Mary (1648) and a son, John (1651). For a period of about two years, the whole Powell family, evicted from Oxford because of their royalist sympathies, joined the Miltons in their large house in the Barbican. After their return to Oxford, the Milton family moved into a smaller house in Westminster. There Mary gave birth to another daughter, Deborah

(1652), but died a few days later. Her son, John, died a month or so later. In this period, too, Milton's father and father-in-law both died.

The thread that links all the spheres of Milton's activities, and is central to *Paradise Lost,* is the authority of man over man. Both God and Satan are seen as monarchs, and the relationship between Adam and Eve explores their relative authority and influence from several interesting angles. In many passages Milton expresses republican ideas and sentiments. One of the most direct passages occurs in Book 12 where Michael presents his vision of a libertarian society endangered by rejection of reason:

> Reason in man obscur'd, or not obeyd,
> Immediately inordinate desires
> And upstart Passions catch the Government
> From Reason, and to servitude reduce
> Man till then free.
>
> (12.86–90)

Milton, then, despite the failure of the republican cause, retained until the end an essentially republican view of human society. More broadly, we see him here upholding the rule of reason that he held supreme in religious as in civil regulation.

Blindness

The changes, both general and personal, in his circumstances – the restoration of Charles II and the onset of blindness – did not interrupt Milton's literary work. With the help of amanuenses, he was able to proceed, albeit with greater difficulty and more slowly. But the focus of his work began to alter. He continued to write political works: he published his *Defensio pro se* (defence of himself) in 1655; in 1659 he published *A Treatise of Civil Power in Ecclesiastical Causes* and his *Ready and Easy Way To Establish a Free Commonwealth*; and in 1660 he published *The Likeliest Means to Remove Hirelings out of the Church.* This was also the year in which two of his earlier publications, the *Defensio pro populo Anglicano* and *Eikonoklastes* were publicly burned.

His domestic life continued to be turbulent. In 1656, four years after the death of Mary Powell, Milton was married again, to Katherine Woodcock, who in 1657 bore a daughter named after her. Both mother and daughter died in the early months of the following year.

However, different kinds of writing began to occupy more of his time. He continued to write poetry, translated psalms, must presumably have continued to write his *History of Britain*, though it was not published until 1670, and he made a start on his large work on Christian teaching, *De Doctrina Christiana*, which was not discovered and published until 1825.[11] This was also the period in which he began to compose *Paradise Lost*. Milton's habit of work is well known. In the early hours of each day (he speaks in the Invocation to Book 9 of the muse inspiring him each night), he composed some forty or fifty lines of verse, and would dictate them mid-morning[12] to anyone available. The detailed processes of proof-reading and editing came later.

Blindness was the condition under which *Paradise Lost* was written, and also forms a part of the subject. He speaks directly about it at the beginning of Book 9, as we have noted. Furthermore, we hear echoes of its effects in the complaints of Satan condemned to hell, and of Adam and Eve ousted from Paradise. Milton's epic is therefore an intensely personal poem as well as a public one. The experience and thought it collates were dear to his heart. The poem encapsulates ideas that Milton had developed in his political and religious writings: his thoughts on marriage, divorce and the relation between the sexes; his views about the nature of kingship, authority and obedience; and his opinions about organised religion. It also touches on the scientific and philosophical concerns of his time: on the nature of the unseen world, on the structure of the universe, on navigation and discovery. Above all, it pays homage to the writers of the past, whom he had studied intensively in his early years, among them Homer, Virgil, Dante, and Shakespeare. It is truly a life's work.

Last Years

During the writing of *Paradise Lost*, Milton married for the third and last time, in 1663. He and his new wife, Elisabeth Minshull, moved from the threat of plague in London to a cottage at Chalfont

St Giles in Buckinghamshire, which is now, as his only remaining place of residence, open to the public as a Milton museum. There he completed *Paradise Lost*, and there they escaped the plague. Milton's father's house, in Bread Street in London, however, did not escape the Great Fire of 1667.

The publication of *Paradise Lost* in the year of the Great Fire did not end Milton's work. The revised poem was published a year later, and the 12-book second edition after a further six years. During the same period, Milton was writing his *Accidence Commenc't Grammar,* published in 1669, the *History of Britain*, published in 1670, the *Art of Logic* in 1672, *Of True Religion, Heresy, Schism and Toleration* in 1673, *Epistolae Familiares* ('familiar letters' or 'letters to friends') and *Prolusiones* (prolusions, his college exercises) in 1674.

Poetic work occupied him too. There is about it a sense of closure. The religious enterprise that had begun with *Paradise Lost* was completed with the publication in 1671 of *Paradise Regained*. The same year saw the appearance of his biblical drama, *Samson Agonistes*, thus fulfilling his early ambition of writing a tragedy on an epic theme. A second edition of his poems was published with an additional essay as *Poems, &c. upon Several Occasions by Mr. John Milton: Both English and Latin, &c. Compos'd at several times. With a small Tractate of Education to Mr Hartlib* was published in 1673, and *Paradise Lost*, of course, found its final twelve-book form in the second edition of 1674.

That same year Milton died and was buried near his father on 12 November at St Giles, Cripplegate.

8

The Context of *Paradise Lost*

In this chapter we consider the influences that shaped *Paradise Lost*. The Renaissance period at the end of which the poem was written witnessed an extraordinary surge in human culture, taking in the arts, religion, science, politics, education and philosophy, all of which find expression in the poem. Finally we discuss the influence of the poem on later times.

It is interesting that the Renaissance period, generally agreed to have occupied the fourteenth to the seventeenth centuries, beginning in Italy, and percolating to England much later, in the sixteenth century,[1] is embraced by two literary works on roughly comparable topics: Dante Alighieri's *La Divina Commedia*, written during the first quarter of the fourteenth century, and *Paradise Lost*, written three centuries later. Dante's poem is clearly a Renaissance piece: it is in Italian, and not Latin, and indeed was instrumental in confirming Tuscan as the standard language of Italy; it illustrates the rediscovery of ancient learning in that the classical Roman writer Virgil acts as Dante's guide, and it contains many figures from classical times; it takes an independent and critical view of the religious authority and political turmoil of his age; like Milton, as well as alluding to the learning of the past, Dante touches on the scientific knowledge of his contemporaries. Like Milton's poem, Dante's deals with a religious theme on an epic scale, recounting Dante's journey through purgatory, hell and heaven; allegorically, it deals with the journey of the soul towards heaven. However, it remains mediaeval in many respects: its cosmology is mediaeval, and so is its theology. Nowhere in *La Divina Commedia* do we find the idea that is central to Milton that God's handling of the world needs justifying to men. That is to say, the concept of humanism – the centrality of human experience – is much more developed in Milton's poem, and is essential to it.

We proceed, now, with a brief review of the perceptions that underpinned Milton's work, and of the literature he drew on and built on.

Literary Antecedents

The most important of all influences on *Paradise Lost* is patently the Bible. Milton knew and studied the Geneva Bible of 1560 and the King James Authorised Version that appeared in 1611. The ideas and phrasing of these, just as much as their narrative, underlie Milton's poem. It is well worth studying the biblical originals that Milton was familiar with; several editions of the poem, the Teskey edition among them, contain the most relevant parts of the Bible as an appendix. If you are working on your own, you need to look at least at Genesis 1–9 and 11–12, Exodus 13–14, 19–29, 24 and 40, Job 26 and 38, Psalms 104, 114 and 148, Isaiah 6–7, 9 and 40, Ezekiel 1, Matthew 1, Mark 12–13, Luke 1, John 1 and 3, Acts 13, Romans 3 and 6, 1 Corinthians 11, 15, and Revelation 4–6, 12, 20–2.

Classical writings were the other root influence on Milton. The pastoral style of Vergil's *Eclogues* and other classical works inspired much Renaissance writing, including Spenser's *The Shepheardes Calendar* and *The Faerie Queene*, and Sidney's *Arcadia*. Milton often employed the pastoral mode, in *Lycidas* for one notable example. In *Paradise Lost*, he calls on the pastoral style for the description of the Garden of Eden in Books 4 and 9.

The epics and comparable works of the ancient Greek and Roman writers are still more important, for Milton alludes in various ways to the *Odyssey* and *Iliad* of Homer, the writings of Hesiod, the *Aeneid* of Virgil, Lucan's *Pharsalia*, Ovid (*Metamorphoses*), and Lucretius (*De rerum natura*). Among the modern epics, we can find in *Paradise Lost* echoes of Ariosto (*Orlando furioso*, 1516), Tasso (*Gerusalemme Liberata*, 1581; *Il Mondo Creato*, 1592–4).), Du Bartas (*La Sepmaine; ou, Creation du monde*, 1578), Camoens (*Os Lusiadas*, 1572) and Spenser (*The Faerie Queene*, 1590, 1596). Milton discusses Spenser in *Areopagitica* (Teskey, 350), and refers not infrequently to Chaucer, but not all his influences are so evident. We find echoes of Ariosto in several parts of *Paradise Lost*.[2] There are echoes also of Tasso,[3] and of both Tasso and Horace in Book 2.170–4. Urania (1.6; 7.1) appears as the muse of poetry in Du Bartas, who is also referred to in Book 3.373. Milton owes much to Spenser, too, for example in the 'golden chain' at 2.1051 and the waters of the creation at 3.11; the allegorical portraits of Sin and Death look back to Spenser's Errour.[4]

Despite these echoes, and there are many, Milton did not see his influences as models to be followed. In his introductory note on the verse of *Paradise Lost* Milton rejects the rhyme favoured by Ariosto, Tasso and Spenser as unsuitable for a serious subject, and prefers to look for a model to the unrhymed hexameters of the ancients. He eschews the subject-matter of his immediate predecessors, too. In Book 9.34–7 – with contemptuous alliteration – he rejects for his subject matter the 'tilting Furniture [and] tinsel Trappings' of such knightly romances.

However, he does owe much to his immediate precursors. In particular, he shares the mingling of pagan and religious material, or at least secular and religious material, that we find in *The Faerie Queene*, and, going back much earlier, in *Beowulf*. (Note, however, that Milton had no access to the text of *Beowulf*, which did not become available until long after his death. It is not, therefore, that he knew and learned from *Beowulf*: it is rather that Milton's poem shares in a traditional feature of epic writing that *Beowulf* exemplifies in the Christian world.)

Among less direct influences, the most important is surely Shakespeare, who died when Milton was eight years old. The republic was no friend to the theatre, but not all Puritans objected as strongly as William Prynne, the chief instigator of the movement against theatre. Milton himself had attended the theatre, and drafted dramatic works, including a dramatic version of the Genesis story. The extent to which he was influenced by Shakespeare may be gauged from the fact that his first published poem was an elegy 'To Shakespeare'. Milton, of course, adopted the principles of the republican era, and *Paradise Lost* contains a soundly puritan condemnation of the immorality of 'Mixt Dance, or wanton Mask, or Midnight Bal' (4.768); yet Milton had himself in earlier years penned the masque *Comus* for private performance, and his last published poem was nothing less than a verse drama, *Samson Agonistes*. More significant than these facts, however, is the powerful dramatic vividness everywhere apparent in *Paradise Lost*. The war in Heaven that follows on Satan's rebellion is already foreknown: yet it is presented as a real, violent and spectacular struggle of doubtful outcome. Milton dramatises the domestic world of Adam and Eve, too. Behind the formal requirements of the relationship between Adam and Eve, we sense a lively and realistic sense of the sources of conflict between men and women. In Satan we find Macbeth writ large. Macbeth's ambition is matched by that of Satan. Satan's desperate heroism when he resolves 'Evil be thou my Good' (4.110) replays Macbeth who says that he is now 'in blood / Stepp'd in so far that, should I wade no more, / Returning were as tedious as go o'er',[5] and who finally confronts his nemesis with reckless abandon: 'Lay on, Macduff, / And damn'd be him that first cries, "Hold, enough!"'.[6] Satan's finest speeches are, in effect, Shakespearean soliloquies that give Satan the strong semblance of human conflicts and passions: 'Thus while he spake, each passion dimm'd his face / Thrice chang'd with pale, ire, envie and despair, (4.114–15). Iago, too, lies behind the envious cynicism of Satan. If we recall an earlier play, Marlowe's *Doctor Faustus*, we find more of Satan in the tortured human mind of Faustus than in Mephostophilis.

Another important element in the literary world of the era appears, from all the evidence we have, to have passed Milton by: he seem to have had little interest in the metaphysical movement in poetry. It is not impossible that he had little or perhaps even no knowledge of it, and there is no incontrovertible evidence as far as I know that he had ever read a poem by John Donne, or any other among the metaphysical poets. It is hardly conceivable, however, that he and Andrew Marvell (1621–78) – his contemporary, a late metaphysical, his friend and secretary, instrumental in saving him from execution, author of the prefatory poem 'On Paradise Lost' to the 1674 edition – can have failed to exchange the odd word on the subject of poetry. However, we can find, if we look for them, echoes of Donne in Milton's poem, as we can find echoes also of Sidney, Marlowe, and other Renaissance writers. Be that as it may, the trademark of the metaphysical poets, the metaphysical conceit, has no place in *Paradise Lost*: the canvas is too broad. Milton's speciality is not the specific or minute: it is the

general – the 'Miltonic vague' as it has been called – of infinite suggestion, of the imaginative power of broad colour, light and sound.

Science

Milton was a mathematician as well as a poet, and his interest in the
science of the natural world is everywhere apparent in the poem. The
structure of the whole has a mathematical order, and the geographical
knowledge of his time is apparent in references to places as far distant as
China, India and Norway. Nevertheless, the scientific developments of
Milton's era go largely unnoticed in *Paradise Lost*, with one very important exception: changes in humankind's perception of the structure of
the universe in the Renaissance period are evident in the poem.

The structure of the universe forms a constant theme in the poem.
We find many references to the constellations and stars (including a
vivid description of the stars in Book 5.620–7), falling stars, comets,
the moon, Venus, and, most often, the sun. We also find references to
the zodiac in Book 10.675–9 and elsewhere.

What were Milton's views of the universe? He had met Galileo, and
was well aware of the conflicting theories of the universe; the discoveries of Copernicus, Brahe and Kepler were already well known. Milton
refers to Galileo in comparing Satan's shield with 'the Moon, whose
Orb / Through Optic Glass the Tuscan Artist views / At Ev'ning from
the top of Fesole' (1.287–9) and in 'the Glass / Of Galileo [which]
less assur'd, observes / Imagind Lands and Regions in the Moon'
(5.261–3). In the poem, dealing as it does with the creation, Milton
treads a careful path, touching on both Ptolemaic and Copernican
theories. In Book 8, which begins with a discussion about the structure of the universe, Raphael, who as an angel would certainly know
the truth, explicitly avoids the issue when he advises Adam:

> Whether the Sun predominant in Heav'n   160
> Rise on the Earth, or Earth rise on the Sun,
> Hee from the East his flaming rode begin,
> Or Shee from West her silent course advance
> With inoffensive pace that spinning sleeps
> On her soft Axle, while she paces Eev'n,

And bears thee soft with the smooth Air along,
Sollicit not thy thoughts with matters hid,
Leave them to God above, him serve and feare;
Of other Creatures, as him pleases best,
Wherever plac't, let him dispose: joy thou   170
In what he gives to thee, this Paradise
And thy faire Eve; Heav'n is for thee too high
To know what passes there; be lowlie wise:
Think onely what concernes thee and thy being;
Dream not of other Worlds, what Creatures there
Live, in what state, condition or degree,
Contented that thus farr hath been reveal'd
Not of Earth only but of highest Heav'n.

                                                        (8.160–78)

Raphael's advice sounds odd from the pen of Milton. Where Raphael counsels not seeking after the mysteries of the universe ('Sollicit not thy thoughts with matters hid'), Milton was clearly very much in sympathy with those who did seek after them, accepting the discoveries of Galileo and his fellow astronomers, objecting to the authority of the clergy, and disputing the rights of kings. However, the world Milton depicts in *Paradise Lost* is largely pre-Copernican, and the poem as a whole presumes a Ptolemaic, geocentric universe, and uses the Ptolemaic language to describe it. For example, Book 3 refers to 'the fixt, / And that Crystalline Sphear whose ballance weighs / The Trepidation talkt, and that first mov'd' (3.481–3); and the conclusion of Book 3 refers to the distinction between wandering and fixed stars (3.718–21), and to Satan's descent to the earth from 'th'ecliptic' (3.740) of the Sun's orbit. In Book 3, again, God views Satan coasting the wall of heaven before alighting on the outermost wall of the universe (3.70–4).

Milton's world was not the geocentric mediaeval world, though that older world is the one he chose to represent in *Paradise Lost*. More startlingly, it was also not an exclusively anthropocentric world: in Book 8, there is a fleeting speculation on the subject of extra-terrestrial life:

                        ...other Suns perhaps
With thir attendant Moons thou wilt descrie
Communicating Male and Femal Light,   150

Which two great Sexes animate the World,
Stor'd in each Orb perhaps with some that live.

(8.148–52)

The possibility of life in other worlds was a subject of popular debate in the seventeenth century as it is now, and was then fuelled by the Copernican revolution. However, we see it here in a strangely medi-aeval dress, in the perspective of a correspondence of sun and moon with male and female principles. A Renaissance work *Paradise Lost* is, therefore, but it retains mediaeval modes of thought.

The seventeenth century overflowed with ideas, but they did not necessarily win immediate (if any) acceptance. William Harvey's theory of the circulation of the blood, *De Motu Cordis* (On the Motion of the Heart and Blood), had been published in 1628, and as early as 1616 it had been suggested that man was descended from apes. Thus there were ideas, and there was experimentation. But there was not necessarily approval. Lucilio Vanini, the Italian philosopher and early evolutionist who dared link man and ape, was condemned, tortured and burned at the stake for his views. Less sensationally, people's ideas about their world were slow to change. For Milton and his contemporaries, the world was still essentially Aristotelian. There were four elements – air, fire, earth and water (cf. 3.715) – from which all that existed was constituted. Human psychology consisted of a balance among four corresponding humours – blood, yellow bile, black bile, and phlegm – and psychologi-cal theory was based on the ancient ideas of Galen and Hippocrates.

Politics

Politically, Milton's England was in a state of ferment, and Milton was in the middle of it, casting himself in the role of a spokesman for the republican cause he resolutely supported. In the period 1641–60 he spent much of his time writing tracts on behalf of the republicans and serving in Oliver Cromwell's government. His essays on the principles of commonwealth (*The Tenure of Kings and Magistrates*, 1649), on the unsanctioned rule of kings (*Eikonoklastes*, 1649), on the defence of the regicide (*First Defence*, 1651, and *Second Defence*, 1654), and against monarchy (*The Readie and Easie Way to Establishing a Free*

Commonwealth, 1660) make his position clear. He rejected the absolute authority of kings, and was willing to sanction regicide to remove rulers who resolutely refused to devolve their power. He supported instead the republican organisation of states such as Venice, Holland, and Switzerland. As an ancillary, he also rejected the authority of state over church, as of bishops over clergy.

Clearly, Milton's republican sentiments were deeply ingrained. He had learned them from the classics, from his studies of the ancient civilisations of Greece and Rome, and he crystallised them in the course of his European tour. There were influential voices arguing a different case. Thomas Hobbes, a most influential writer for his own and later times, argued in *Leviathan*, published in 1651, that civilised life could only derive from absolute rule. Without rule, he famously said, human existence would be 'solitary, poor, nasty, brutish, and short'.[7] Milton could hardly have been more strongly opposed to this view. Later in his career, he discovered that the English republicans in practice fell short of his expectations, and harboured reservations both about Cromwell himself, and about the constitution of parliamentary England. He nevertheless remained staunchly faithful to his own republican ideals.

In *Paradise Lost* we can find several echoes of Milton's republican principles. In his explanation of 'The Verse' that prefaces the poem, he seems to suggest that the very form of the poem reflects the republican ideal by offering 'an example set ... of ancient liberty recover'd to Heroic Poem from the troublesom and modern bondage of Rimeing' (Lewalski, 10). In the poem itself we find Satan exhorting his followers in the language of the republican platform. He complains that 'Another now hath to himself ingross't / All Power, and us eclipst under the name / Of King anointed' (5.772–4), eschews 'Knee-tribute yet unpaid, prostration vile' (5.779), and asserts proudly that 'Orders and Degrees / Jarr not with liberty (5.789–90). However, this does not mean that Milton sympathises with Satan. Satan's response to his damnation in Hell is to claim dominion over his new realm: 'High on a Throne of Royal State' he occupies a 'bad eminence' (2.1–6).

The Garden of Eden, however, is a true republic. Adam and Eve are 'not equal' (4.296), yet work together in perfect amity to manage their world. In their looks there is 'Truth, Wisdome, Sanctitude severe and pure, / Severe, but in true filial freedom plac't; / Whence true autoritie in men' (4.293–5). Authority, in Milton's view, is God's, and only what derives from God is proper to men. Anything else is tyranny. Like the faithful angels, Adam and Eve offer obedience to God and His laws freely and willingly. There is freedom in this servitude. The Fall, however, destroys this easy balance: as Michael points out to Adam in Book 12, 'Since thy original lapse, true Libertie / Is lost, which alwayes with right Reason dwells / Twinn'd' (12.83–5).

Milton's republicanism is idealistic. It is almost synonymous with liberty. In the republic that Milton envisages, each individual is free from oppression, and free to contribute to the common wealth. The very title of his 1660 pamphlet, *The Readie and Easie Way to Establish a Free Commonwealth*, indicates his opinions and his hopes – though by this time, his ideas about the practical organisation of the republic had altered considerably. It is clear in *Paradise Lost* that the claims of kings are spurious, ultimately rooted in mere vanity; only in a republican world can paradise be recreated. After the Fall, mankind is bedevilled with ambitious tyrants 'not content / With fair equalitie, fraternal state' (12.25–6). We should notice, too, that Paradise, like the Republic, fails, and is ultimately destroyed in Noah's flood according to Michael's account in Book 12.

Religion and Theology

The political ferment of Milton's period was matched by religious conflict. The Puritans were reformers in both political and religious spheres, dedicated to stripping away artificial laws, barriers and principles, and to strengthening the essential. Milton expounded his opinions in pamphlets arguing against the structure of the official government of the English church (*Of Prelatical Episcopacy*, 1641; *The Reason of Church Government*, 1641; *The Likeliest Means to Remove Hirelings out of the Church*, 1659), and in his *De Doctrina Christiana*, published posthumously.

Milton's religious writings are various and extensive, but his ideas may be summed up simply:

- He believed in the absolute authority of the Bible simply interpreted.
- He rejected any hint of idolatry.

- He rejected the association of church and state, and argued for disestablishment.
- He objected to the principle of authority vested in the organised structure of the English church, and wanted to abolish the structure of clerical authority.
- He believed that clergy should be unpaid volunteers.
- It follows that religion for Milton was a matter between a man and his God.

For Milton, hence, simplicity was the key. As we have seen, *Paradise Lost* contains a parody of the kind of religious ceremonial associated with Catholic practice: this was for him a form of idolatry. The great council in hell, and the building of Pandemonium reflect the gross magnificence of Rome, its overblown ceremonial and heavyweight organisation; the speeches of the fallen angels as they consult about their plight represent the ponderous discussions of Cardinals and Bishops in the Vatican. In contrast, the religious observances of Adam and Eve are marked by simplicity; their prayer in Book 4 (724ff.), shows the spontaneity and brevity proper to an 'adoration pure / Which God likes best' (4.737–8). Of course, this directness of worship issues from the innocence reflected in their unashamed nudity; after the Fall, they cannot appear before their God without shame, and cannot address Him without the consciousness of guilt.

From the theological point of view, Milton's Christianity was far from orthodox. It appears from *Paradise Lost* that he did not adhere to the doctrine of the Trinity: that is, that God comprises three persons – the Father, the Son, and the Holy Spirit – all present from the beginning. He was rather a Unitarian. For him, the Father is the origin of all things, and he fashioned the Son from his own being. As for the Holy Spirit, the third element in the Trinity scarcely rates a mention in the poem, occurring only as an inspirational principle, the counterpart of Urania, or as the dove-like spirit in the first of the invocations, and possibly as the 'Comforter' of 12.486.

Milton believed in predestination, but not in its simple, Calvinist form. For Calvin, man behaves precisely according to God's plan, and thus each of us is preselected for salvation or damnation. Milton, as he makes clear in *Paradise Lost*, believed in free will: God knew from the beginning that Adam and Eve would fail to adhere to his command to eschew the fruit of the Tree of Knowledge, but they were still free either to eat or not; this explains the temptation scenes, which show first Eve, then Adam, voluntarily ignoring what they have been told, and choosing to contravene God's single prohibition. God made His creatures 'just and right, / Sufficient to have stood, though free to fall' (3.98–9); the matter is fully discussed in Book 3, 95–128. Milton's position is Arminianist*: salvation is guaranteed for those who obey God's will. In the way he depicts Adam and Eve as living and worshipping in simple style, Milton also reveals his leanings towards the antinomian view: he did not believe in distinguishing between clergy and laity, did not believe in formal expressions of faith such as Sunday services; for him, inner piety was sufficient. We have noted that earlier in life he had been destined for Holy Orders: given his views, it is unsurprising that he disappointed his father's expectations.

Milton did not hold the orthodox dualist view of creation. That is, he did not distinguish spiritual and material modes of existence as separate states; he did not perceive people as having a spiritual identity as distinct from their physical reality; the soul was not distinct from the body. He was a monist: the spiritual and physical worlds were for him a single continuity. Thus in *Paradise Lost*, angels, conventionally considered to be entirely spiritual entities, experience something akin to sexual desire (8.622ff.), and Raphael can eat with Adam and Eve (5.433ff.). Conversely, Adam and Eve may hope gradually to refine themselves in their devotion to God until such a point that they can become as angels. There is thus no absolute frontier where the material ends and the spiritual begins: one can move towards, and shade into, the other. There is therefore no limit to the potential development of Adam and Eve: it is open to them to aspire to the realm of the refined spirits. This is important for the temptation scene in *Paradise Lost*, since it brutally stresses the emptiness of Satan's argument. When Satan tempts Eve, he offers merely a short cut – and, of course, an illusory one – to the higher existence to which she may aspire in the fullness of time. The rebel angels can have sex too, in their own way: Death is the progeny of the evil union of Sin and Satan; love is another matter, however, and there is a note of envy in Satan's reference to Adam and Eve 'Imparadis't in one anothers arms' (4.506).

Marriage and Related Matters

Milton's position in the world of sexual politics is a difficult one. He has often been accused, not to say convicted, of misogyny. His opinions concerning divorce scandalised his contemporaries, and still seem radical in ours. His own adventurous marital history may have something to do with this. He was married three times, living separately from his first wife, Mary Powell, for a period of three years. However, it was chiefly his writings that awakened the concern, shock, horror and ire of his contemporaries.

Four pamphlets constitute the major evidence of Milton's view of divorce: *The Doctrine and Discipline of Divorce* (1643), *Judgment of Martin Bucer* (1644), *Tetrachordon* (1645) and *Colasterion* (1645). These pieces carefully reinterpret scripture to give authority to a much more relaxed view of divorce than was conventional. Of course, divorce had only become possible as a result of the Reformation: the Church of Rome did not recognise it. However, Milton went much further than his contemporaries in arguing that divorce should be available on grounds of incompatibility. He argued that there was nothing godly about a bad marriage, which placed greater burdens on the partners than they would experience unmarried. Milton was perceived in effect as advocating divorce on demand.[8]

In fact, Milton's idea was to support the happiness of both partners in a marriage. He asserts that a primary aim of marriage is 'the apt and cheerfull conversation of man with woman, to comfort and refresh him against the evil of solitary life'.[9] In Adam and Eve we see the principle in practice. They enjoy an easy companionship, 'talking hand in hand' (4.689), and a sexual union blessed by God, which is the 'sole proprietie, / In Paradise of all things common else' (4.752–3). In Adam's eyes, Eve is the 'Sole partner and sole part of all these joyes' (4.410), whose company would make even the harshest labours sweet. Such is the relationship that inspires Milton's impassioned hymn, 'Haile, wedded Love' (4.750). How different, then, their relationship after the Fall. As we have seen in Chapter 6, Adam concurs in Eve's transgression, for 'we are one, / One Flesh; to loose thee were to loose my self' (9.958–9). The immediate effect of his decision to join her in disobedience is the awakening of lust:

> Carnal desire enflaming, hee on Eve
> Began to cast lascivious Eyes, she him
> As wantonly repaid; in Lust they burne

$$(9.1012–14)$$

Here Adam takes the lead, where Eve did in the case of eating the fruit, and as Adam followed her in eating the fruit, so now Eve matches him in lust, which she 'As wantonly repaid'. From there they descend to mutual recrimination, Adam blaming Eve, Eve blaming Adam for having allowed her to have her way in going off to labour on her own, until Adam, 'incenst' (angry: the word contains its own inherent irony!) exonerates himself and blames 'Ingrateful Eve' (9.1162,4) for all their woes. Thence Book 9 ends with Milton's summation of the change in their relationship that we have previously analysed. This, evidently, is the negation of what Milton understood by a good marriage: it is a torture for both the parties to it, and contains no virtue.

A significant feature of this breakdown in the relationship is its mutuality, its reciprocality. There is no suggestion here of inequality in blameworthiness. In lust they 'burne' together. In argument, Eve gives as good as she gets. There is no sense of her as an inferior partner.

The position of the woman in this microcosmic society, however, is unclear in the poem as a whole. When first introduced, Eve is presented as a secondary creation both in time and in importance. She is created for Adam's benefit, and he is her author – for she is fashioned from his rib – as much as God is. Naturally, therefore, Adam's primary relationship is with God, and hers is with Adam – 'Hee for God only, shee for God in him' (4.299). Their personalities are distinct: Adam is designed for 'contemplation...and valour' (4.301), while Eve has 'softness...and sweet attractive grace' (4.298); his noble visage suggests 'Absolute rule', where hers implies 'Subjection...coy submission' (4.308–10). The description falls into line with the common acceptance in Milton's era that in general women were the inferior sex, designed primarily for the bearing of children and the support of their husbands. As Raphael puts it in Book 7, 'Male he created thee, but thy consort Femal for Race' (7.529–30); Eve's function, thus, is required for preservation of the species, and not, it sometimes seems, for much else. She is, for instance, excluded from the discussions of Raphael and Adam about the nature of the universe – she is restricted to picking fruit and serving lunch – and it is Adam and not she who is warned of Satan's plans.

Milton thus gives an impression that is anathema to feminists. Charlotte Brontë summed up the feminist view wittily in *Shirley*:

> Milton was great; but was he good? His brain was right; how was his heart? He saw heaven: he looked down on hell. He saw Satan, and Sin his daughter, and Death their horrible offspring. Angels serried before him their battalions: the long lines of adamantine shields flashed back on his blind eyeballs the unutterable splendour of heaven. Devils gathered their legions in his sight: their dim, discrowned, and tarnished armies passed rank and file before him. Milton tried to see the first woman [but] It was his cook that he saw.[10]

Charlotte Brontë was great, too, but she evidently harboured a somewhat warped view of Eve, for the Eve we meet in the poem is a dynamic character. Though she appears submissive in the earlier parts of the poem, the Fall stems from her refusal in Book 9 to accede to Adam's wish that they should continue to work together. She meets his polite and loving insistence with 'sweet austeer composure' (9.272). Later, when Satan tempts her, he tempts her with the promise of power and knowledge – an escape from her 'low and ignorant' (9.704) state to be as the gods in wisdom – and when she takes the fruit, she seizes upon it as 'This intellectual food' (9.768). Returning to Adam with what she fondly supposes to be her good news, she urges him to eat of the fruit too so that 'equal Lot / May joyne us, equal Joy, as equal Love' (9.881–2). Of course, her invitation to Adam to raise himself to her new level reveals her complete misreading of her situation; but her words also reveal by implication her earlier dissatisfaction with her secondary status. Whatever else she may have been or have become, Eve shows herself to be far other than merely the cook.

Despite her claim to equality, however, Milton presents Eve at this point as a lesser being than Adam. It is not just that Eve asks the questions, while Adam gives the answers: Milton presents Eve as a weaker nature. From the beginning, when she has to be recalled by Adam from her absorption in her own reflection before she is capable of perceiving his excellence, Eve needs him for guidance. Thus she happily accepts her subordinate position when Adam and Raphael have important matters to discuss. In this context, her determination to go off and work on her own may look more like wilfulness or a desire to assert herself than genuine independence of spirit; and Adam, after all, is shown by the aftermath to be right. It may be, too, that Eve is by her nature – intrinsically weaker than Adam's – more susceptible to temptation than Adam would have been. In contrast, Adam's reaction to her account of the temptation confirms his strong-mindedness:

> Adam, soon as he heard
> The fatal Trespass don by Eve, amaz'd,
> Astonied stood and Blank, while horror chill
> Ran through his veins, and all his joynts relax'd;
> From his slack hand the Garland wreath'd for Eve
> Down drop'd, and all the faded Roses shed
>
> (9.888–94)

In these lines, Milton establishes a link between Adam and the natural world that represents him as the voice of reason. The faded roses reflect his disappointment in Eve. He is stricken with horror, shock and fear to the depths of his being. The garland with which he meant to honour her as the queen of Eden lies forgotten. His words to her express a world of defeat as he contrast her, 'fairest of Creation, last and best / Of all Gods Works' (9.886–7) with her fallen state, 'Defac't, deflourd, and now to Death devote' (9.901); the alliteration and repeated 'de-' prefix reflect vividly the depth of his despair. He understands at once the full meaning of her error: she is 'lost,' he moans, and repeats, 'lost' – and at this point he believes that he is lost with her.

Milton's own view is more violently expressed a little later. There is no avoiding the fact that Eve succumbs to the serpent's temptation, and thus betrays both God and Adam. Milton bitterly associates her with 'the Harlot-lap / Of Philistean Dalilah' (9.1060–1); as such, she is the cause of the downfall of Adam, who matches 'Herculean Samson' (9.1061).

The structure of the poem, however, suggests a different assessment of Eve. At the end of Book 12, Eve has, if anything, a higher status than Adam. It is she who makes the closing speech. In it, she proclaims her future mission with confidence and pride:

> ... though all by mee is lost
> Such favour I unworthie am voutsaft,
> By mee the Promis'd Seed shall all restore.
>
> (9.620–2)

Though he makes no answer (for the angels are waiting to expel the pair from the Garden) Adam feels 'well pleased' (9.623) at her words. Here Eve acknowledges her fault and her unworthiness – that is, both her specific transgression in succumbing to temptation, and the inherent, abiding imperfection of her nature. In doing so she achieves a new human dignity and stature. Of course, in that very endorsement of Eve's words by Adam's silent approval we may perceive an implicit assumption of Adam's superiority; but the Eve of the conclusion is a very different character from a mere partner of Adam in enjoying the fruits of Paradise.

It is dangerous to try to generalise about social attitudes of bygone eras. In Milton's time, as now, there were all sorts of shades of opinion on the subject of the social status of women. By virtue of its subject matter *Paradise Lost* clearly occupies a traditional position in the spectrum of opinion. The most conservative Puritan position drew on the view the Bible expressed succinctly in the Book of Timothy:

> Let a woman learn in silence with all subjection. But I suffer not a woman to teach, nor to usurp authority over the man, but to be in silence.
>
> (1 Timothy 2:11–12)

This is an extreme view, and seems to be supported by Adam when he tells Eve where her best duty lies:

> nothing lovelier can be found
> In woman, then to studie houshold good,
> And good workes in her Husband to promote
>
> (9.232–4)

In Adam's eyes, Eve exists as a subordinate whose function is to support him. He is a careful patriarch, looking after the interests of his spouse. He takes it upon himself to advise her for her own good that she should work with him, and not separate herself. The terms of Milton's description, when 'domestick Adam in his care / And Matrimonial Love' (9.318–19) tries to dissuade her, show that Adam sees it as his responsibility to guide her. From this point of view, Eve is essentially secondary. Thus it is that not only is she excluded from Adam's conversation with Raphael: she does not hear at first hand his warning of Satan's plot; and thus also she does not hear Michael's promise of the second coming. She is in Adam's eyes secondary and subordinate.

Clearly, then, if Eve emerges from the poem as a stronger character, it is not by virtue of Adam's perceptions, but through those of Milton. Adam is loving, generous, and essentially repressive. Milton, by contrast, illuminates strengths in Eve. In his writings on divorce, as in his work as a poet, Milton shows himself to be more egalitarian in the matter of sexual politics than we might expect.

The Influence of *Paradise Lost*

Paradise Lost was recognised in Milton's own lifetime as a significant achievement, and the poem has retained its fame, if not its status, ever since. It has always generated conflicting responses.

Among the first to respond to the poem was John Dryden, who published his own stage version, *The State of Innocence, and Fall of Man*, in 1677 (libretto written in 1674). Ironically, in view of Milton's opinion about verse, Dryden introduced rhyme into his version, having received Milton's permission to do so. He turned Milton's poem on its head politically, by using Satan to represent Oliver Cromwell; Dryden was a royalist.

In the eighteenth century, the mock-epics of Pope, a classicist to rival Milton himself, brought satire to the epic form in the *Dunciad* and *The Rape of the Lock*. Both adapt the Miltonic style to satirise trivial events and achieve an effect of mild ridicule or strenuous mockery in a mock-epic style.

The Romantic poets were much possessed by Milton. He figures more or less significantly in poems by Blake (*The Marriage of Heaven and Hell*) and Wordsworth (*London, 1802*); and Milton and Satan were topics of discussion among writers like Blake, Shelley, Coleridge, Burke, and Johnson. Keats felt displeased with *Hyperion* because he had failed in the writing to escape Milton's influence.

One of the works of the nineteenth century most heavily influenced by *Paradise Lost* is Mary Shelley's novel, *Frankenstein*. She refers to the poem in the Preface, alludes to it several times in the course of the novel, and selects this for the epigraph to the 1818 edition:

> Did I request thee, Maker, from my Clay
> To mould me Man, did I sollicite thee
> From darkness to promote me...?

$$(10.743–5)$$

Paradise Lost is one of the few works of literature that the monster studies, and he compares himself explicitly with Satan.[11] In one of the key scenes the monster stares at his own reflection in a pool of water:

> I had admired the perfect forms of my cottagers – their grace, beauty, and delicate complexions; but how was I terrified when I viewed myself in a transparent pool! At first I started back, unable to believe that it was indeed I who was reflected in the mirror; and when I became fully convinced that I was in reality the monster that I am, I was filled with the bitterest sensations of despondence and mortification.[12]

Here the language ('started back' particularly) as well as the situation offer a close parallel with Eve's reaction to seeing her own reflection in a pool. We may, indeed, see *Frankenstein* in general as a reworking of the ideas of *Paradise Lost*, exploring the nature of the relationship between creator and creature. This is hardly surprising, since Shelley is reported to have been reading Milton's poem aloud while Mary was writing the book.

Closer to our own time, the poem has continued to stir the imagination of creative artists. Perhaps the best-known example is Philip Pullman's trilogy *His Dark Materials*,[13] which draws on Milton, and takes its title from Book 2 of *Paradise Lost*, where Satan's vision of Chaos reveals that all must remain in utter confusion of the elements 'Unless th' Almighty Maker them ordain / His dark materials to create more Worlds' (2.914–15). The North American title of the first volume, *The Golden Compass*, is from Book 8, where God 'took the golden Compasses, prepar'd / In Gods Eternal store, to circumscribe / This Universe' (8.225–7). Other book titles taken from the poem are *In Dubious Battle* (John Steinbeck), *Precious Bane* (Mary Webb), and *Thrones, Dominations* (Dorothy L. Sayers). Milton's famous resonant oxymoron, 'darkness visible' (1.63) has many offspring, including William Golding's 1979 novel, *Darkness Visible*, a memoir of the same name by William Styron (1989), and another about Freemasonry by William Hannah (1952); it is also the name of a track by the American band Altered State, and in a modified spelling, *Darknesse Visible*, of a piano piece by Thomas Ades. Milton's influence on William Golding, however, is broader and harder to pin down than a mere title. His work is imbued with themes of innocence and corruption, and no doubt Milton's Beelzebub was in his mind when he fixed on the title of *The Lord of Flies* for his most famous work. This survey is by no means exhaustive: we can find allusions to *Paradise Lost* in many other writers, from James Joyce (especially in *A Portrait of the Artist as Young Man*) to J. R. R. Tolkien.

The poem has proved an inspiration for musicians into our own times. *Paradise Lost* provided a significant part of the libretto of Haydn's *Creation* (1798), and inspired an opera of mixed renown by Penderecki.[14] The British heavy metal band Paradise Lost, from Halifax, has released a number of albums since the beginning of the 1990s, often featuring material from Milton's poem, including CDs entitled *Lost Paradise* (1990), *Icon* (1993) and *Paradise Lost* (2005). The American progressive metal band Symphony X have relied heavily on Milton, with a CD named *Paradise Lost* (2007), and others called *Iconoclast* (2011) and *The Damnation Game* (1995). Another group, The Cradle of Filth, released a video, *Babalon A.D. (So Glad for the Madness)* (2003) that draws on the ideas of *Paradise Lost*. The film *The Devil's Advocate* (1997), quotes from the poem ('Better to reign in Hell, then serve in Heav'n', 1.263) and has Al Pacino playing the protagonist whose name is John Milton – ironically, since he is actually Satan.

Over the centuries the poem has inspired a number of artists and illustrators, including William Blake, Gustav Doré, Henry Fuseli, Eugéne Delacroix, Francis Hayman and Salvador Dali among others.[15] It has also influenced writers of graphic novels like Neil Gaiman (the *Sandman* series) and Mike Carey's (the *Lucifer* series).

More generally, the influence of *Paradise Lost* on everyday language is hard to judge, because it shares so much of its phrasing with the Authorised Version of the Bible. However, the word 'Pandemonium' (1.756) is clearly from the poem, since Milton invented it, as is the phrase 'all Hell broke loose' (4.918) which, though forms of it appeared earlier, owes its popularity to Milton.

Unusual Miltonic usages have affected our language – whether for good or ill, depends upon one's point of view. In Part One, we noted compound epithets such as 'Heav'n-warring Champions' (2.424), Sail-broad Vannes' (2.927), 'high-climbing hill' (3.546), 'arch-chimic sun' (3.609), 'half-rounding guards' (4.862), 'night-warbling Bird' (5.40), 'love-labour'd song' (5.41), 'Fruit-trees overwoodie' (5.213), 'Shee...Vertue-proof' (5.384), 'double-founted stream' (12.144). Compounds using 'arch-' particularly (as in 'th' Arch-Enemy', 1.80, 'th' Arch-fiend', 1.156, 'Arch-Angels', 3.325, 'th' arch-fellon', 4.179) are still in common use today, frequently to describe arch-criminals, even though the usage sounds a little old-fashioned – more Moriarty than Hannibal Lecter.

Another frequent usage is the inversion of the meanings of words by adding a negative prefix: 'Unrespited, unpitied, unrepreevd' (2.185), 'Swarm populous, unnumber'd as the Sands' (2.903), 'in unapproached light' (3.4), 'the false dissembler unperceivd' (3.681), 'with eyes / Of conjugal attraction unreprov'd' (4.492–3), 'Like Teneriff or Atlas unremov'd' (4.487), 'Nor are thy lips ungraceful,' (4.218), 'All perfet good unmeasur'd out' (5.399), 'Unwearied, unobnoxious to be pain'd' (6.404), 'the vast immeasurable Abyss' (7.211), 'sighs now breath'd / Unutterable' (11.5–6). Sometimes Milton uses a double negative to create the effect of understatement: 'Astoreth...In Sion also not unsung' (1.438–42); 'Not uninvented' (6.470), 'Not unperceav'd of Adam' (11.244), 'Dismiss them not disconsolate' (11.113).

The 'dis-' prefix is also used widely: 'disarraid' (3.396), 'disjoine' (3.415), 'distemperd, discontented thoughts' (4.807), 'discompos'd' (5.10), 'disrelish' (5.306), 'disburd'ning' (5.319), 'disincumberd' (5.697), 'discontinuous wound' (6.329), 'displode' (6.345), 'dispeopl'd' (7.151), 'Disparted' (7.241), 'disproportions' (8.27), 'discount'nanc't' (8.553) 'discount'nanc't both, and discompos'd' (10.110) 'disinherited' (10.821), 'disconsolate' (11.113), 'distrust and all dispraise' (11.166). Some such compounds were first minted by Milton: 'disespous'd'

(9.17), 'inabstinence' (11.476) and 'disinthrone' (2.229) fall into this category according to Lewalski (xviii). Sometimes Milton enhances the effect of negation by piling up a whole series:

> I now must change
> Those Notes to Tragic; foul **dis**trust, and breach
> **Dis**loyal on the part of Man, revolt
> And **dis**obedience: On the part of Heav'n
> Now alienated, **dis**tance and **dis**taste,
>
> (9.5–9)

And 'disobedience', of course, is the negative from which the entire poem all begins, in respect of both its theme and of its first line.

Conclusion

It is clear, then, that *Paradise Lost* is deeply embedded in our culture, whether religious, political, social or linguistic. So frequently has it inspired writers and musicians and artists of later generations that its fame cannot soon fade. If anything, its power will surely continue to grow. As evidence of the broader influence of Milton, we have the Milton Society of America, the John Milton Society for the Blind, founded by Helen Keller in 1928. It is, of course, impossible to say quite how far Milton has influenced the English language we now speak. But one wonders, would such a verb as 'disrespect' have been so easy to invent without the precedent of Milton?

9

Some Critical Approaches

Paradise Lost, though always recognised since its first publication as an important work, has aroused divergent responses in its readers as to both its subject and its style. The vast field of criticism is equally diverse. In this chapter, we will concentrate on recent criticism after a brief review of earlier criticism.

Early Criticism

As we noted in the previous chapter, John Dryden was among the first to seize upon *Paradise Lost* as a suitable subject for adaptation, producing his own operatic version of the story. He was also among the first to pick out what he, among many others, perceived as the main weakness of Milton's work: the primacy of Satan. While acknowledging Milton as a genius and as his master, he yet suggests that he could only be considered a successor to Homer and Virgil 'if the Devil had not been his hero, instead of Adam; if the giant had not foil'd the knight, and driven him out of his stronghold, to wander thro' the world with his lady errant; and if there had not been more machining persons than human in his poem'.[1] According to Dryden, therefore, Milton got the balance of his poem wrong in several ways, but firstly, and most importantly, in making its hero Satan instead of Adam.

Thus was born the debate that dominated the earlier period of criticism of *Paradise Lost*. How are we to assess a poem that condemns as wholly evil the character that dominates its most vivid moments? Has it not shot itself in its cloven foot?

William Blake – another strong admirer of Milton's genius – modifies the difficulty in *The Marriage of Heaven and Hell* thus:

> The reason Milton wrote in fetters when he wrote of Angels & God, and at liberty when of Devils & Hell, is because he was a true Poet and of the Devils party without knowing it.[2]

Here Blake makes two points in one. First, that Milton's poetic imagination took flight when he wrote about Satan, but was constrained when he wrote of God and the angels, because Satan is essentially a subject better suited to poetry. Second, he also suggests that Milton was unaware of the effect to which he was victim.

Percy Bysshe Shelley took a very different view. For him, Milton was very well aware of what he had done, and had done it with the intention of throwing down a gauntlet in the face of convention:

> Milton's poem contains within itself a philosophical refutation of that system, of which, by a strange and natural antithesis, it has been a chief popular support. Nothing can exceed the energy and magnificence of the character of Satan as expressed in 'Paradise Lost.' It is a mistake to suppose that he could ever have been intended for the popular personification of evil ... Milton's Devil as a moral being is as far superior to his God, as one who perseveres in some purpose which he has conceived to be excellent in spite of adversity and torture, is to one who in the cold security of undoubted triumph inflicts the most horrible revenge upon his enemy, not from any mistaken notion of inducing him to repent of a perseverance in enmity, but with the alleged design of exasperating him to deserve new torments. Milton has so far violated the popular creed ... as to have alleged no superiority of moral virtue to his God over his Devil. And this bold neglect of a direct moral purpose is the most decisive proof of the supremacy of Milton's genius.[3]

Shelley seems to wish here to package Milton as the pioneer of a revolutionary movement against authority and against convention – to make him a standard-bearer for Shelley himself. Satan here is no mere villain who has got out of hand: he is not only the most vivid character; he is first and foremost the moral hero of the poem. This character is very much Shelley's own Satan, and to that extent wildly distorted. From a more objective point of view it is hard indeed to feel that Milton has not alleged moral superiority to God; he tells us in almost every line where God and Satan are opposed that God is superior; even Satan himself acknowledges the fact.

The debate on Satan fuelled criticism for many years. By the time Grierson's *Cross-Currents in the English Literature of the XVIIth Century* appeared in 1929 the debate had crystallised. Critics distinguished a moral poem from a poetic poem: according to this perception, Satan is poetically the most powerful character; in the moral structure, however, he nevertheless remains merely the antagonist – the temporarily successful but ultimately powerless antagonist – of mankind. For Grierson, 'There is no doubt that Satan is Milton's greatest creation' whose domination of the first two books 'far surpasses[es] in interest all that follows'.[4] It is difficult to see Milton's poem as a success in the light of this perception, and – needless to say, perhaps – many have found cause to disagree with Grierson's assessment. What of the relationship between Adam and Eve? What of the portrait of the Garden of Eden? What of the temptation scene? What of the bitter aftermath of the Fall? What of the conclusion? Do these not at least bear comparison with the early books? These obvious reservations aside, Grierson's thesis is a persuasive one. *Paradise Lost* in his view expresses two Miltons: a poet, whose imaginative visions of Satan and the Garden and its inhabitants are richly drawn, and so compelling as to occupy the foreground of the poem as a whole; and, equally, a thinker whose thesis about justifying the ways of God to man constantly runs counter to, and tries to hold in check, the more ebullient poetic material.

Milton's language has been the other main focus of critical attention. Samuel Johnson, whose opinion of *Paradise Lost* was distinctly ambivalent, commented thus in his essay on Milton in *Lives of the Poets*:

> Of him, at last, may be said what Jonson says of Spenser, that 'he wrote no language,' but has formed what Butler calls a 'Babylonish dialect,'

in itself harsh and barbarous, but made by exalted genius and extensive learning the vehicle of so much instruction and so much pleasure, that, like other lovers, we find grace in its deformity.[5]

Despite this almost violent criticism, Johnson goes on to accept 'the faults of his diction' (ibid.) and to excuse them on the grounds of Milton's compensating virtues. However, Johnson's criticisms extend beyond matters of style. He further disparages Milton on the grounds of the lack of human interest in the poem, producing in summation of his opinion one of the more elaborate among his celebrated aspersions:

> *Paradise Lost* is one of the books which the reader admires and lays down, and forgets to take up again. None ever wished it longer than it is. Its perusal is a duty rather than a pleasure.[6]

Although, on the other hand, he apologises for failure to quote much Milton, because 'of selecting beauties there had been no end' (ibid.), Johnson's portrait as a whole savours of damning with faint praise: he is constantly glorying in Milton's virtues, only to undercut his commendations with an equal battery of complaints. It is difficult to reconcile his strictures with his general comment that 'Milton ... was a genius that could cut a Colossus from a rock'.[7]

In the twentieth century, critical opinion about Milton's style was dominated largely by T.S. Eliot's notorious theory of the 'dissociation of sensibility'[8] – that is, the differentiation of thought and feeling, or of sense and sound – that he believed occurred in the seventeenth century. We can see echoes of this theory in the view of Grierson outlined above that Milton the thinker clashed with Milton the poet. Eliot approved the particularity of the Metaphysical poets such as John Donne, for whom, he asserted 'A thought ... was an experience; it modified his sensibility'. Equally, he disapproved of the style of Milton as 'unsatisfactory', saying that 'His language is ... artificial and conventional ... Thus it is not so unfair, as it might at first appear, to say that Milton writes English like a dead language'.[9] However, this kind of criticism was not new: it goes back a long way, before Johnson, at least as far as Addison in his *Lives*, where, among various criticism of Milton's verse, he concludes that 'Our Language sunk under him, and was unequal to that Greatness of Soul, which furnished him with such glorious Conceptions'.[10] As far as Eliot was concerned, it is worth remembering that he was speaking as a poet, about the effect the example of Milton might have on the work of a practising poet, rather than attempting a general critical assessment; it is worth remembering, too, that Eliot revised his opinion in a later essay on Milton.[11]

Into the melting pot of all the theoretical critical stances that the Milton debate spawned in the twentieth century, Stanley J. Fish introduced in 1967 his *Surprised by Sin*.[12] This essential analysis of *Paradise Lost* tried to unite the polar extremes of thought on the poem – those who believed the poem to be orthodox in its message, and those who believed that Milton to be unconsciously supporting the Satanic side – by suggesting that the effect of Milton's method is to inveigle the reader into sympathising with Satan in order to realise his fallen nature. That is, the reader who feels drawn to side with Satan against God thereby reveals himself to be infected with Original Sin. If the moral point of *Paradise Lost* seems unclear, it is the reader who is confused, and not Milton, and he is confused because of his incapacity to make innocent judgements. Fish's thesis is almost ancient history now, but is so influential that it is worth spending a little time on.

Stanley Fish: *Surprised by Sin* (1967)

The opening chapter of Fish's book is titled '"Not so much a teaching as an intangling": Milton's Method in *Paradise Lost*'. This quotation comes from Milton's *Tetrachordon*, one of his tracts on divorce, and implies how Fish's thesis differs from those that had gone before: he posits a high degree of consciousness in Milton's guiding of the reader's response to his text. It is not that Milton was of the devil's party without knowing it: on the contrary, Milton knew exactly how he was making Satan appear attractive, and did it with the aim of deflating the reader's confidence in his judgement. Fish announces his argument with clarity in three postulates: the reader is the focal point and subject of the poem; Milton's intention is to make the reader conscious of his fallen state; Milton's method is to re-enact the drama of the Fall in the mind of the reader – to 'intangle' him in Adam's sin.

According to Fish's theory, Milton engages in a consistent campaign of 'reader harassment'[13] – the phrase is adapted from Johnson's *Life* – in which he involves the reader in Satan's predicament, encouraging sympathy or even admiration (see Shelley's view above), only to confront him with his own error. Thus he tries to 'worry his reader, to force him to doubt the correctness of his responses'.[14] Fish takes the speech beginning at Book 1.84 where Satan calls to Beelzebub, 'But O how fall'n!' for an example of the way in which Milton engages our sympathies with Satan's strength of spirit in adversity, with his indomitability, with his leadership – all qualities we are inured to admire. The speech closes (a point Fish does not mention) with Satan's reference to God as holding 'the Tyranny of Heav'n' (1.124). At once Milton denies the moral polarity set up here in the following lines:

> So spake th' Apostate Angel, though in pain,
> Vaunting aloud, but rackt with deep despare
>
> (1.125–6)

Here, then, we see the undercutting of the reader's sympathetic response to Satan in Milton's flat dismissal of Satan as 'th' Apostate Angel' and in the implied vanity and self-delusion of 'Vaunting aloud'.

Milton's procedure is a subtle one, though dependent on the reader's preconceptions. By identifying Satan at the beginning of the speech as the foe, the enemy of mankind, he encourages the reader to feel secure in assigning moral evaluations of the characters in the poem. But such security is dangerous, for it leads us to underestimate the power of evil: we think we know where it lies, so we can ignore it. But then, unexpectedly, it draws us into interest, thence into acceptance, and, ultimately, into imitation. This is exactly what happens to Eve: she knows not to eat the fruit of the Tree of Knowledge, she is confident that she will come to no harm on her own, she is suspicious of the serpent, yet she is entranced by the superficial attractiveness of its appearance and its arguments; and she eats. Thus the reader, like Eve, may be 'surprised by sin'. Fish offers a variety of different scenarios in which this pattern, or a similar pattern, occurs; he is particularly interesting on the subject of the comparison between Satan's spear and a Norwegian pine that we considered in Chapter 3, for example. He draws in Milton's use of time and sequencing, his use of classical allusions, the concept of the 'good temptation',[15] his monistic view of the world and the concept of heroism to form a cohesive view of the whole poem, and argues it with detailed analysis of specific episodes.

Fish has not been without his opponents, to say the least, but there is broad agreement that his thesis has dominated *Paradise Lost* criticism for the last half-century. It is almost impossible to discuss the poem without referring to it.

Feminist Antagonism

In view of the magnitude and complexity of *Paradise Lost,* it is hardly surprising that modern criticism is copious and diverse, unsurprisingly. There are large areas of discussion of Milton's theological and philosophical ideas, his religious and ecclesiastical views, the structure and chronology of the poem, its language and style, Milton's use of sources, the political and cultural context of the poem, and the biographical background of the poem, to mention only the most obvious areas of scholarship.

In the space available here we cannot attempt to deal with criticism in general. One important point of focus in the broad panorama of discussion, however, is the question of gender. This is a question that, alongside Fish's thesis, has dominated discussion of the poem since 1979, when Sandra M. Gilbert and Susan Gubar published their influential *The Madwoman in the Attic*, and it is one on which our selected modern critical essays express diverse points of view.

Concerning themselves mainly with Jane Austen, Charlotte Brontë (whose *Jane Eyre* provided the title for the volume), George Eliot and Emily Dickinson, Gilbert and Gubar argue that Milton's portrayal of Eve expresses a patriarchal, or masculinist, or indeed misogynistic stranglehold from which women writers in the nineteenth century had to struggle to free themselves. Though their book sparked a renewed controversy, their ideas have a well-defined pedigree in feminist criticism going back almost two centuries.

Feminist disparagement of Milton has a long and honourable history. Mary Wollstonecraft's *Vindication of the Rights of Women* (1792) summarises Milton's Eve in these scathing terms:

> ... when [Milton] tells us that women are formed for softness and sweet attractive grace, I cannot comprehend his meaning, unless, in the true Mahometan strain, he meant to deprive us of souls, and insinuate that we were beings only designed by sweet attractive grace, and docile blind obedience, to gratify the senses of man when he can no longer soar on the wing of contemplation.[16]

The cornerstone of Wollstonecraft's argument is that women are in no sense inferior to men, but only appeared so because of their being deprived of the appropriate education. We can indeed see the seeds of this view in *Paradise Lost*: all the intellectual business is Adam's; Eve takes care of the cakes.

In the nineteenth century, Wollstonecraft's daughter, Mary Shelley, enunciated a different view of the argument in her portrait of the monster in *Frankenstein* (1818), who may be interpreted as an analogy of Eve. Generated on the whim of a prior being, Doctor Frankenstein, he/ she is envisaged as monstrous, misunderstood, doomed to remain an intruder in the world/ Paradise until finally ostracised or cast out. As we saw in Chapter 8, the monster feels in sympathy with Milton's poem. A more discursive brief commentary dating from thirty years later we have already noted above in Charlotte Brontës *Shirley* (1849).

In the twentieth century, the fire of discontent reached white heat in Virginia Woolf's impassioned essay, *A Room of One's Own* (1929). In controlled but vitriolic prose she denounces the long marginalisation or suppression of women, inventing an inspired imaginary sister, Judith, for Shakespeare – a sister even more gifted than her male counterpart, but suppressed, as her successors are condemned to spend their days in the confines of the kitchen sink. She also invented the concept of 'Milton's bogey' (bogey: a malignant spirit)[17] to focus the idea that the male-dominated culture presents a well-nigh impassable obstruction to the development and progress of women in the arts as in society.

It is from Woolf that Gilbert and Gubar took the title for Chapter 6 of *The Madwoman in the Attic*: 'Milton's Bogey: Patriarchal Poetry and Women Readers'. They spend some time analysing the meaning of Woolf's ambiguous phrase – does it refer to Milton or to Eve? – and conclude that 'both [Milton] and the creatures of his imagination constitute the misogynistic essence of what Gertrude Stein called "patriarchal poetry"'.[18] This is a fascinating and stimulating chapter in a colourful book, but Gilbert and Gubar did not claim to be Milton experts: for them, their theme takes precedence over analysis of the individual subject.

Taking her cue in turn from them, Christine Froula picked up the theme in her essay entitled 'When Eve Reads Milton: Undoing the Canonical Economy' (1983). She takes as her epigraph the brief passage from 1 Timothy 2: 11–12 that we quoted in Chapter 8, and, while recognising that the world she inhabits has changed much from that which Woolf inhabited over half a century earlier, nevertheless insists that '[Milton's] emphatic suppression of the female in his transformation of Genesis is integral to his authority in patriarchal culture, pre-enacting the silencing of Eve and the Fall which follows upon her violation of the orthodox prohibition of knowledge'.[19] Like Gilbert and Gubar, however, Froula is pursuing her own thesis rather than exploring Milton. They see Eve not as a representation of the feminine principle, but rather as a masculine misrepresentation of it.

Perhaps ironically, the effect of the strenuous antagonism to Milton voiced by the feminist critics has been to stimulate closer analysis of the role of Eve in the poem, and to discover that its misogynistic qualities may have been overstressed. The three essays we explore below take different aspects of Eve's role in the poem; but all fail to castigate Milton for misogyny. We will explore them in order of publication. The second essay, by Karen L. Edwards, treats the subject directly, aiming particularly at Milton's conception of marriage. In the third essay, Theresa DiPasquale interprets Milton's poem in the light of biblical sources. We begin with Nick Davis, who takes a different theme as his starting point, but introduces gender as a significant element in it.

Nick Davis: 'Milton Swallows Chaos' (1999)

Nick Davis's discussion comes from his *Stories of Chaos: Reason and its Displacement in Early Modern Narrative*[20] in which he explores the treatment of chaos in *Sir Gawain and the Green Knight*, *The Faerie Queene*, *King Lear* and *Paradise Lost*. He begins the chapter on *Paradise Lost* by relating Milton's concept of chaos to that of Plato's *Timaeus*. Essentially both Plato and Milton see chaos as a state of randomness or lawlessness in which 'there is no regular proportion of cause and effect, and indeed no consistent direction of causation implying movement' (160). The world as we see it represents the order imposed on the primordial chaos by the agency of a supreme power – in Milton's case, the Christian God.

In Plato's view, chaos was a prior creation with its own characteristic features. Milton's chaos, in contrast, is a completely formless and incomprehensible state. Milton represents chaos by means of vague generalities. He associates it often with night and darkness. More specifically, he refers to the 'the loud misrule / Of Chaos' (7.271–2), and 'the waste / Wide Anarchie of Chaos damp and dark' (10.271–2). His most vivid description uses the sea as a metaphor:

> the vast immeasurable Abyss
> Outrageous as a Sea, dark, wasteful, wilde,
> Up from the bottom turn'd by furious windes
> And surging waves, as Mountains to assault
> Heav'ns highth, and with the Center mix the Pole.
>
> (7.211–15)

However, at different points in the poem Milton uses the word chaos to mean different things. Sometimes it is the raw material from which the Creator brought the world into being, and sometimes it is the region in which Satan and his angels make their home; sometimes it is the gap between heaven and earth.

Nick Davis focuses on two versions of chaos: the absolute chaos that denies order, time and sequence, the chaos from which the universe was formed; and the tendency towards disorder that characterises the world of order and constantly nibbles at its edges, working towards tipping it again into absolute chaos. Chaos, or disorder, or the appearance of it, he sees as intrinsic in the created world, even in the perfect society of God and His angels. He speaks of the harmony of heaven, quoting 'the minstrelsy of heaven' (6.168) and the complex dance of the angels, as evidence of a concept of 'deterministic chaos' (161). The perception of angels is different from the perception of men, who cannot see the greater pattern in the creation around them.

Adam and Eve, therefore, do not at once adjust to divine regulation. Adam has to be encouraged to 'direct our knowledge ... whereon ... By steps we may ascend to God' (5.508–12); he spends much of his time in contemplation, working out how the universe reflects God's order. Equally, Eve has to be withdrawn from narcissistic contemplation of her own image before she sees Adam as the expression of God's beauty. She asks Adam about why the stars should shine when there is no one to see them. Most pointedly, Davis quotes Book 8.25–38, where Adam expresses his confusion about the disproportion, superfluousness, restlessness and repetition of the universe as he perceives it. All these suggest, from Adam's point of view, disorder; and Raphael's advice to Adam on the subject is merely that he should not concern himself with large questions, but confine himself to admiring Eve and busying himself in the garden. The possibility of chaos, in the sense of disruption of God's order in the world, is thus kept constantly before us; in Davis's view, a significant element of this tendency to disorder derives from Adam's difficulties in adjusting to gender differentiation. Davis finds in both Adam and Eve an essential narcissism in their perception of the world: they see themselves as its centre, and only gradually come to realise, largely by means of adjusting their own relationship, that their perception is only partial.

Davis shows how the poem expresses chaos or disorder in a range of modes of experience. One of the questions that Raphael specifically evades is the Galileo question, which brings a contemporary parameter to the dichotomy between order and disorder. The mediaeval world was orderly, with man in the middle; the post-Copernican world pushes man to the periphery. Davis stresses the importance of Galileo as the only contemporary Milton mentions, and suggests that his telescope illuminates a newly discovered disorder in the universe; in the poem, the point is reflected in the comparison between Satan's shield and the spots on the moon. The representation of Satan and the demons expresses chaos, of course, in a variety of ways. Chaos appears particularly in the distempered passions that disfigure Satan's countenance – from which 'heav'nly minds ... Are ever clear' (4.118–19) – and in the association of the demons and Satan with gunpowder. Davis completes the link by suggesting the similarity between a telescope and a gun: both point to disorder. The poem expresses chaos in its language, too. The recurrent motif of error, or wandering, or maze, shows how the universe – and Adam and Eve with it – constantly tests the boundaries of order.

However, from the point of view of the creator, these tendencies to disorder – Davis collates them under the theological term 'errancy' (174) – constitute merely details modifying a foreknown pattern. Davis, leaning towards determinism, quotes the passage in Book 11.90–3 in which God looks upon Adam's confusion after the Fall, refers to Adam's 'motions', and confirms that 'His heart I know, how variable and vain', and points out the double meaning of 'motions': emotions, but also puppet shows. This leads him to discuss the question of conditional freedom: when Adam and Eve do the will of God, they are essentially behaving as the puppets of God; when they act independently ('self-left'), they behave in ways 'unconstrainedly erratic [and] have become full participants in chaos' (180). That is, the pattern of creation is visible to God, but hidden from Adam and Eve, who are left to struggle towards, but not to achieve, perception of the pattern of which they are a part. They cannot, for example, understand what death is, beyond 'some dreadful thing, no doubt' (4.426). They are not in a position to understand God's plan, nor the nature of their own freedom.

Satan, in contrast, knows full well the outcome of his plot and the absolute defeat he and his followers have suffered. However, for his own political ends he pretends to the rebel angels and to himself that they can still act against God. Thus they set up in opposition to Heaven a 'parodic counter-order' (178) in hell: they build Pandemonium, and plan their countermeasures against God's new creation. Ultimately, nevertheless, there is no salvation for them.

For Adam and Eve, salvation remains a possibility. They have fallen, but they are not eternally doomed. The point of Nick Davis's title is that in the errant act of eating the apple they have metaphorically swallowed chaos. In deviating from God's law, they have condemned themselves and their successors to a world of errancy, and consciousness of it.

Equally, in framing his account of the Fall, Milton had to absorb the nature of error, of sin, of deviation. In accepting error as part of the human lot, he, too, swallowed chaos.

I have simplified much in this discussion of Nick Davis's chapter on *Paradise Lost*. It is densely argued, but lightened by moments of humour. It has its fair share of postmodern critical abstraction and nods towards Lacan and 'différence' (160), and thus may appeal rather to the academic than the student. However, his is a fruitful view, and draws into the analysis of Milton's treatment of chaos many facets of the poem, including the scientific elements, gender relationships, several theological themes, and a number of stylistic features of the poem, including some elements of its imagery. He also refers (though scantily) to Milton's prose writings as background for his analysis of the poem. The discussion brings depth to the central issue of the Fall and its meaning for us and for the protagonists of the poem.

Karen L. Edwards: 'Gender, Sex and Marriage in Paradise' (2007)

The essay by Karen Edwards, a chapter from the widely available collection, *A Concise Companion to Milton*,[21] treats gender as a central topic in *Paradise Lost*. It is also much more straightforward and stylistically direct than Nick Davis's treatment of chaos.

Edwards takes as her starting point the first description of Adam and Eve in which Milton sums up their different relationship with their creator in the phrase 'Hee for God only, shee for God in him' (4.299), and explores the controversy the line has awakened, rejecting interpretations that see Milton as either an extreme misogynist or as a modern feminist. She also considers the statement that Adam and Eve 'Not equal ... seemed' (4.496), noting, as we did in Chapter 5 in Part 1 of this book, the difficulty of interpreting the meaning that Satan's perspective brings to the scene: which elements in the description should we attribute to Satan, and which to Milton? Her conclusion is that right interpretation of the description depends on an analysis of Milton's view of marriage.

For its discussion of marriage, the essay makes interesting links between Adam's description of Eve in Book 8 ('Bone of my Bone, Flesh of my Flesh, my Self', 8.495) and Milton's views of divorce as expressed in *Tetrachordon*, and his analysis of biblical passages such as St Paul's First Epistle to the Corinthians. What emerges is not a simple view of marriage. Edwards notes the concern with hierarchy common to Milton's contemporaries, and its supreme importance in Milton's portrayal of heaven and hell, but stresses that Milton shares his contemporaries' belief that a woman may prove superior to a man in respect of virtue or capability. 'Wisdom,' she says, 'may outrank masculinity' (148) – an idea fully explored in the DiPasquale essay discussed below. Given this context, she interprets the 'Not equal' status of Adam and Eve not as a hierarchical description, but as a way of recognising the harmonious differentiation of their capabilities and qualities. These differences are reflected in the different ways in which Adam and Eve recount their origins – Adam in Book 8, and Eve in Book 4 – in passages that Edwards analyses lightly but persuasively. Crucially, she concludes, both natures are essential: the whole – marriage – is greater than the sum of its parts. Their inequality makes them, together, complete.

From this point, Edwards turns to showing how Adam and Eve, who have been closely comparable in behaviour and ideas up to this point, begin to diverge after Eve's Satan-inspired dream in Book 4. The divergence begins when Adam and Eve discuss her strange and worrying dream. Despite her acceptance of Adam's argument of her blamelessness, Eve is reduced to tears by the stress of her experience, and these, the first tears shed in paradise, imply that her residual feelings about her dream are not accessible to Adam. This implied separation of feeling takes a more defined form in the disagreement between Adam and Eve in Book 9 over whether they should work together or independently, and then takes material form when they finally part to pursue their separate labours. This episode is another critical crux which Edwards explores succinctly, showing in brief how variously the words and behaviour of the couple have been interpreted. Is Eve asserting her independence, whether fittingly or otherwise, or is she rather moved by the desire to work more efficiently? Does Adam in disagreeing with her overvalue his masculine power to protect, or does he truly evaluate the dangers attendant on their separation? And, in acceding to Eve's will, does he reveal love-inspired weakness, or show confidence in her, or show mature judgement of the needs of their relationship? There are many facets to this scene and many possible interpretations of it, but none can ignore the divergence of opinion and will that it enacts.

This scene is crucial to the argument of the essay. Edwards presents the disagreement between Adam and Eve as a dispute of evenly-balanced alternatives, a natural disagreement which might have, conceivably, a different outcome. Thus the blame for the outcome is shared: the decision to separate is not Eve's alone; thus Eve cannot be solely to blame for the fall that results from the separation; thus, too, Milton opposes the ancient misogynistic tradition of Eve's culpability.

A similar sharing of blame attaches to the eating of the fruit of the tree. If Eve's was the first fall, Adam's was the more self-conscious. Eve needs to be tempted, where he does not. However, Edwards shows that in the aftermath of the Fall, as the pair alternate between lust and conflict, Adam places the blame wholly on Eve in a long misogynistic speech (10.720–844). But this underlines Milton's different view, for Eve's refusal to accept rejection, and her repeated pleas for forgiveness ultimately bring about her hard-won reconciliation with Adam.

Edwards thinks of this reconciliation as support for the prophecy that 'Heav'nly love shal outdoo Hellish hate' (3.298). Even though Adam and Eve must inhabit a post-lapsarian world in which good and evil, pleasure and pain are equally mixed, living lives fraught with difficulties, their future is one they share in mutual support. Edwards finds specific significance in the idea that Eve becomes pregnant only after leaving Eden: only after the Fall can Adam and Eve achieve emotional maturity. Eve's pregnancy, she says, is 'the surest sign that the physical, emotional and spiritual fulfilment provided by a loving marriage in a fallen world is *also* a "Fruit of that Forbidden Tree"' (159).

Though brief, the essay covers a great deal of ground. Sparely argued, it focuses chiefly on a few scenes that Edwards discusses with selectively detailed analysis. She pursues her thesis with lightness of touch, without minimising the significance of alternative interpretations. The effect is not to convince – which I think is not really her aim – but to stimulate further thought and study on the part of the reader. This is a thoroughly readable essay likely to make a strong appeal to students of Milton.

Theresa DiPasquale: 'Eve and Wisdom in *Paradise Lost*' (2008)

Theresa DiPasquale's essay is part of a chapter on Milton in her book *Refiguring the Sacred Feminine*.[22] Her purpose is to explore how 'the tradition of the sacred feminine' (1) enshrined in the Old and New Testaments, and developed in the writings of the early theologians of the Christian church, is revised in the work of Donne, Lanyer and Milton. According to tradition, the relationship between God and Man is gendered: 'God is the father, bridegroom, king; the human soul and the church ... are daughter, bride and consort' (1). This simple relationship, however, is complicated by the biological differentiation between men and women and its attendant differentiation of outlook, feeling, duties, rights and abilities. DiPasquale considers Reformed theology to have diminished the influence of the feminine – especially as expressed in the figurehead of the Blessed Virgin. Each of her three selected poets, in contrast, 'portrays the feminine as a reflection of the divine, and woman herself, at her best, as an agent of redemption or conduit of grace' (2).

DiPasquale thinks Milton, who was 'politically, ecclesiastically and theologically radical' and to that extent independent of both Calvinist and Roman Catholic orthodoxies, well positioned to encourage his readers to appreciation of the sacred feminine. The Eve of his poem is, she says, a 'portrayal of woman as an earthy type of heavenly Wisdom, and of divine grace' (5). Her approach to her subject is intertextual, but not systematically so: she alludes to the cultural history of the feminine and of Mary the Mother of Jesus, and to the image of Sapientia or Wisdom in the Book of Proverbs. She notes that Milton chooses to root his argument about the freedom God gives to men in the human relationship of marriage that is bound up with issues of freedom and obedience; and she argues that in portraying the pre-lapsarian relationship between Adam and Eve, Milton adopts as a model the relationship between Solomon and Wisdom as expressed in the Book of Proverbs, the Song of Solomon and the Book of Wisdom. She indicates parallels between Adam and Solomon, pointing out, for example, the echoing of the Song of Songs in the opening of Book 5 of *Paradise Lost*. She suggests that Eve's function is similar to that of the wife of a devoted husband in the Book of Proverbs: she does not personify wisdom, but her relationship with her husband both enacts and evidences his devotion to wisdom.

We may wonder at this point how DiPasquale intends to deal with the centrality of Eve in the Fall. In the event, she spends much more of her time on the positive elements in Eve's story.

The specific discussion of *Paradise Lost* begins with Milton's portrayal of the marriage of Adam and Eve in Book 4.750–70. In particular, DiPasquale stresses that love and marriage are identified, and quotes the vivid imagery employed by Milton. She argues that rather than underlining any hierarchy in the union, the passage portrays Adam and Eve as equally in thrall to love, mutually transported and delighted. They reflect, she suggests, the nature of God that appears at the beginning of the poem in the image of pregnancy: a God combining both masculine and feminine, and creating the world out of chaos as if by divine parthenogenesis. DiPasquale contends that if he is to justify the ways of God to men, Milton first deals with the fact that men and women are different, and were different before the Fall as well as after. Alluding to the different origins of Adam and Eve – he made from God, she from Adam – DiPasquale points out that hierarchical difference of gender occurred in the Garden of Eden from the beginning.

In contrast with the conventional view of Eve as a secondary figure in the poem, DiPasquale stresses her dynamic power. Eve is no mere object of admiration or desire; rather, she constantly challenges Adam and thus deepens his perceptions. She is first to express herself in the form of autobiography; her questions about the stars inspire Adam's inquiry of Raphael; and she explains Adam's knowledge of Eden when he asks her to provide food for Raphael. Thus she acts as an intellectual stimulus. In another aspect, Eve, as the fruitful mother of mankind, reflects the fruitfulness of the Garden. She carries within her the tree of human life and thus reflects the wisdom of the Book of Proverbs which represents Wisdom as 'a tree of life to them lay hold upon her'.[23]

DiPasquale underpins her discussion with close analysis. She analyses persuasively one of the crucial parts of the poem, in which Eve acknowledges that 'beauty is excell'd by manly grace / And wisdom, which alone is truly fair' (4.489–91). DiPasquale points out the doubt about whether 'manly' qualifies both 'grace' and 'wisdom', and inclines to think that it does not: in her view beauty is excelled by grace, and beauty is also excelled by (feminine) wisdom which alone is truly beautiful. Of course, it is possible to interpret the line the other way. However, DiPasquale supports her argument by alluding to the invocation to Urania at the beginning of Book 7, where Milton speaks of his muse as the sister of wisdom. She points out, further, the parallel between Milton's description of the second person of the Trinity as 'the Son both of God and Man' whom the Father refers to as 'my wisdom' and his description of Eve as 'Daughter of God and Man'. Eve is thus 'the earthly portrait of both the heavenly Wisdom and the earthly' (265).

Turning to another aspect of her rich analysis of Eve, DiPasquale points to the ambiguous or oxymoronic phrasing Milton frequently applies to Eve when he describes her 'sumissive Charms', 'obsequious Majesty', and 'modest pride'. The reticent power implied in these phrases emerges from her behaviour. Her choosing to work separately from Adam is not an error of judgement, but reveals her self-sufficiency. Equally, she is not excluded from Adam's discussion with Raphael; rather, she shows her independence and her devotion by excusing herself so that she can later have the pleasure of hearing from Adam what has been discussed.

How, then, given the large potency of this portrayal of Eve, does DiPasquale explain Eve's part in the Fall? In large part, she seems to suggest, Eve succumbs to temptation because she trusts the serpent's account of his achieving wisdom. She is seduced by the promise of wisdom. DiPasquale adduces the sexual overtones of the scene and suggests that Eve's act, intended to achieve wisdom for herself, constitutes a violation of her own identity. Her language renders Experience as an aggressor, a male principle that threatens femininity.

The immediate effect of her fall is that Eve ceases to be self-sufficient. Where previously she sought solitude, she now needs Adam's company. The Fall brings loss of freedom, and specifically of sexual freedom; thus the way is opened to the sexual licence that Milton refers to on several occasions in the course of the poem. Adam's view of Eve changes accordingly when he follows her example in eating the fruit: he 'sunders the bond that unites him with Wisdom even as it warps and adulterates the bond that unites him with Eve' (279). He tries to make excuses for his lapse, but at the same time reveals that he recognises the changes in Eve. DiPasquale uses another instance of detailed analysis to make the point persuasively when she comments on the idea in Book 9 that Adam is 'not deceiv'd' but 'fondly overcome with Female charm': 'fondly', she points out, means foolishly, and thus shows that Adam is submitting to folly, the opposite of wisdom; it does not mean love.

Love is the theme that concludes DiPasquale's discussion. She shows how Adam, now fallen, expresses bitter resentment against Eve, only to be answered with her assurance that she feels for him sincere love and heartfelt reverence. In a gesture that prefigures the sacrifice of the Son, she offers to undertake his punishment on herself. In a recurrence of Eve's sapiential character, once again Adam learns from her, and relents. The renewal of their relationship points towards the possibility of salvation. Specifically, we may see Eve as a precursor of Mary, the mother of the Saviour; and in Adam's love for his wife, we may see the rebirth of wisdom.

DiPasquale's essay is a pleasure to read. It will appeal to students as well as to academics. Her view of Eve is perhaps not entirely consistent, and there are moments when her argument is less than clear; how, for instance, does she explain the regeneration of Eve's sapiential character? But as a whole, hers is a stimulating and enjoyable essay, refreshingly clear in its expression and structure.

Notes

1 Milton's Conception in *Paradise Lost*

1. The invocations are known alternatively to some writers as 'Proems' (the terms used for the introductory lines of the Homeric epics), though most prefer to reserve this term for the prose 'Arguments' that precede each of the 12 books in the revised 1674 edition of the poem.
2. These matters are dealt with in Chapter 7 of this book. See, for example, Fowler pp.1–4, and the Introduction and Appendix in the Lewalski edition.
3. *Paradise Lost* [Audio CD]. Read by Anton Lesser. Naxos AudioBooks; unabridged edition (2005).
4. Fowler, p. 3n.
5. Consider the use of 'into' in Tennyson's 'The Charge of the Light Brigade': 'Into the valley of Death / Rode the six hundred' or Milton's own 'Into the heart of Eve his words made way' (9.550). The word is popular in the mass media, presumably, because of its connotations of investigation and examination, as in 'report into', 'conference into', survey into', and so on.
6. Online editions of Samuel Butler's translation of the *Iliad* and *Odyssey* of Homer may be found at: http://www.online-literature.com/homer/iliad/0/ and http://www.online-literature.com/homer/odyssey/1/.
7. I have avoided using the rhetorical terms that would have been familiar to Milton and his contemporaries but are largely unknown nowadays. These are mostly taken from Greek, and include such terms as brachologia, ecphonesis, erotema, epizeuxis, hirmus, ploce, prosonomasia, prosopopeia and synathroesmus. Fortunately, these terms can be adequately substituted by reference to repetitions or reversals or rhetorical questions of one kind or another. Some of the Renaissance terms are comparatively well known, however, and feel safe to use: antithesis, oxymoron, simile, synonym, for example. It is possible to analyse Milton's verse in terms of its Renaissance rhetoric, and some critics have done so. See, for example,

J.B. Broadbent's 1959 essay, 'Milton's Rhetoric' (in Alan Rudrun (ed.). *Milton*. Macmillan and Company Limited, 1969). There are examples of these terms in Appendix B.

8. See Wordsworth's Preface to *Lyrical Ballads* (1798). The phrase used here is what appears in the Preface, but the form often used is 'the common language of men'. In the ranks of popular misquotations this ranks only slightly lower than 'Play it again Sam', 'Come up and see me sometime' and 'Alas, poor Yorick, I knew him well'.

2 The Epic Structure of *Paradise Lost*

1. Milton's cosmology is self-contradictory in *Paradise Lost*. The matter is discussed in chapter 8 of this book.

3 God, His Son, and the Realms of Light

1. But they did not discuss how many angels could fit on the head of a pin. This debate appears to be a parody, and an unjust one.

2. For a notable example, look at *The Canterbury Tales*. Chaucer discusses the topic with humorous convolutedness in *The Nun's Priest's Tale*, ll.150–6:

> But what that God forwoot moot nedes bee,
> After the opinioun of certein clerkis.
> Witnesse on hym that any parfit clerk is,
> That in scole is greet altercacioun
> In this mateere, and greet disputisoun,
> And hath been of an hundred thousand men.
> But I ne kan not bulte it to the bren
> As kan the hooly doctour Augustyn,
> Or Boece, or the Bisshop Bradwardyn,
> Wheither that Goddes worthy forwityng
> Streyneth me nedely for to doon a thing, -
> 'Nedely' clepe I simple necessitee;
> Or elles, if free choys be graunted me
> To do that same thing, or do it noght,
> Though God forwoot it er that was wroght;
> Or if his wityng streyneth never a deel
> But by necessitee condicioneel.

(F. N. Robinson, ed. *The Complete Works of Geoffrey Chaucer*. 2nd edn. Boston and New York: Houghton Mifflin; Oxford: Oxford University Press, 1957, p. 203)

3. John Calvin, Arminianism and predestination. Predestination takes two principal forms:

    (a) Unconditional predestination: the elect are preordained by God and will be united with him in heaven. This is the Calvinist view.

    (b) Conditional predestination: the elect are those who repent and serve God; they are free to choose how to live, even though God already knows their decision. This is the view that defines Arminianism.

4. Arianism. The view advanced by the fourth-century theologian Arius that God is distinct from the Son, and the Holy Spirit, who were created by God. Orthodox Christianity upholds the Trinity: the three persons in one God were all present from the beginning. (Take care not to confuse Arianism with Aryanism, which refers to the racial views of the Nazi ideologists!)

5. Thus Michael means 'who is like God', Raphael 'health of God', Gabriel 'strength of God', Ithuriel 'discovery of God', Abdiel 'servant of God', Uriel 'light of God', Uzziel 'strength of God', and Zophiel 'spy of God'. The exceptional 'Zephon' means 'searcher of secrets'. There are different ways of rendering the Hebrew; these definitions are from the Glossary in the Teskey edition.

6. The subject has been much discussed, and biblical authority is equivocal. Matthew 22:30 and Mark 12:25 suggest that marriage is not compatible with angelic life. Angels are referred to as male throughout the Bible except in Zechariah 5:9, where they are winged women. 1 Corinthians 15:44 distinguishes between physical bodies and spiritual bodies. However, angels do eat in Genesis 18:8.

4 Satan, the Rebel Angels, and their World of Darkness

1. The precise meaning of the simile is unclear. It may refer either to the recoil that occurs when a cannon is fired, or to the backfiring of a badly primed cannon.

2. Marlowe: *Doctor Faustus* (ed. Roma Gill. London: Ernest Benn Ltd., 1965), I.iii.76. Mephostophilis amplifies later (II.i. 1213):

    > Hell hath no limits, nor is circumscribed
    > In one self place; but where we are is hell,
    > And where hell is, there must we ever be.

3. There are far too many references to list here. Among the most significant are:

   Christ as the good shepherd, John 10:14; The church compared to 'the sheep of thy pasture', Psalms 74:1. Lambs are often referred to as sacrificial victims (for example, Jeremiah 11:19 refers to the famous 'lamb ... to the slaughter'), and Christ is called 'the lamb of God' (John 1:29).

4. Milton is not even criticising those of any religious persuasion other than his own; he is expressing his individual view that clergy should not be paid — should not be hirelings in that specific sense. He believed that clergy should be amateurs, gaining their income from other sources than their religious duties. In 1659 Milton wrote a tract entitled *Considerations touching the likeliest means to remove hirelings out of the church*. See Fowler, 227n.

5. Cormorants are by no means always evil in literature. They are used to symbolise a variety of ideas, and are often used in heraldry. In Charlotte Brontë's novel *Jane Eyre*, a cormorant is used to refer to the cruel Mrs Reed. Wilfrid Wilson Gibson's poem, *Flannan Isle* refers to 'three queer, black, ugly birds—/ Too big, by far, in my belief,/ For cormorant or shag' (*Collected Poems* by Wilfrid Wilson Gibson, published by The Macmillan Company, New York, 1923).

6. In lines 200–1 Milton introduces the odd idea that the Tree of Life, if it had been 'well used' would have been 'the pledge / Of immortality'. Clearly, Satan is immortal by nature, and had he been otherwise, could not have used the tree in any way to gain immortality. The line is perhaps best treated as a general reference to the betrayal of God's will and the abuse of God's trust in the temptation and Fall.

7. The word 'crew' appears frequently. Some of the more vivid examples are: 'horrid crew' (1.51), 'banished crew' (4.573), 'rebellious crew' (4.952), 'hapless crew' (5.879), 'wicked crew' (6.277), 'atheist crew' (6.370), 'cursed crew' (6.806) 'monstrous crew' (11.474).

5   Adam, Eve and their Perfect Paradise

1. The point Milton makes here is more explicit in *Areopagitica* (see Teskey, 84n).

2. This is not to say that there are not those qualities in Milton that are likely to touch the sensitivities of even the less ardent among feminists.

3. This hair style can be seen in portraits of Cromwell such as Samuel Cooper's (http://en.wikipedia.org/wiki/File:Oliver_Cromwell_by_Sam-

uel_Cooper.jpg) and of Milton himself, such as William Faithorne's (http://www.npg.org.uk/collections/search/portraitLarge/mw118608/John-Milton).

4. See Lewalski, 100n (brief) and Fowler, 238n (not so brief).
5. See chapter 8 for a discussion of Milton's monism. Essentially, he sees the spiritual and material worlds as a single continuum, so that it is theoretically possible for Adam and Eve to move from a physical reality to a spiritual reality. Of course, access to the spiritual world is available according to Christian belief to all men, but only after death, and through the agency of the supreme Christian sacrifice of the Saviour on the cross. Adam and Eve, being immortal, have not access to that means, and being pre-lapsarian, have no need of it.

6   The Fall and its Aftermath

1. See book 4.988 and book 6.188 & 191.
2. Teskey (502n) suggests that the folds of the serpent's body rise up like spires, as if it is a moving castle. Fowler, less fancifully, thinks that 'spires' is a metrical equivalent for 'spirals' (p. 499n). Lewalski offers 'coils'. Whichever way we interpret the word, the architectural implication remains.
3. The double meaning of 'wanton' appears, for example, in the description of Eve's hair as 'wanton ringlets' (4.306), but the word is more often used in the poem to mean 'lustful', as for example in 'wanton passions' (1.454) and 'wanton masque' (4.768).
4. Such incongruous relationships still have the power to move. Consider the violent public reaction to the scene in which Mary Jane Watson kisses Spiderman in the film *Spider-Man* (2002).
5. Cf. Lewalski, Barbara Kiefer. *Milton and Idolatry. SEL Studies in English Literature 1500–1900* – Volume 43, Number 1, Winter 2003, pp. 213–32. See, for example, Adam and Eve entertaining Raphael, 5.451–2
6. For a discussion of monism, see chapter 8.
7. For example, 'Thus when with meats and drinks they had suffic'd / Not burd'nd Nature' (5.451–2).
8. For example, Fortunatus's version of the *Pange Lingua*, specifically the section beginning 'Crux fidelis' (faithful cross), and the *Vexilla Regis*, specifically the stanzas beginning 'Arbor decora et fulgida' (O lovely and refulgent Tree). You can find complete versions of these hymns at the website http://www.preces-latinae.org/thesaurus/Hymni.
9. This is how the marriage service appears in the 1549 version:'I *N.* take thee *N.* to my wedded husbande, to have and to holde from this day

forwarde, for better, for woorse, for richer, for poorer, in sickenes. and in health, to love, cherishe, and to obey, till death us departe: accordyng to Goddes holy ordeinaunce: And thereto I geve thee my trouth.'

10. 'All animals are equal, but some animals are more equal than others'. George Orwell: *Animal Farm*. The word 'doublethink', however, is from *1984*.

11. See Teskey, 302n.

12. There is no evidence that Milton read Donne's poems, though he seems to have disapproved of the Metaphysical approach to poetry. Written around the turn of the fifteenth and sixteenth centuries, Donne's poems were published posthumously in 1634, so there is, equally, no reason to assume that Milton did not know of them.

13. See 4.321, 689, 488–9 and 739. Contrast 9.385, where she withdraws her hand from Adam's and goes off alone to the scene where she will succumb to temptation, and 9.1037, where Adam seizes Eve's hand and takes her off to seal their guilt in lust.

7 Milton's Life as it Relates to *Paradise Lost*

1. Gordon Campbell, ' Life Records', in Thomas N. Corns, ed. *A Companion to Milton*. Blackwell Publishing Ltd., 2001, 2003.

2. Anna Beer, *Milton: Poet, Pamphleteer and Prophet*. London: Bloomsbury Publishing Ltd, 2008.

3. These quotations from *The Reason of Church Government Urged Against Prelaty* (1642) are all from the introductory material to Book 2. You can find the document in the Norton edition of *Paradise Lost* edited by Scott Elledge (Norton & Company 1975), p. 292 or on the internet in the Online Library of Liberty: http://oll.libertyfund.org/?option=com_staticxt&staticfile=show.php%3Ftitle=1209&chapter=78007&layout=html&Itemid=27.

4. Cf. Lewalski, xv; Teskey, xviii.

5. Cf. Fowler, 1–5; Lewalski, 341–3.

6. See also, particularly, 3.589, 5.262.

7. *Galileo Galilei. Abjuration*, 22 June 1633.

8. Maria describes him as 'a kind of puritan' in II.iii.6.

9. See http://www.constitution.org/milton/tenure_kings.htm.

10. See http://www.britannica.com/shakespeare/article-260518.

11. The authorship of this work has been disputed. However, the ideas expressed in it match those expressed in *Paradise Lost* well. (See Michael

Bryson, 'The Mysterious Darkness of Unknowing', in *From 'Paradise Lost: A Poem Written in Ten Books': Essays on the 1667 First Edition*. Eds. Michael Lieb and John Shawcross. Pittsburgh, PA: Duquesne University Press, 2007. pp. 183–212.)

12. See Fowler, 4–5; Lewalski, 217n.

8 The Context of *Paradise Lost*

1. Of course, such broad generalisations are always open to question and revision both in detail and total. See, for example, the ' Renaissance' entry in the *Oxford Dictionary of Literary Terms*.
2. See 1.16; 3, Proem, 16; 3.440ff.; 4.156–9.
3. See, for example, 2.41; 2.709–11; 5.266–76.
4. See *The Faerie Queene* 1.1.14–15, 2.7.46 and 1.1.39.
5. Shakespeare. *Macbeth* III.iv.
6. Ibid., V.viii. In connection with the general point, look particularly at Satan's speeches at 1.84ff, 1.242ff, 4.32ff, 4.356ff. It is interesting to note that *Paradise Lost* contains a specific echo of Macbeth in 10.496, where Adam is referred to as 'Not of woman born'—like Macduff.
7. Thomas Hobbes, *Leviathan*, chapter 13.
8. For a brief but informative discussion of Milton's views on marriage, see Annabel Patterson, 'Milton: Marriage and Divorce' in Thomas M.Corns (ed.), *A Companion to Milton* (London: Blackwell, 2001), pp. 279–93.
9. Preface to Book 1 of *The Doctrine and Discipline of Divorce*. You can find this on the internet, for example at http://www.saylor.org/site/wp-content/uploads/2011/07/The-Doctrine-Discipline-of-Divorce.pdf.
10. Charlotte Brontë, *Shirley*, chapter 18.
11. Cf. Mary Shelley, *Frankenstein*, chapter 15.
12. Ibid., chapter 12.
13. Philip Pullman: *Northern Lights* (1995, published as *The Golden Compass* in North America), *The Subtle Knife* (1997), and *The Amber Spyglass* (2000).
14. Krysztoff Penderecki: *Paradise Lost* (commissioned 1976, premiered 1978). The libretto is by Christopher Fry.
15. You can find many of the illustrations on the internet. Many are collated at http://myweb.stedwards.edu/georgek/milton/icon.htm. You can also see Delacroix's *Milton dictating 'Paradise Lost' to his Daughters* at http://www.artofeurope.com/delacroix/del14.htm, and Dali's engravings at http://www.martinlawrence.com/dali_paradise_lost.html.

9   Some Critical Approaches

1. John Dryden, 'Dedication' to his translation of Virgil, the *Aeneis*.
2. William Blake, Note to the section on 'The Voice of the Devil' in *The Marriage of Heaven and Hell*. Quoted in Teskey, 389.
3. Percy Bysshe Shelley,: *A Defence of Poetry*.
4. H. J. C. Grierson, *Cross-Currents in the English Literature of the XVIIth Century*, 1929, p. 258.
5. Samuel Johnson, 'Milton'. *Lives of the Poets*.
6. Ibid. More fully, the passage runs: 'The want of human interest is always felt. *Paradise Lost* is one of the books which the reader admires and puts down, and forgets to take up again. None ever wished it longer than it is. Its perusal is a duty rather than a pleasure. We read Milton for instruction, retire harassed and overburdened, and look elsewhere for recreation; we desert our master, and seek for companions.'
7. Boswell, *Life of Samuel Johnson*, IV.
8. T. S. Eliot, 'The Metaphysical Poets' (*Selected Essays*, 1921).
9. T. S. Eliot, 'Milton 1(1936)', in *On Poetry and Poets*. London: Faber, 1957; New York: Farrar, Straus and Cudahy, 1957.
10. Thomas Addison, *The Spectator*, No. 297. Saturday, 9 February 1712.
11. T. S. Eliot, 'Milton 2 (1947)', in *On Poetry and Poets*. London: Faber, 1957; New York: Farrar, Straus and Cudahy, 1957.
12. Stanley Fish, *Surprised by Sin: The Reader in* Paradise Lost. London, 1967. Cambridge, 1998.
13. See Alan Rudrum (ed.), *Milton*, MacMillan and Company Ltd., p.104.
14. Ibid., p.105.
15. Ibid., p.129. The good temptation is not the same thing as the *felix culpa*, but an interesting parallel.
16. Mary Wollstonecraft, *Vindication of the Rights of Women* (1792), chapter 2. The text is available in several locations online, for example, http://classiclit.about.com/library/bl-etexts/mwollstone/bl-mwoll-vin-2.htm.
17. Virginia Woolf, *A Room of One's Own*, Chapter 6, pp. 117–18. The text is available online at http://ebooks.adelaide.edu.au/w/woolf/virginia/w91r/contents.html.
18. Sandra M. Gilbert and Susan Gubar, *The Madwoman in the Attic* (1979), p. 188.
19. Christine Froula,. 'When Eve Reads Milton: Undoing the Canonical Economy'. *Critical Inquiry*, 10 (1983), p. 160. The text is available online: http://www.hu.mtu.edu/~rlstrick/rsvtxt/froula1.pdf.

20. Nick Davis, 'Milton swallows Chaos'. In *Stories of Chaos: Reason and its Displacement in Early Modern English Narrative*. Aldershot, Brookfield, VT, Singapore, and Sydney: Ashgate, 1999.
21. Karen L. Edwards. 'Gender, Sex and Marriage in Paradise'. In Angela Duran (ed.), *A Concise Companion to Milton*. Oxford: Blackwell Publishing Ltd 2007, pp. 144–60.
22. DiPasquale, Theresa M. 'Eve and Wisdom in *Paradise Lost*'. *Refiguring the Sacred Feminine: The Poems of John Donne, Aemilia Lanyer, and John Milton*. Pittsburgh, PA: Duquesne University Press, 2008, pp. 254–83.
23. Proverbs, 3.18.

Glossary

Alliteration

At its simplest, alliteration occurs when successive words begin with the same letter. But it also occurs in closely neighbouring words, can occur at the beginnings of syllables within a word, and can extend over whole sentences. Look, for example, at 1.249–52: 'Farewel happy Fields / Where Joy for ever dwells: Hail horrours, hail / Infernal world, and thou pro-foundest Hell / Receive thy new Possessor'. Here the alliteration begins with 'f' 'Farewel' alliterates with 'Fields') and modulates to 'h'. The triple h-alliteration is emphasised by the repetition of words. But notice too that the 'f' sound echoes into the second part of the quotation in 'Infernal'and 'profoundest'.

Anti-episcopalian

Episcopalian refers to government of the church by bishops, to which Milton was strongly opposed.

Antinomian

The term refers to a religious doctrine (antinomianism) according to which faith is the sole basis for salvation and, conversely, the moral codes of specific religious doctrines have no relevance to the hope of salvation. The antinomian position held appeal after the Protestant Reformation because it justified rejection of the authority of the Church of Rome. Critics of the antinomian position, however, objected that it allowed a rejection of all moral law and constituted in effect an encouragement to licentiousness.

Apostrophe

We are not speaking here of a punctuation mark. In its other sense, an apostrophe is a speech made to a thing, or to a person not present or not directly addressed. Often, it begins with 'O'. For example, in Satan's address (or apostrophe) to the sun at 4.35–7: 'to thee I call, / But with no friendly voice, and add thy name / O Sun, to tell thee how I hate thy beams'. In the verbal form, we say that Satan apostrophises the sun. Later in Book 4 Milton speaks as if directly to Adam and Eve: 'Ah gentle pair, yee little think how nigh / Your change approaches' (4.366–7). Shortly after, Satan apostrophises them, all unaware of his presence: 'Hell shall unfould, / To entertain you two' (4.381–2). These three situations are all different, but all exemplify the apostrophe: the common factor is that the object of the address is unaware of being addressed.

Apposition

The use of two nouns (or noun phrases) standing next to each other that each make independent sense but are used together to amplify the meaning. There is a double example when Adam first speaks to Eve: 'Adam first of men/ To first of women Eve' (4.408–9).'first of men' stands in apposition to 'Adam', and 'Eve' stands in apposition to 'first of women'. Each term in the appositional phrase helps to define the other.

Assonance

Assonance is a repetition of vowel sounds that excludes consonants, and thus falls short of rhyme. So 'eight' rhymes with 'late', but shares only assonance with 'rain'. Consider 11.228–31: 'I descrie / From yonder **blaz**ing Cloud that **veil**s the Hill / One of the heav'nly Host, and by his **Gate** / None of the meanest, some **great** Poten**tate**'. Here we have assonance in 'blazing... veil... Gate' and rhyme in 'Gate... great... Potentate'.

Bathos

Originally coined by Alexander Pope to mean an unintentional and ridiculous descent from the great to the trivial. Contrast *anticlimax* (as at the end of Book 4) where the author deliberately reduces the importance of a character or event. Nowadays, bathos is often used for comic purposes. (Take care to distinguish this word from 'pathos'!)

Caesura

A pause in the middle of a line of verse, where the sense breaks naturally. It is a mark of good versification that the position of the caesura (or caesurae – there may be more than one, as in several lines in the example below) varies from line to line, thus avoiding a mechanical effect. Milton is especially noted for his handling of the caesura, as in these lines from near the end of Book 4:

> The latter quick up flew, // and kickt the beam;
> Which Gabriel spying, // thus bespake the Fiend.
> Satan, // I know thy strength,// and thou knowst mine,
> Neither our own but giv'n; // what follie then
> To boast what Arms can doe, // since thine no more
> Then Heav'n permits, // nor mine, // though doubld now
> To trample thee as mire: // for proof look up
> And read thy Lot in yon celestial Sign
> Where thou art weigh'd, // & shown how light, // how weak,
> If thou resist.

Notice that the caesura in the second line, which follows an unstressed syllable, is a feminine caesura. The masculine caesura, which follows a stressed syllable, is much more common.

Caricature

In writing, a caricature is a description that exaggerates some selected feature(s) to create a comic or grotesque effect. It is the literary equivalent of a graphic cartoon.

Decasyllabic

The metrical line of ten syllables in which *Paradise Lost* is cast. Often these lines are regularly iambic in pattern, but often not! Both of the following are decasyllabic lines, and both are regularly iambic:

> Unshak'n, **unseduc'd**, unterrifi'd (5.896)
> Ye **Hills** and **Dales**, ye **Rivers**, **Woods**, and **Plaines** (8.275)

This line is also regular, but contains elisions, single syllables where we might expect two, as marked with italics:

> Of **high** coll*ate*ral glor*ie: him* **Thrones** and *Powers* (10.86)
> (The word 'powers' is often spelt 'powrs' in *Paradise Lost*.)
> This, on the other hand, is decasyllabic but not a regular iambic:
> **Not** to know **mee arg**ues your **selves** un**known** (4.830)

Milton's use of the decasyllabic line is flexible, therefore. He uses it with freedom, adapting it for dramatic effect or for clarity of meaning.

Dental

The terms refers in this book specifically to consonants of the dental plosive variety: that is, 'd' (voiced) and 't' (unvoiced). There are several kinds of dental sounds. In English the other most common dentals are the dental fricatives, both written 'th' but distinguished by being either voiced ('this') or unvoiced ('thin'). The intensifying effect of repetition of 'd' sounds may be seen in the following lines from Book 2:

> Through all the Empyrean: **d**own they fell
> **D**riv'n hea**d**long from the Pitch of Heaven, **d**own
> Into this **D**eep....

> (2.771–3)

Diction

The way in which ideas are expressed. The term is probably most often used to refer to a writer's choice of vocabulary. Consider the difference between, say, *almighty* (Old English) and *omnipotent* (Latin in origin): the decision to use one or the other is diction. Then think of all the other terms used for God, such as 'Power' (4.412), 'Thunderer' (6.491), 'Threatner' (9.687), 'Forbidder' (9.815): each has its particular force for which it is selected in its context. The term includes the relative complexity of words – polysyllabic or simple, and also the relative complexity of sentence structure. (Outside the sphere of literary criticism, however, *diction* is used to mean the way a person speaks.)

Dissimile

A simile that picks out the differences instead of the similarities between two terms. When Pandemonium is built, for example, Milton stresses its wonders by comparing other palaces unfavourably

> ... **Not** Babilon,
> **Nor** great Alcairo such magnificence
> Equal'd in all thir glories

$$(1.717–19)$$

Elision

The omission of a sound in a word or phrase. Usually, this means omitting a syllable in a word, or between successive words. Milton often omits a syllable in such words as 'wandring', adventrous', and 'Heav'n'. He also habitually omits a syllable when a word ending with a vowel is followed by a word beginning with a vowel. Thus he regularly speaks of 'th' Omipotent' or 'th' Almighty'.

Ellipsis

Basically, a gap. Specifically, the word has several meanings. It may refer to an omission marked by three dots, as frequently in this book where I begin or end a quotation in mid-sentence. Omission of words or syllables as a device of versification, however, is a very common characteristic of *Paradise Lost*. One of the most dramatically effective examples appears at the close of Book 4:

> ... The Fiend lookt up and knew
> His mounted scale aloft: nor more; but fled
> Murmuring, and with him fled the shades of night.

$$(4.1009–10)$$

The two words 'nor more' actually signify 'and Satan wasted no more time in talking'. One example we considered in our discussion is the account of Eve, who 'knew not [that she was] eating Death' (9.792). Another appears in Adam's account, where he speaks of the birds in Eden: 'Joyous [were] the Birds' (7.515).

Enjambement (or enjambment) and End-stopped

Continuing the sense from one line of verse to the next without a pause. This is a key feature of fluent, varied versification. For example:

Thus I have told thee all my State, and **brought**
My Storie to the sum of earthly bliss
Which I enjoy, and must confess to find
In all things else delight indeed, but **such**
As us'd or not, works in the mind no change,
Nor vehement desire, these delicacies
I mean of Taste, Sight, Smell, Herbs, Fruits, & Flours,
Walks, and the melodie of Birds;

(7.521–8)

The clearest examples here, where line 1 carries through to line 2, and line 4 to line 5, are shown in bold. In contrast, lines 5 and 7 are very clearly **end-stopped** – that is, there is a natural pause, marked by a comma, in the sense at the end of the line.

Epic Simile

An extended comparison, often beginning with a phrase like 'as when', and containing a number of different terms. See Chapter 2 for a full discussion.

Epithet

An adjective or descriptive phrase, or a reference to a person or thing by its properties. This God may be called 'Father of Mercie and Grace' (3.401) or 'th' Eternal Father' (5.246) or 'Creator wise' (10.889). See **Transferred epithet** below.

Epos

A story concerning the deeds of a hero. This is the noun from which the word *epic* is formed. More broadly, an epos can be the story of the life of any person *treated as* a hero, which is how we may think of *Paradise Lost* as in a sense the epos of Milton.

Euphemism

Minimising uncomfortable, embarrassing, or offensive ideas by dressing them up (or down!) in language that seems less harmful. For example, Eve refers to her sin mildly and neutrally as 'my change' (9.819), and when she thinks of becoming superior to Adam as an effect of her having eaten the forbidden fruit, she thinks of this as 'a thing not undesireable' (9.824), when she might instead have said, perhaps, 'an advantage I want'.

Hyperbole

An exaggeration or overstatement of facts. Consider this description of the whale: Leviathan / Hugest of living Creatures, on the Deep / Stretcht like a Promontorie sleeps or swimmes, /And seems a moving Land, and at his Gilles / Draws in, and at his Trunck spouts out a Sea' (7.412–16). Whales are large, but they are not in actuality as large as an isthmus; nor do they spout seas.

Iamb, Iambic, Iambic Pentameter

An iamb is a metrical foot consisting of an unstressed and a stressed sylla-ble. A metrical line of five successive iambs is called an iambic pentameter. The name 'E**laine**' is an iamb. Repeat it five times and you have an iambic pentameter.

The iamb is one of several different kinds of poetic feet. Most two-syllable British first names, unlike 'Elaine', are trochees – the reverse of an iamb – like '**Dun**can' or '**Kath**ryn'. (So what is your first name? Iamb or Trochee? Or is it perhaps something else, such as a dactyl, like '**Oli**ver' or '**Jenn**ifer', or an amphibrach like 'A**lex**is' or 'Ca**ssand**ra'). Note, however, that the metre is independent of words: thus we can construct an iambic pentameter out of 'A**lex**is, **Paul**, Ca**ssand**ra, **Kath**ryn, **Jane**'. See also **Spondee** below.

Inflection

A rise or fall in pitch. The word *aspire* has a rising inflection because nor-mally the second syllable is higher in pitch than the first. The term may apply to sentences, too. Questions usually have an upward inflection. Note that inflection does not have to match metrical pattern. *Aspire* is an iamb, but so is *descend*, which usually has a falling inflection. In these examples, the inflection matches the meaning, but that is often not the case. Meaning may conflict with inflection, in, for example, a question such as 'Would you rather go down to the beach [rising] or up to the lighthouse? [falling]'.

Inversion

Used in two senses:

a) Metric inversion: reversal of the normal metric pulse, for example, beginning a line with a trochee instead of an iamb.
b) Syntactic inversion: a reversal of the natural order of words in a phrase or sentence for emphasis or clarity: 'Mee damp horror chill'd' (5.65).

Latinate

The richness of the English language derives largely from the range of its sources. Many volumes of writing have been devoted to the study of the complexities of is derivation. Here we can only state the broad essentials. The language spoken in England until the Middle Ages was a mixture of northern European languages (Germanic, Norse, Icelandic). Old English is not easily intelligible today. But it is the origin of our modern words for the basics of life: meat, bread, birth, life, death; these words tend to be brief and hard-hitting. After the Norman Conquest, the language was enriched by a huge influx of words from the Mediterranean region, mainly French, but also Italian and Spanish, the so-called *Romance* languages. These words, used for chivalry and courtly love, are frequently longer and more seemingly sophisticated – flowery, even: the ruling Normans used them as a matter of course; the subjugated native population used Old English. Thus we have *pork* for *pig*, *beef* for *cow*: the stinking animals were English; the aromatic art of cooking them was French. Further, the Romance languages derived in turn from ancient Greek, and more directly from Latin, which percolated into the language also through the medium of the Church of Rome. Thus *Renaissance* is a French word for the Old English *rebirth*, and we may, if we choose, spell it the Latin way: *Renascence*. The process of enrichment developed further in the Renaissance period of wide travel, discovery: the British voyagers plundered words as well as goods and people. By the time of Shakespeare, the English language was in more or less the form it takes now. The effect is that we have many different words for similar things. However, those different words have different impact. Old English feels direct and simple. Romance words feel more ceremonial, more cerebral. Contrast, for example, *motherly* with *maternal*. Note, though, that there is no hard-and-fast rule. Sometimes the Old English can seem more ornate than the Romance equivalent: contrast *betrothed* (Old English) and *engaged* (French). One of the ways in which Milton controls our response in *Paradise Lost* is by careful selection of the language that will touch us with more than surface meaning. See also **Periodic** below.

Metre, Metrical Foot

Metre in poetry is the organisation of stressed and unstressed syllables in a line of verse. A metrical foot is one unit of two or three stressed and unstressed syllables. A number of feet (usually four, five or six) make up a line of poetry. We may think of the verse of *Paradise Lost* as built from iambic pentameters; that is, each line consists of five iambic feet (see **Iamb** above). However, the poem is very irregular, also using trochees (one stressed and one unstressed syllable) or dactyls (one stressed and two unstressed syllables). For this reason, some people prefer to call the verse **Decasyllabic** (see above).See also **Spondee** below.

Monism, Monistic

Monism is the view that perceives existence as a single substance, as opposed to the dualistic view that thinks of reality as divided into material and spiritual. The matter is discussed in chapter 8.

Oxymoron, Oxymoronic

A specific variety of Paradox in which two terms that seem contradictory are linked: 'darkness visible' (1.63), 'pretious bane' (1.692), 'bad eminence' (2.6), 'honor dishonorable' (4.314).

Paradox, Paradoxical

An apparent contradiction: 'numbers without number' (3.346), 'Evil be thou my Good' (4.110), 'regular / Then most, when most irregular they seem' (5.623–4).

Periodic

Periodic sentences are those in which the essential meaning becomes clear at the end. They are longer, more involved, and therefore harder to follow, than simple sentences. However, they can make a point far more effectively by making us wait for the conclusive statement. For example, a barrister may say to a jury, 'I can prove conclusively that the man in the dock is guilty of murder'. This is a simple sentence, clear and to the point. Another barrister may prefer to say, 'That the man in the dock in the guilty party, that the man before you held the knife, that it was he who stabbed the victim repeatedly, that he did so in the full knowledge of what he was doing, and that he was moved merely by greed – all these points I will prove to you conclusively'. This is a periodic sentence, in which the meaning appears at a climactic point. Such sentences are often described as having *suspended* syntax: the full meaning is held in suspense until the final words. Periodic, or suspended, sentences are associated with the classical languages, in which the formal convention was to place the verb at the end of a sentence, no matter how many other components preceded it. Thus a Latin sentence might take the form *subject–adjective–subordinate clause–adverb–verb*. The *Aeneid* (one of the models for *Paradise Lost*) begins with two suspensions (verbs italicised):

> Arma virumque *cano*, Troiae qui primus ab oris
> Italiam, fato profugus, Laviniaque *venit*
> litora.
>
> (Vergil, *Aeneid*, ll.1–3)

Dryden's translation avoids the first suspension to create an English order, and only partly retains the second suspension (same verbs italicised):

> I *sing* of arms and the man who of old from the coasts of Troy *came*, an exile of fate, to Italy and the shore of Lavinium.
>
> (Dryden, *Aeneis*, p. 1)

Old English, despite its inflected structure, was more direct in its structure as well as its vocabulary; the order might be *object–verb–subject*, but was much more likely to be *subject–verb—object*, with the verb normally in the middle. Most capable writers, Milton among them, are very clever at mingling periodic and simple structures for dramatic effect, or for clarity of meaning, or to suggest character – or simply for variety. There are and have been, however, writers who studiously avoid periodic sentences (Hemingway, for example).

Personification

Strictly, treating an inanimate object or an abstract idea as if it were a person. In Book 7 Milton personifies the abstract idea of: 'Thou with Eternal Wisdom didst converse, / Wisdom thy Sister, and with her didst play' (7.9–10). In Book 2, Milton treats night as a person: '... with him Enthron'd / Sat Sable-vested Night, eldest of things' (2.961–2). (This is one of a sequence of personifications of figures including rumour, chance and discord.) The term may also refer more loosely to treating an idea or object as something living. In Book 6, for example, the idea of victory is brought to life: 'at his right hand Victorie / Sate Eagle-wing'd' (6.762–3). Here we may imagine either a person with eagle wings, or simply an eagle.

(Note, by the way, that an object cannot personify an idea. For example, the Berlin Wall could not personify oppression – despite the pronouncement of a well-known political figure. That would be symbolism.)

Plosive

A consonant pronounced by stopping and then releasing the airflow, with a mildly *ex-plosive* effect. In this book I use the term only for the consonants *b* and *p*, the labial (that is, made with the lips) consonants, though it may also refer to *d*, *t*, *g* and k, which are not made with the lips.

Pre-lapsarian, Post-lapsarian

Lapsarian refers to the Fall. Anything that occurred before it is pre-lapsarian, and anything after is post-lapsarian.

Prosodic

Used here as shorthand to indicate the aspects of Milton's language that are to do with rhythm, stress, metre and versification, as distinct from grammatical structure or syntactic structure.

Protestant

See Reformation.

Reformation, Protestant, Roman Catholic

Briefly, the Reformation came about in Western Europe in the sixteenth century in an effort to correct perceived abuses in the practices of the (Roman Catholic) Church of Rome. Its origin was marked by Martin Luther's publication of his *Ninety-Five Theses* in 1517. It resulted in the development of a range of Protestant movements that stressed, to a greater or lesser extent, simplicity and individuality. Influential figures like John Knox and John Calvin developed their own brands of Protestantism. Among the different Protestant groups that emerged and diverged were Lutherans, Baptists, Congregationalists, Anglicans, Presbyterians and Methodists; new shades of belief continue to arise today. Despite the diversity of Protestantism, rejection of the authority of Rome unites all Protestants. Although papal infallibity was not formally declared until 1870 it was assumed from the earliest times (at least from 1070). A primary thesis of Protestantism was to reject the supreme authority assumed by the Church of Rome, and to rely instead on the Bible as the absolute source of religious truth. Inevitably, this placed responsibility for interpretation of the Bible on influential exegetes, and indeed on the individual believer.

Rhetoric, Rhetorical question

Rhetoric is essentially the art of persuasion. Think of the word as a hold-all term containing all the tricks and devices of language that one can use to carry an argument. It includes imagery, exclamations, irony, and so on. Appendix B illustrates some less well-known devices. One of the most widely used of these devices is the rhetorical question.

A **rhetorical question** is used for effect rather to elicit an answer. It may be addressed to a thing, or to the universe in general, or the answer may be too obvious to require saying. Often a rhetorical question is a preface to another stage in an argument, or to a summary of what has been said. In hell, Satan puts rhetorical questions to his fellow rebels to awaken their resistance and stimulate their energy. He concludes 'who can think submission?' and presuming the answer 'no one', at once concludes 'Warr then' (1.661). On the threshold of the new world, Satan has a soliloquy in which he uses rhetorical questions to argue out his own situation as when he asks 'which way shall I flie / Infinite wrauth, and infinite despaire? (4.73–4) simply to confirm for himself that he has no alternatives. When he tempts Eve, in contrast, Satan in the serpent uses successions of rhetorical questions to encourage Eve to scorn the prohibition against eating the forbidden fruit:

>   ... wherein lies
> Th' offence, that Man should thus attain to know?
> What can your knowledge hurt him, or this Tree
> Impart against his will if all be his?
> Or is it envie, and can envie dwell
> In heav'nly brests?

>   (9.725–30)

Contrast Gabriel's interrogation of Satan: 'Why hast thou, Satan, broke the bounds prescrib'd / To thy transgressions...?' (4.878–9). He wants an answer.

Roman Catholic, Church of Rome

See Reformation.

Spondee

A metrical foot consisting of two long or stressed syllables. Obviously, it will only occur as a variation from some other metre consisting of stressed and unstressed syllables, and normally has an effect of emphasis. Sometimes whether a pair of syllables are treated as a spondee or some other metrical foot is a matter of interpretation. However, the first two syllables of the third line of the following extract (stressed syllables marked by italics) can only be a spondee:

> *Well* have ye *judg'd*, well *end*ed *long* de*bate*,
> *Syn*od of *Gods*, and *like* to *what* ye *are*,
> **Great things** re*solv'd*.

>   (2.390–2)

Here the irregularity underlines the power and greatness of which Satan wishes to make the rebel angels fully conscious.

Symbolism, Symbolic

Using an object or physical state to represent an idea. For example, Satan's disfigurement represents his inner corruption; light and dark are regularly associated with good and evil.

Syntax, Syntactical

Syntax is the grammatical organisation of sentences. It includes word order, which in *Paradise Lost* is often Latinate. This means that Milton uses many tricks of Latin, such as placing an adjective after noun it describes, as when the rebel angels reduce their 'shapes immense' (1.790), or when Adam and Eve leave Eden with 'wandring steps and slow' (12.648), or when the light of hell is described as 'darkness visible' (1.63). Often he reverses subject and verb, or uses one part of speech for another.

Transferred Epithet

An adjective that applies logically to one subject is attached grammatically to a different but related subject. Thus Milton transfers the adjective 'impious' from Satan to his 'impious Crest' (6.188), and exchanges noun and adjective in referring to 'the watrie calm' (7.234) instead of calm water. In another extraordinary example, 'th' innumerable sound / Of Hymns' (3.147–8), the epithet demands a plural noun, but has only a singular: it is actually the hymns that are innumerable.

Appendix A: Characteristics of Epic

Note: these features are not a prescription: they are rather observations of the nature of the classical epics. See chapter 2 for detailed discussion of some of the ways in which Milton adapts the classical conventions.

General Structure

The subject is large: an inclusive event of great national or human or universal importance.

The events involve decisive deeds of valour or gallantry.

The settings used embrace a broad range, extending even into hell or heaven as well as over great stretches of the human world.

Battle scenes include broad general action with much focus on the machinery of chariots and weapons.

Individual confrontations have decisive significance.

Supernatural forces mingle with the human action.

The epic story opens *in media res* – that is, 'in the middle of things', when the story is already at a climactic point. History and prophecy draw in the past and the future, and reference is made to events elsewhere in the story.

Opposing forces in armed battle are catalogued, paying special attention to the generals.

Councils of war are held in which the main characters express their views.

Epic pageants and games occur.

The Characters

The protagonists, fitting the grandeur of the subject matter, are heroic in their stature, whether morally or physically. They may have superhuman traits.

The characters undertake epic journeys, including a journey to the underworld.

The Style

The style of writing is appropriate to the subject: elevated, even ceremonial. When the protagonists speak, they speak in a formal, heightened style.

The writer invokes the help of the Muse to inspire his creative abilities.

Epic simile, or Homeric simile, a formal simile extended by detailed parallels, is employed to give weight to the theme.

Standard epithets, particularly in appositional phrases, are repeatedly used to describe the main characters.

Inversions of normal word order occur.

Milton's Adaptation of the Epic Form

His theme is even greater than those used in the classical epics.

He pays more attention to the characters' internal conflicts.

Correspondingly, the focus shifts away from physical battle.

Milton's moral world is much more complex.

The journey to the underworld becomes a vision of hell.

Appendix B: Milton's Rhetoric

In Milton's time, rhetoric was an important subject in its own right, and he was familiar with formal rhetorical patterns in a way that we today are not. Here, to understand better the way Milton thought about his writing, we illustrate a selection (by no means exhaustive) of the patterns he uses in *Paradise Lost*. The terms are still in use today, but are less well known than those in the Glossary, which are not repeated here. Several of the terms defined below have simpler modern equivalents, or else are more usually described as repetitions or parallelisms of one kind or another.

Anadiplosis. Repetition of the last word of one clause or phrase at the beginning of the following clause or phrase: 'I formd them **free**, and **free** they must remain' (3.124); 'from the bottom stir / The **Hell** within him, for within him **Hell** / He brings' (4.19–21); 'guiltie **shame**, dishonest **shame** / Of natures works' (4.313); 'Heav'n is **high**, / **High** and remote to see from thence distinct' (9.810).

Anaphora. Repetition of the same word or group of words at the beginnings of successive clauses or phrases: 'Is **this the** Region, **this the** Soil, the Clime,/ Said then the lost Arch Angel, **this the** seat?' (1.242–3); 'Shall we then live **thus** vile, the race of Heav'n / **Thus** trampl'd, **thus** expell'd?' (2.194–5).

Anastrophe. Reversal of word order: 'Creatour him they sung' (7.259) for 'they sang [his praises as] creator'.

Antanaclasis. Repetition of a word in two different senses: '**Fruitless** to mee, though **Fruit** be here to excess' (9.648); 'O Father, **gracious** was that word which clos'd /Thy sovran sentence, that Man should find **grace**' (3.144–5), '**highly** they rag'd /Against the **Highest**' (1.667–8), 'As one great Furnace **flam**'d, yet from those **flames**' (1.62).

Anthimeria. Using one part of speech for another: 'when they list, would creep,/ If aught disturb'd thir noyse, into her woomb,/ And **kennel** there' (2.656–8).

Antimetabole. Repeating words in reverse order (mirror repetition in plain English!):

> Of Providence, **Foreknowledge**, **Will**, and **Fate**,
>
> Fixt **Fate**, free **will**, **foreknowledge** absolute (2.560–1)
>
> The **Hell within him**, for **within him Hell** (4.419)

Asyndeton. Omission of conjunctions: 'Is this the Region, this the Soil, the Clime ... the seat ... this mournful gloom' (1.242–4); 'Him God beholding from his prospect high, / Wherein past, present, future he beholds' (3.77–8). The opposite – using too many conjunctions – is called **Polysyndeton**.

Antonomasia. A specific variety of periphrasis, in which a title, epithet, or descriptive phrase is used instead of a proper name. For example, Milton refers to Adam and Eve as 'our Grand Parents' (1.29), or to God as 'th' Omnipotent'.

Aphaeresis. Omission of the first syllable of a word: 'I sdeind subjection' (4.50).

Auxesis. Nowadays we usually call this climax. Ordering ideas according to increasing importance: 'Whether upheld by strength, or Chance, or Fate' (1.133); 'there to pine / Immovable, infixt, and frozen round' (2.601–2).

Catachresis. At its simplest, a mixed metaphor: 'what heart of Rock could long / Drie-ey'd behold?' (11.490–1).

Chiasmus. A reversal of terms, like **Antimetabole**, but the logical relations between the terms shaped like a cross. Easier to illustrate than define! For example, 'If then his Providence / Out of our evil seek to bring forth good, / Our labour must be to pervert that end, / And out of good still to find means of evil' (1.162–5).

Ecphonesis. An exclamation, sometimes indeed called an *exclamatio*, suggesting a spontaneous surge of strong emotion, and usually commencing with a cry of 'O': 'But O how fall'n!' (1.84); 'O shame to men!' (2.490); 'O unexampl'd love' (3.410); 'our Seed (O hapless Seed!)' (10.965).

Ellipsis. Omission of a word (or words) that are more or less essential to the sense and must be supplied by the reader. There are numerous instances in *Paradise Lost*, for example: 'without Love [there can be] no happiness', 'But I can now [say] no more' (8.631). 'Nor [did he say] more' (4.1014), 'Lives ther [anyone] who loves his pain?' (4.888); 'O [most] Sovran, vertuous, [and] precious of all Trees' (9.794).

Epanalepsis. Starting and ending a statement with the same word: 'So man, as is most just/ Shall satisfie for man' (3.294–5); 'Sweet is the breath of morn, her rising sweet' (4.641); 'thou to mee / Art all things under Heav'n, all places thou' (12.616–17).

Epistrophe. Repetition of the same words at the ends of successive clauses or phrases: 'What though the field be lost? / All is not lost' (1.105–6).

Erotesis. We usually call this a rhetorical question. Asking a question, not to elicit an answer but to imply an assertion: 'who can think Submission?' (1.661). Often a rhetorical question marks a turning point in an argument. A related device, called *hypophora*, uses a question as a starting point for an explanation. We might view 'What though the field be lost?' (1.105) as either erotesis or hypophora.

Hyperbaton. Deviation from normal word order: 'High on a throne of royal state ... Satan exalted sat'.

Hysteron-proteron. A reversal of logical order of elements in a phrase (A variety of **Hyperbaton**): 'Inexplicable / Thy justice seems.' (10.754–5) – a device familiar from the *Star Wars* films.

Litotes. A specific variety of understatement, in which an affirmative is expressed by denying a negative: 'In Sion also not unsung (1.442), 'that strife / Was not inglorious' (1.624–5), 'Not uninvented that, which thou aright' (6.470), 'A thing not undesireable' (9.824), 'Not unperceav'd of Adam' (11.244).

Meiosis. We usually call this understatement. There are several instances in the dialogue between Satan and Gabriel at the end of Book 4, where each tries to win moral ascendancy. Gabriel, for instance, ironically calls Satan a 'courageous Chief, / The first in flight from pain' (4.920–1), and sums him up antithetically as 'no Leader, but a lyar trac't' (4.949).

Onomatopoeia. Use of words whose sound echoes the sense: 'A dismal **universal hiss**, the **sound**/ Of public **scorn**' (10.508–9), '**ceasless hiss**' (10.574), 'great laughter was in Heav'n / And looking down, to see the **hubbub** strange / And hear the **din**' (12.59–61).

Periphrasis. A circumlocution, often used in *Paradise Lost* to create an effect of solemnity, particularly when instead of a proper name, Milton refers to characters by means of a descriptive phrase (see **Antonomasia**). However, Milton uses the device freely throughout the poem, as when he refers to nine days as 'Nine times the Space that measures Day and Night / To mortal men' (1.50–1).

Paronomasia. Use of words alike in sound but different in meaning: 'O **Eve**, in **evil** hour thou didst give eare / To that false Worm' (10.1067–8), 'I see the tenor of Mans **woe** / Holds on the same, from **Woman** to begin' (11.632–3). Nowadays we use the term 'pun', althoughpuns for us usually have a humorous aspect.

Pleonasm. A variety of repetition, in which words of similar meaning are used together Sometimes this can be merely a pointless redundancy of words, but may be used for emphasis: 'fate inevitable' (2.197), 'racking torture' (11.481).

Polyptoton. Repetition of a word in different forms: 'Father, who art Judge / Of all things made, and **judgest** onely right' (3.154–5).

Polysyndeton. Employing a greater number of conjunctions than strictly required: 'Havock **and** spoil **and** ruin are my gain (2.1009); 'armd with ice / And snow **and** haile **and** stormie gust **and** flaw' (10.687–8). This longer example illustrates **Anaphora**, too:

> All is not lost; the unconquerable will,
> **And** study of revenge, immortal hate,
> **And** courage never to submit or yield:
> **And** what is else not to be overcome.

> (1.106–9)

Prosopopoeia. Applying human qualities to inanimate things or abstract ideas. Nowadays we usually call this personification: for example, 'the gorgeous East with richest hand / Showrs on her Kings Barbaric Pearl & Gold' (2.3–4), 'fickle Chance' (2.233), 'Skie lowr'd, and muttering Thunder, som sad drops / Wept' (9.1002–3).

Synathroesmus. A series of adjectives: 'The Firmament, expanse of **liquid, pure, /** **Transparent, Elemental** Air' (7.264–5).

Syncope. Omitting a syllable from the middle of word: 'adventrous'. (The term for omitting a syllable from the end of a word is **Apocope**.)

Synecdoche. Substitution of a part or a substance for a whole, one thing for another, or a specific name used for a generic: '**bend thine eare** / To supplication' (11.30–1) means 'listen sympathetically to the prayers of Adam and Eve'.

Sample Analysis

Here, now, is an extract, the beginning of Book 4, analysed according to its rhetorical structure:

O For that warning voice, which he who saw	*Ecphonesis*
Th' Apocalyps, heard **cry** in Heaven **aloud**,	*Pleonasm*
Then when **the Dragon**, put to second rout,	*Antonomasia*
Came **furious** down to be reveng'd on men,	*Anastrophe, Anthimeria*
Wo To The Inhabitants On Earth! that now,	
While time was, **our first Parents** had bin warnd	*Asyndeton (2),*
	Antonomasia

The coming of thir secret foe, and scap'd — *Asyndeton ([Of] The Coming)*

Haply so scap'd his mortal snare; for **now** — *(Anadiplosis*
Satan, **now** first inflam'd with rage, came down, — *(Anadiplosis*
The Tempter ere th' Accuser of man-kind,
To wreck on **innocent frail** man his loss — *Synathroesmus*
Of that first Battel, and his flight to Hell:
Yet not rejoycing in his speed, though bold,
Far off and **fearless**, nor with cause to boast, — *Prosopopoeia*
Begins his dire attempt, which nigh the birth — *Asyndeton ([and] Begins)*

Now rowling, boiles in his tumultuous brest,
And like a devillish Engine back recoiles
Upon himself; horror and doubt distract
His troubl'd thoughts, and from the bottom stirr
The **Hell within him**, for **within him Hell** — *Epanalepis, Antimetabole*

He brings, **and round about him**, **nor from** Hell — *Pleonasm*
One step no more then from himself can fly
By change of place: Now **conscience wakes despair** — *Prosopopeia*
That slumberd, wakes the bitter memorie
Of **what he was, what is, and what must be** — *Auxesis, Anaphora*
Worse; of **worse** deeds **wors**e sufferings must ensue. — *Anadiplosis*
Sometimes towards Eden which now in his view
Lay pleasant, his grievd look he fixes sad, — *Anastrophe, Anthimeria*

Sometimes towards Heav'n and the full-blazing Sun,
Which now **sat high in his** Meridian Towre: — *Prosopopeia, Ellipsis*
Then much revolving, thus in sighs began.
O thou that **with surpassing Glory crownd**, — *Apostrophe, Periphrasis*
Look'st from thy sole Dominion like the God
Of this new World; at **whose sight** all the Starrs — *Prosopopeia*
Hide thir diminisht heads; to thee I call, — *Prosopopeia*
But with no friendly voice, and add thy name
O Sun, to tell thee how I hate thy beams — *Ecphonesis, Apostrophe*
That bring to my remembrance from what state
I **fell**, how glorious once **above** thy Spheare; — *Antithesis, ellipsis([I was] once)*

Till Pride and worse Ambition **threw** me down — *Prosopopeia*
Warring in **Heav'n** against **Heav'ns matchless King**. — *Anadiplosis, Antonomasia*

Further Reading and Bibliography

Editions of *Paradise Lost*

The edition used for this book is *The Poetical Works of John Milton, Edited after the Original Texts*, edited by H. C. Beeching (Oxford: Clarendon Press, 1900). This edition is available online at http://www.gutenberg.org/files/1745/1745-h/1745-h.htm. It is also the basis of the much-reprinted edition of Milton's poems edited by W. Skeat (Oxford University Press, 1904 & *sequ.*)

The following three editions of *Paradise Lost* are specifically designed for students:

Prof. Alastair Fowler, ed. *Milton: Paradise Lost* (Longman Annotated English Poets). Longman, revised 2nd edition, 2007.

Barbara K. Lewalski. *John Milton: Paradise Lost*. Oxford: Wiley-Blackwell, 2007.

Gordon Teskey, ed. *John Milton: Paradise Lost*. 3rd Edition (Norton Critical Edition). New York: W. W. Norton, 2005.

You can also find a well-annotated online text at the Milton Reading Room:

http://www.dartmouth.edu/~milton/reading_room/contents/index.shtml.

Biographical Works

Barbara Lewalski. *The Life of John Milton*. Oxford: Blackwell Publishing, 2003. (The biography I used for this study.)

A. N. Wilson. *The Life of John Milton*. Oxford: Oxford University Press, 1983.

There is also a brief, faintly interactive and quite diverting online biography in the 'Darkness Visible' website at: http://www.christs.cam.ac.uk/darknessvisible/miltons_life.html.

Basic Guides to the Poem

Harry Blamires. *Milton's Creation: A Guide through Paradise Lost*. London: Methuen, 1971.

You may wish to view a parallel-text online version of the original poem alongside a modern English paraphrase at: http://www.paradiselost.org/novel.html. The first few modernised lines of each book are immediately available, but note that there is a small fee for the complete 'novel' of each book.

Good general introductions to the study of *Paradise Lost* are these brief student's guides:

David Kearns. *How to Study Milton*. London: Macmillan, 1993. (Selective, and not exclusively confined to *Paradise Lost*.)

David Loewenstein. *Milton: Paradise Lost*. Cambridge: Cambridge University Press, 1993, 2004.

General Criticism

Beer, Anna. *Milton: Poet, Pamphleteer and Patriot*. London: Bloomsbury Publishing Ltd, 2008. (Chapter 17: 'Epic, 1667'.)

Belsey, Catherine. *John Milton: Language, Gender, Power*. Oxford: Basil Blackwell Ltd, 1988.

Brontë, Charlotte. *Shirley*, 1849.

Corns, Thomas N. ed. *A Companion to Milton*. Oxford: Blackwell Publishing, 2001, 2003.

Danielson, Dennis, ed. *The Cambridge Companion to Milton*. Cambridge: Cambridge University Press, 1989.

Davis, Nick. *Stories of Chaos: Reason and its Displacement in Early Modern English Narrative*. Aldershot, Brookfield, VT, Singapore, and Sydney: Ashgate. 1999 (Chapter 6: 'Milton Swallows Chaos').

DiPasquale, Theresa M. *Refiguring the Sacred Feminine: The Poems of John Donne, Aemilia Lanyer, and John Milton*. Pittsburgh, PA: Duquesne University Press, 2008. (Milton 3: 'Eve and Wisdom in *Paradise Lost*'.)

Duran, Angelica, ed. *A Concise Companion to Milton*. Oxford: Wiley-Blackwell 2011.

Dyson, A.E. and Lovelock, Julian, eds. *Milton: Paradise Lost: A Casebook*. London: Macmillan 1973.

Edwards, Karen L. 'Gender, Sex and Marriage in Paradise'. In Angela Duran (ed.), *A Concise Companion to Milton*. Oxford: Blackwell Publishing Ltd 2007, (pp. 144–60).

Elledge, Scott, ed. *Paradise Lost: An Authoritative Text, Backgrounds and Sources, Criticism*. New York: W.W.Norton & Company Inc., 1975.

Fish, Stanley E. *Surprised by Sin: The Reader in Paradise Lost*. Cambridge, MA: Harvard University Press, 1967.

Flannagan, Roy. *John Milton: A Short Introduction*. Oxford: Blackwell Publishing, 2002.

Froula, Christine. 'When Eve Reads Milton: Undoing the Canonical Economy'. *Critical Inquiry*, 10 (1983), pp. 142–64.

Gilbert, Sandra M ; Gubar, Susan. *The Madwoman in the Attic: The Woman Writer and the Nineteenth-Century Literary Imagination*, 2nd edn; Yale University Press: New Haven and London, USA and UK, 2000. 1979.

Kean, Margaret. *John Milton's Paradise Lost: A Sourcebook*. New York: Routledge, 2005.

Maresca, Thomas E. *Three English Epics: Studies in Chaucer, Spenser, and Milton*. Lincoln, NE and London: University of Nebraska Press, 1979.

Pullman, Philip. *Introduction, Paradise Lost*. Oxford University Press, 2005.

Ricks, Christopher. *Milton's Grand Style*. Oxford: Clarendon Press, 1963.

Rudrum, Alan, ed. *Milton: Modern Judgements*. London: Aurora Publisher Incorporated & Macmillan and Company Limited, 1969.

Wollstonecraft, Mary. *A Vindication of the Rights of Woman*. London, (1792).

Woolf, Virginia. *A Room of One's Own*. New York and London: Hogarth Press, 1929.

Index